# The Japanese Comfort Women and Sexual Slavery during the China and Pacific Wars

*War, Culture and Society*

**Series Editor**: Stephen McVeigh, Associate Professor, Swansea University, UK

*War, Culture and Society* is a multi- and inter-disciplinary series which encourages the parallel and complementary military historical and socio-cultural investigation of 20th- and 21st-century war and conflict.

**Published**:
*The British Imperial Army in the Middle East*, James Kitchen (2014)
*The Testimonies of Indian Soldiers and the Two World Wars*, Gajendra Singh (2014)
*South Africa's 'Border War'*, Gary Baines (2014)

**Forthcoming**:
*Cultural Responses to Occupation in Japan*, Adam Broinowski (2016)
*Jewish Volunteers, the International Brigades and the Spanish Civil War*, Gerben Zaagsma

# The Japanese Comfort Women and Sexual Slavery during the China and Pacific Wars

Caroline Norma

Bloomsbury Academic
An imprint of Bloomsbury Publishing Plc

B L O O M S B U R Y
LONDON · OXFORD · NEW YORK · NEW DELHI · SYDNEY

**Bloomsbury Academic**

An imprint of Bloomsbury Publishing Plc

| | |
|---|---|
| 50 Bedford Square | 1385 Broadway |
| London | New York |
| WC1B 3DP | NY 10018 |
| UK | USA |

**www.bloomsbury.com**

**BLOOMSBURY and the Diana logo are trademarks of Bloomsbury Publishing Plc**

First published 2016

**British Library Cataloguing-in-Publication Data**
A catalogue record for this book is available from the British Library.

ISBN: HB: 978-1-4725-1247-5
ePDF: 978-1-4725-1125-6
ePub: 978-1-4725-0780-8

**Library of Congress Cataloging-in-Publication Data**
A catalog record for this book is available from the Library of Congress.

Series: War, Culture and Society

Typeset by Integra Software Services Pvt. Ltd.

*Dedicated to the South Korean prostitution survivors group Moongchi,
in solidarity and admiration.*

# Contents

# Acknowledgements

So many things about this book and my life, except their flaws and faults, are due to radical feminists and our allies. You all deserve to be individually listed here, but, trying not to succumb to that kind of liberalism(!), I hope naming your organizations will show some of my gratitude for your daily support and conversations, strength, hard work and resistance. I owe a particular debt to sisters and comrades involved with the Anti-Pornography and Prostitution Research Group, Asha, Coalition Against Trafficking in Women Australia, Coalition Against Trafficking in Women International, Collective Shout, National Solidarity for Resolving the Problem of Prostitution, Nordic Model Australia Coalition, People Against Pornography and Sexual Violence (PAPS), Pink Cross Foundation Australia, Project Respect, Salim Center, *Seibouryoku no kai*, Spinifex Press, Taipei Women's Rescue Foundation (TWRF), Violence Against Women in War Research Action Center, Women's Action Museum, and the Women's Human Rights Commission of Korea (WHRCK). There are women outside of these organizations whose long-standing friendship and collaboration enriches my life, including Emma Dalton, Helen Pringle, Mary Sullivan and Caroline Taylor. While writing the book I was humbled to receive sponsored speaking invitations from PAPS, TWRF and the WHRCK, and I would like to sincerely thank their members. Okano Yayo kindly hosted me at Doshisha University, and Hiroshi, Saeko and Itsuki Nakasatomi were beyond kind and generous in their hosting of me in Kyoto; I am always grateful for their solidarity. Mark Selden and Norma Field at *Japan Focus* have been similarly kind and encouraging. I received sabbatical funding from the School of Global, Urban and Social Studies to complete the book's writing, for which I owe particular thanks to the School's Dean, Professor David Hayward, whose support I have benefited from consistently since January 2011. I also owe thanks to my colleagues in the Translation and Interpreting Program at RMIT, and the Director of the Centre for Global Research, Dr. Damian Grenfell, for painstakingly reading manuscript drafts. My PhD student, Kate Phelan, was also a wonderful reader, and has been a fun interlocutor over the past four years. I am lucky to have her and a whole group of brilliant PhD students to work with at RMIT. My days at the university would not be the same without Melissa Slee and the other members of the best branch committee of the National Tertiary Education Union.

In the mechanics of research and writing, Tony Foley and his team at RMIT's Document Delivery service have been extraordinarily helpful, and I was lucky to have the editorial guidance of Rhodri Mogford and Emma Goode at Bloomsbury. I also thank *War, Culture and Society* series editor Stephen McVeigh for having confidence in my project from the start. I would lastly like to convey thanks to the unnamed reviewer of my manuscript, not just for being so generous with my ideas and words, but for the wisdom and good sense they sent with the review.

Many fond thanks to Russell Spencer and Ursula Groves for close-range care and everyday support, and for the many baked sweet things I adore. I am very grateful to both of you. Love to my two precious nephews Sacha and Emile, and thanks to their doting father Shane Newberry who is a Japanese linguist of skill I can only dream of. Gratitude and love to their mother and wife, and my younger sister, psychiatrist Jillian Spencer, whose company is important to me beyond words, and whose example of intelligence, drive and common sense is one we all aspire to. Jill, thanks for being there for me during these years of writing.

# Introduction: The First Victims

Whether we were 'comfort women' or 'sexual service providers', when, now, I look back forty years and think about how many of us died in huge numbers in the most inhuman of circumstances, I'm just overwhelmed by its stupidity (Japanese comfort station survivor, Shirota Suzuko, speaking in 1986).[1]

Serial penetration by many men is not a mild form of torture. Just the tears at the vaginal opening feel like fire applied to a cut. Your genitals swell and bruise. Damage to the womb and other internal organs can also be tremendous … [B]eing used as a public dumping ground by those men left me with deep shame that I still feel in the pit of my stomach – it's like a hard, heavy, sick feeling that never entirely goes away. They saw not just my completely helpless, naked body, but they heard me beg, and cry. They reduced me to something low and disgusting that suffered miserably in front of them … Even years later, it has taken tremendous courage for me to put these words on the page, so deep is the cultural shame … (US military prostitution survivor, Suki Falconberg, writing in 2006).[2]

The sexual slavery system of the Japanese military during the China and Pacific wars (1937–1945) interned tens of thousands of women of different nationalities, with Korean women the most widely known victims. Less well known is the trafficking of Japanese women into military brothels or 'comfort' stations throughout the two wars. This book describes the history of Japanese women enslaved in military brothels in Japan, Okinawa, Japan's colonies and occupied territories, and overseas battlegrounds. They were the first victims of the 'comfort women' system of sexual slavery operated by the Japanese military with support from the Japanese bureaucracy, but have been mostly sidelined in research and activism taking place since 1990. As the book shows, Japanese women were trafficked into comfort stations throughout the China and Pacific wars, and while the full picture of their historical experience has not been captured in English before now, it tells us a great deal about the military sexual slavery system and its origins and causes.

Information on Japanese victims of military sexual slavery has been in the Japanese-language media since the 1970s, but only one woman of Japanese nationality is widely recognized as a comfort station survivor. Her biography was published in 1971 under the pseudonym 'Shirota Suzuko' and she became publicly active as a survivor under her own name in the 1980s. She recounted her experience to newspaper reporters, went on radio, and raised money to build a modest memorial shrine in Japan to victims of the military system. The shrine remains today in Chiba prefecture near the women's shelter where Shirota lived from 1965 with other survivors of prostitution. Before her death in 1993, she was quoted in a newspaper expressing happiness that South Korean survivors of the military sexual slavery system had spoken out publicly.

Shirota's feelings of solidarity with survivors of military sexual slavery from other countries are well justified on the basis of her own experience of the system. As a teenager, she was trafficked into comfort stations on Taiwan and Truk during the war years for sexual use by both Japanese military officers and rank-and-file troops. She lived in the comfort stations with women from Korea, as well as with women trafficked from civilian sex industries on Japan and Okinawa. Her biography records that she was approached by brokers to travel to Taiwan while in a civilian brothel in Tokyo, and accepted the offer in order to escape crushing debt. She had been sold into a geisha venue by her father at age 17, and he took out further loans against her subsequent trafficking into a brothel, and then again when she was trafficked into a naval comfort station on colonial Taiwan. Shirota and the seven other Japanese women trafficked with her were all 'sex industry women',[3] and they ended up on a Taiwanese island hosting twenty naval comfort stations that were managed by Japanese operators. Shirota's station alone interned fifteen women. Their movement outside the venues was heavily restricted, and they were subjected to regular venereal disease examinations, for which station managers bribed military medical staff to let them pass.[4] Shirota recalls that weekends in the brothel were terrifying: soldiers would line up in droves and 'jostle' to get their turn, which meant the women were used by up to fifteen men each day on Saturdays and Sundays. For Shirota, this was like living a nightmare in which she had to 'fend off wild beasts coming at me one after the next'.[5]

While the experience of Japanese survivors of military sexual slavery might be different from that of women of other nationalities for the fact they were more often trafficked into comfort stations directly from civilian brothels, this book highlights the fundamental similarity of their experience. This common experience was primarily of prostitution and other forms of sexual violence in the stations, but extends to other aspects: for example, Shirota's life after military sexual slavery had much in common with that of other survivors. She continued to be prostituted after the war in civilian venues, specifically by American occupying soldiers in Japan. Reflecting on this experience, Shirota said, 'at any rate, I felt I existed to be used by men for profit and for fun, that's a woman's lot, I just felt like my body was a throwaway object'.[6] Like most other survivors of the military system, Shirota was left with little money, psychological trauma and in poor physical health after her experience of the comfort stations (and in civilian prostitution before this from the age of 17), and this left her vulnerable after the war to trafficking into 'camptown' prostitution (i.e. prostitution by military men in peacetime).[7] Katharine Moon notes in her 1997 discussion of postwar Korean camptown prostitution that 'former comfort women ... worked as GI prostitutes [and were] among the first generation of kijich'on [camptown] sex workers',[8] and this fate was common for Japanese survivors as well. Regardless of the pathway that led women into the wartime comfort stations – whether it was manipulation, abduction, or trafficking out of civilian brothels – their health, welfare and life-course outcomes, irrespective of nationality, were depressingly the same. At least two Japanese survivors are known to have committed suicide after returning home.

A number of Japanese women are described in media articles and books as survivors of the military system, but these women do not necessarily self-identify as survivors, their experiences have not always been well documented, their identities have sometimes been unknown, and they have rarely spoken in public using their own names. Nonetheless, Japanese women are referred to repeatedly in the survivor testimony of women of other nationalities, especially Koreans.[9] There has been no estimate made of the number of Japanese women prostituted through the military system, but the broad consensus is they were a minority of victims. Qiu Peipei writes that,

[b]ased on the evidence gathered by Chinese researchers since the 1990s ... from 1937 to 1945, the comfort women replacement rate was much higher than previously thought, approximately 3.5 to 4., which brings the estimated total number of comfort women up to either (1) more than 360,000 (3,000,000 Japanese soldiers/29 × 3.5 = 362,068 women) or (2) more than 400,000 (3,000,000 Japanese soldiers/29 × 4.0 = 413,793 women). In terms of nationalities ... about 140,000 to 160,000 of the total number of comfort women were Korean and ... 20,000 were Japanese, with several thousand being from Taiwan and Southeast Asia and several hundred coming from European countries. The rest were Chinese women who numbered about 200,000.[10]

While this book does not necessarily seek to challenge such numerical estimations, it does urge reconsideration of the longstanding view that Japanese women were infrequent victims of the system. Their early trafficking into comfort stations out of civilian sex industries in Japan, Korea and Taiwan; their widespread prostitution and trafficking on the Chinese mainland and elsewhere as '*karayuki*' before the military system began operating; and their on-going trafficking into military stations throughout the years of war, including on Okinawa, is likely to mean their numbers were not insignificant. Japanese women were found in stations all over Asia and the Pacific, including as far out as Burma and Rabaul, throughout the years of war, including in the final months in large numbers on Okinawa. They were also prostituted, together with Korean women, through stations created on Japanese soil during the war years, and particularly after 1944 when a domestic network of 'comfort facilities' (*ian shisetsu*) were set up under a policy of the Home Ministry, as is described in Chapter Three.

The experiences of Japanese survivors, including those of Shirota Suzuko, are described throughout this book, and particularly their histories of civilian prostitution (in Japan, colonial Korea and Taiwan, and Okinawa) before being trafficked into comfort stations. In most of the cases, Japanese survivors were sold into prostitution as girls, and entered comfort stations after being bought out of debt bondage by brokers and traffickers acting for the military, or when civilian brothels were converted into military stations. Many did not survive the ordeal, and those who returned home sometimes faced early death from disease or suicide. A former nurse who worked at a venereal disease sanatorium in Fukuoka and cared for a Japanese returnee from a mainland comfort station at the end of the war recounted to researchers in 2005 her memory of this patient before she died. The woman (whose name is unknown) had been sold into prostitution by her parents, and was in a local brothel when she was approached by a broker to travel to a wartime comfort station in China on the promise her debts would be paid off and she would receive a regular income. As a result of this experience, according to the nurse,

> she was physically and mentally scarred, spoke very little, and her mind seemed far away … she had late-stage syphilis, and the infection had permeated her mucous membranes. Her lips were peeling off and pus was leaking from her skin … There was no penicillin … Her hair had already fallen out …[11]

Nonetheless, the nurse mused, the woman's short stay in the sanatorium before her death had probably been the first and only time in her life she would have had 'the chance to experience a day lived in peace without imposition from other people, and without being humiliated, beaten, or caused physical pain'.[12]

No Japanese woman has received compensation for these kinds of outcomes of the military system (nor for similar outcomes of civilian prostitution, for that matter); indeed, Japanese survivors were specifically excluded in a financial 'atonement' scheme administered by a Japanese semi-governmental agency in 1995. They are nowhere mentioned in the two reports of the United Nations Special Rapporteurs published in 1996 (Radhika Coomaraswamy) and 1998 (Gay McDougall), and this omission is inexplicable in the case of the Coomaraswamy report, given it acknowledges stations were set up in Japan, and that Japan was the first source country for women trafficked into mainland stations (but it suggests these women had been Koreans living in Japan). Japanese survivors were not represented at the citizens' show trial held in Tokyo in 2000 (which featured participation by sixty survivors) that assessed the historical culpability of the Japanese government and emperor for wartime sexual slavery. Although, it must be noted, this Women's International War Crimes Tribunal on Japan's Military Sexual Slavery did recognize, as Nishino Rumiko recounts, that

> Japanese victims of the system were women incorporated into the civilian legalised prostitution system of the time, and who were sold into prostitution by impoverished families from disadvantaged rural areas … [and] the military had targeted for trafficking into comfort stations these women as the most vulnerable members of Japanese society.[13]

Nonetheless, Japanese women were excluded from a bill presented to the Diet by the Japan Communist Party in the year 2000 to propose measures for resolution of the wartime sexual slavery problem. The bill proposed that victims be recognized without respect to nationality for the payment of compensation funds, but this clause was eventually amended to exclude Japanese women.[14]

Shirota's valiant efforts in building a memorial shrine in Chiba notwithstanding, there are no public monuments or observance rituals honouring Japanese survivors (there are monuments on Tokashiki and Miyakojima islands, but not specifically for Japanese survivors), and only recently have Japanese women been the subject of a historical materials exhibition at the Women's Active Museum on War and Peace in Tokyo. A major aim of this book, therefore, is to examine why Japanese survivors have been overlooked in the 'justice for comfort women' activism and scholarship that has been continuing in a number of countries since the early 1990s, including in Japan. This aim is addressed in the next chapter.

While most of the book's discussion focuses on Japanese victims of military sexual slavery, this focus is not ultimately determined by nationality. Rather, most Japanese victims of the comfort station system were trafficked from the civilian sex industry – by pimps and brokers operating either in Japan or overseas. It is this prior experience of prostitution before being trafficked into military sexual slavery that guides the focus of the book, and so the experiences of prostituted women of other nationalities are also discussed. While Kinoshita Naoko calls for recognition of non-prostituted Japanese women trafficked into military stations,[15] prostituted victims of military sexual slavery – in other words, women with historical experience of enslavement in both civilian and military forms of prostitution – are prioritized. Reasons for this focus are explained further below.

Having said that, the author is not interested in creating a hierarchy among victims of different forms of prostitution, whether military or civilian. Rather, she follows Yoshimi Yoshiaki's view that

> [t]here is no point debating which was the worse system [between the pre-war legalised brothel system or the comfort station system]. This is because, for the women who were victimised in each of the respective systems, their sexual victimisation was so severe as to be unforgivable. Both were extremely severe systems of sexual slavery and sexual violence.[16]

Accordingly, traditional distinctions drawn between prostituted women and non-prostituted women trafficked into comfort stations are deemed irrelevant to the book's discussion. Historical accounts of women prostituted in comfort stations being subsequently singled out for trafficking into other prostitution systems (and vice versa) illustrate the absurdity of attempting to create hierarchies among comfort station survivors. These historical accounts include Hirai Kazuko's observation that thirteen former comfort women were singled out after the war for trafficking into prostitution to serve invading Russian troops in Dandong, China,[17] as well as Yoshimi's research showing that, on the Indonesian island of Ambon Pulau in 1944,

> [a] list of women with experience as comfort women, prostitutes, women rumoured to be prostitutes, and women who wanted to be comfort women was drawn up … The women rounded up were Eurasian (in this case, women of mixed Caucasian and Indonesian ancestry) and Indonesian.[18]

Further, as recalled by Australia-based Dutch survivor of a comfort station Jan Ruff-O'Herne, survivors were subsequently harassed on the basis of their victimization in comfort stations in exactly the same way civilian prostituted women are denigrated as 'whores':

> The women in the other part of Kramat Camp had been ordered not to make contact with us. Somehow, rumours still spread as to why we were being kept in isolation and cruelly, they gave our camp the name 'Hoeren Camp', meaning, 'Camp of Whores'. They thought we had been voluntary workers in brothels for the Japanese. They also believed that because of this we were being given special treatment and food ... At times, the women from the other part of the camp would shout abusive names at us through the fence and throw messages, written on paper and tied to a stone, over the fence. They addressed us as whores and traitors.[19]

The absurdity highlighted in these accounts is that attempts to differentiate between women trafficked into comfort stations on the basis of prior experience of prostitution are ultimately meaningless, because the same distinction that made women in the civilian sex industry vulnerable to trafficking into comfort stations became the distinction subsequently used to victimize comfort station survivors, regardless of whether or not they had originally been prostituted.

## Structure of the discussion

This book engages centrally with these kinds of historical connections and overlaps between the military comfort station system and various forms of civilian prostitution operating before and during the China and Pacific wars in Japan and overseas. Each chapter considers the military system from a different angle, but always with regards to its historical *civilian prostitution* context: for example, the existing prostitution habits of the creators and users of the military system in the 1920s (Chapter Two); civilian sex industry involvement in the development of the military system, and military mobilization of the homeland sex industry in the 1930s (Chapter Three); the trafficking of women out of civilian prostitution into the military system (Chapter Four); the reliance of the military system on colonial sex industries (Chapter Five); and the mobilization of prostituted Okinawan women for military sexual slavery at the end of the war (Chapter Six). This book is the first attempt in either English or Japanese to recognize and problematize specifically *prostituted* victims of the military system, but its discussion builds on research already expertly undertaken on Japanese survivors of military sexual slavery by feminist historians such as Nishino Rumiko, Onozawa Akane, Yamashita Yeong-ae, Kawada Fumiko and Kinoshita

Naoko. Its conceptual framework relies on Katharine Moon's important 1999 discussion about similarities between the 'comfort women' system and post-war *kijich'on* prostitution in South Korea,[20] and also Hayakawa Noriyo and Fujinaga Takeshi's painstaking and prolific work linking the military scheme to civilian prostitution in Japan and its colonies.

The book's research mostly comes from existing historical scholarship on the comfort station system rather than archival or field-based sources. There is certainly urgent need for research on prostituted victims of the system using primary sources, and Yoshimi notes that research on the military system's 'historical place' within the 'overall prostitution system' (*baibaishun shisutemu*) is unfortunately 'still very far away'.[21] No conceptual framework yet exists to make this research a recognizably productive avenue of inquiry, I would add. The doubly victimized population of prostituted comfort station survivors has not just been overlooked in research on the wartime system to date, these women have been actively sidelined in public and academic discourse. The disproportionate targeting of prostituted women for military sexual enslavement relative to other populations of women is a fact mostly not grasped even in feminist scholarship, let alone in work specifically on the comfort station system.

There does exist, though, first-hand recorded accounts of comfort stations and their victims written by soldiers, journalists, and other men connected to the Japanese military in the China and Pacific wars. This book consults a number of anthologies of these accounts compiled by Japanese historians who have sifted through hundreds of published and unpublished items held in the National Diet Library and other venues to excerpt mentions of the military prostitution scheme. Histories of Japan's 1920s pre-war sex industry are also consulted for their inclusion of information relating to the military or to wartime mobilization. These sources include secondary historical accounts, as well as primary survey reports of the sex industry generated by Japanese public servants and police around the time. In addition to these, a compilation of interviews with people connected to a pre-war brothel district in the city of Sapporo published in the early 1980s is comprehensively referenced for its historical snapshot of the civilian prostitution system that preceded the wartime system. Conversely, the research consults secondary historical sources describing the wartime comfort station system for information relating to Japan's civilian sex industry, its operators, or its victims. In other words, historical sources referring to any civilian prostitution context of the wartime military comfort station system, as well as sources revealing military aspects and connections of the civilian prostitution system, are relied upon in the research of this book.

The thesis of the book that wartime military sexual slavery has origins in the institution of civilian prostitution aligns with an emerging cluster of historical literature that observes institutions, practices, and systems of Japanese militarism and imperialism in the twentieth century as having antecedents in aspects of pre-war Japanese society. Among this scholarship is Tessa Morris-Suzuki's account of Tonohira Yoshihiko's grassroots research showing the existence of a prototype forced labour system on Hokkaido (even using Korean forced labourers) that pre-dates the well-known slave labour schemes of the Japanese military in the China and Pacific wars.[22] Mark Driscoll's account of enslaved labour systems operated by Japanese private entrepreneurs in pre-war China similarly includes the suggestion that these systems were built upon in wartime when the Japanese military developed its mainland forced labour schemes.[23] This growing body of scholarship is interesting for the perspective it develops about the nature of the relationship that existed between war and society in Japanese history. In this perspective, also advanced by the current book, institutions important to military endeavour were forged domestically in peacetime and then developed in wartime in Japan's colonies.

## Underpinnings of the discussion

Late feminist theorist Andrea Dworkin wrote at length about attention owed prostituted women in histories of war and mass murder as first-targeted victims of sexual violence and other atrocities, and her writing in this regard is discussed in the next chapter. In brief, she theorized a social function for prostituted women within military victimized populations as 'scapegoats', which is the theoretical insight that drives the approach of this book. She wrote in groundbreaking terms in 2000 that

> [p]rostitutes were the first: gassed in Poland, sent to Auschwitz ... Auschwitz 1 to 999 were largely if not entirely prostituted women from Ravensbruck ... Prostitutes were also first in another way [i.e. the first to be deported] ... Well, who could care? These are the women left out of any Jewish reckoning with the Nazis – or any feminist reckoning with prostitution: wherever there is racial or ethnic stigmatization, the women of the stigmatized group who are prostituted are the first to be rounded up, shipped off, and forgotten ... This is how to find prostituted women: look at the bottom of the hierarchy – they will be poor relative to those who use them even when wealth is calculated in pieces of bread.[24]

This book takes Dworkin's advice, now more than a decade old, to centrally examine the experience of prostituted victims of the comfort station system. In turn, it examines the system from the viewpoint of their experience. It suggests in the next chapter that prostituted victims have been scapegoated in research and activism on the issue since the early 1990s. In Dworkin's terms, feminists have largely failed to 'reckon with prostitution' in their pursuit of justice for comfort station survivors, in spite of the fact these survivors include prostituted women, and all survivors, regardless of the path that led them into the wartime stations, were victimized through a system of prostitution, albeit a military one.

Not only to understand the experience of prostituted survivors of the military system but also to understand the prostitution experience of all its survivors, this book reassesses existing historical work on the comfort station system. It filters information about the system's links to civilian prostitution already contained in the historical literature. The historiography of the system incorporates frequent reference to civilian sex industries, prostitution entrepreneurs, sex industry practices and conventions, prostitution attitudes and values, and the military trafficking of civilian sex industry victims, but this information is left mostly uncommented upon, or is even cast as irrelevant to historical knowledge about the military system. For example, Hayashi Hirofumi's archival research in 1998 found that,

> [i]n Kuala Lumpur [in 1941], the Quartermaster Corps rounded up fourteen Japanese women who had remained there. Twelve of these women had experience in prostitution and were known as '*karayukisan*' (overseas Japanese prostitutes). These twelve were entrusted with the recruitment of women and the management of comfort houses ...[25]

Yet, neither Hayashi nor any other historian has pursued the probable implication of this observation that the Japanese military recruited people with strong connections to local sex industries (and especially if they could speak Japanese) to broker the trafficking of locally prostituted women into military stations. In this case, the military targeted formerly prostituted Japanese women (who were likely to have been of an older age by the 1940s, after having been trafficked to the Malay Peninsula in the early 1900s as girls).[26] This in itself is a notable fact, but further overlooked is the possibility that the Japanese military took active and systematic steps during the war to arrange the trafficking of women out of civilian prostitution to enter its comfort stations.

The book's discussion draws together snippets of information like this to describe the development and operation of the military system in a way that shows its features to fundamentally reflect and rely on aspects of civilian prostitution. Through emphasizing continuity between the military system and various civilian prostitution systems operating before and during the China and Pacific wars, the discussion poses a challenge to the view that the military system developed uniquely and peculiarly to wartime and battle. This reductionist understanding of the origins of the comfort station system as deriving from 'militarism' and the harsh conditions of war is advocated by the most critical historians of the system, even feminist ones, including Vera Mackie who claims that a 'particular form of masculinity is fostered through military training: an active, aggressive form of masculinity which is seen to need particular sexual outlets'.[27] It is taken as almost axiomatic in both the scholarly and popular literature that men will prostitute women in war and military adventure, but it is not a maxim endorsed in this book. Rather, Antje Kampf's 2008 analysis of the New Zealand military in the two world wars is preferred. She correlates prostitution activity among military personnel quite simply with policies and implementation strategies enacted by military command to prevent or tolerate the behaviour.[28] This alternative understanding, which does not presume any inevitable or universal link between militarism (however 'masculinist' this is in nature) and men's prostitution of women, is reflected in the book's henceforth discussion.

For now, the methodology that guides the book's approach might be provisionally indicated through citing an example of its polar *opposing* approach, as articulated by Kelly Askin in 2001:

> The so-called 'comfort women' of World War II, while clearly victims of sexual violence, have in the past been most commonly referred to as victims of enforced prostitution, although emerging norms deem the crime more appropriately termed sexual slavery. The term 'slavery' is appropriately invoked when victims effectively lose all or partial ownership over their own bodies, being treated as the personal property of the perpetrators or other culpable parties. Referring to the institution as a 'comfort system', naming the venue a 'brothel', or linking the activity to 'prostitution' attempts to transform the crime into something which may have some form of legitimacy by inferring that choice was involved, as if the women and girls participated without coercion or force, received some sort of compensatory benefit, were free and able to leave anytime they chose, or were able to dictate the nature or terms of the sexual services (such as requiring condom use, limiting their number of partners, refusing to participate in certain forms of sex, rejecting persons using physical violence, or demanding specific compensation terms). The former 'comfort women', however, overwhelmingly characterize their treatment as slavery, and tend to reject adamantly any terminology linking their treatment to the word 'prostitution'.[29]

Askin's approach is almost universally adopted by advocates, scholars and activists working towards justice for comfort station survivors today. But it is a view that eschews consideration of civilian prostitution in understanding the history of the system and the experience of survivors, while at the same time trumpeting women's comparative exercise of 'choice' in civilian prostitution on the basis of their supposed ability to 'demand' 'compensatory benefits', and do things like choose customers. While, as discussed in the next chapter, the campaigning of contemporary right-wing defenders of the Japanese military has perhaps understandably caused reactionary thinking to sprout among progressives (e.g. conservatives say comfort women were merely prostitutes, so we must say they were not), this fact does not fully account for the tendency of the progressive position to defend civilian prostitution. If we are truly mindful of survivors in considering the history of comfort station system, how can we comprehend Askin's claim that 'former "comfort women" … tend to reject adamantly any terminology linking their treatment to the word "prostitution"'? For many survivors of the military system, including Shirota Suzuko at the outset of this chapter, it was precisely membership of the prostituted class that prefaced their experience of military sexual slavery, and military sexual slavery prefaced the experience of many more survivors becoming members of the prostituted class thereafter. This overlooked point anchors the discussion of the book overall. It is a thesis succinctly summarized in Suzuki Masahiro's alternatively formulated understanding that

> Japan's sex industry has significant historical origins as an institutionalised system of sexual violence. The idea that girls sold into the industry by their parents were exercising choice is not comprehensible … it was a system of sexual slavery. If we are to seek to identify the differences between the civilian legalised prostitution system and the comfort station system, we have to first acknowledge the slavery of the civilian system … attempts to insist on differences between the two systems are likely to come from proponents who are capitalising on tenets of Japan's contemporary rape/prostitution tolerant culture. It would be better to re-examine the comfort station system from the critical perspective of the rape/prostitution culture circulating in Japan in the pre-war period, as well as the pre-war sex industry.[30]

## Abolitionist terms of the discussion

The way that Askin defines the experience of military sexual slaves as losing 'all or partial ownership over their own bodies, [and] being treated as the personal property of the perpetrators or other culpable parties' is the view taken in this book of the experience of *all* victims of prostitution, regardless of their victimization in either civilian or military systems. This stance resists liberal attempts to split military sexual slavery from its connection to, and origins in, civilian prostitution. Catharine MacKinnon has been writing about these connections since 1993, and suggests military sexual slavery 'is at once both mass rape and serial rape in a way that is indistinguishable from prostitution', and that '[p]rostitution is that part of everyday non-war life that is closest to what we see done to women in ... war'.[31] Connections between the Japanese military sexual slavery system and civilian prostitution in a range of respects are highlighted in the book's discussion, as well as the common experience of victims in both contexts. On this basis, the phrase 'civilian sexual slavery' is coined to mirror the phrase 'military sexual slavery', which are terms I believe accurately describe prostitution from the viewpoint of its victims.

It is an aim of the book to forge an understanding of prostitution in peacetime as a system of 'civilian sexual slavery' in the same way prostitution in wartime is now understood by the United Nations as 'military sexual slavery'. It is the author's hope that reflection on the slavery of the Japanese military system as an historical system of prostitution might inversely spark recognition of the slavery of contemporary civilian prostitution. We might reflect on this fundamental similarity while still being aware of asymmetries, as MacKinnon recognizes in her remark on sexual violence in the 1990s Serbian war that '[t]his war is to rape every day what the Holocaust was to anti-Semitism every day: without the everyday, the conflagration could not exist, but do not mistake one for the other'.[32] In relation to the comfort station system, Morita Seiya distinguishes it on the grounds it was 'more extreme, [operated] on a wider scale, was more debased, and targeted a broader base of women' than prostitution in peacetime but, following MacKinnon, he nonetheless advocates recognition of its essentially identical nature.[33]

Terms commonly used to describe civilian sexual slavery, like 'prostitution' and 'brothel', are used to describe aspects of the military system in this book. It is unfortunately the case that, even taking into account the alternatively formulated descriptions of sexual slavery that have been achieved for the military system since the mid-1990s, as long as these euphemisms remain current for civilian sexual slavery they continue to be useful for describing its military equivalent. The author looks forward to the day when civilian brothels are called 'rape centres' in the way the United Nations has described the wartime comfort stations since 1998, and to the day when someone like former US secretary of state Hillary Clinton insists on replacing the word 'prostitute' with 'civilian sex slave' in the admirable way she corrected a staffer over their use of the term 'comfort woman' in 2012 (Clinton directed the phrase 'enforced sex slave' be used instead).[34]

The language of the book derives from the ideas and history of feminist abolitionism, which goes back at least to the time of the League of Nations. These ideas have been in abeyance for a number of decades, but they are in the ascendency at the time of writing. They are encapsulated in clear, if not blunt, terms in Susan Kay's following description of a prostitution buyer that,

> [l]ike the rapist, he is not concerned with her needs or wants or desires. He does not have to treat her like a human being because she is an object to be masturbated on and in. When we see the violence unmasked and we set aside the money which is used to scapegoat her, his sex is an act of rape …[35]

This kind of understanding of prostitution as a form of sexual violence is being endorsed by a growing list of governments each year, and has recently attracted the support of the European Parliament as well as the Council of Europe, in addition to a cross-party committee of the UK parliament. Views of prostitution as inimical to societies that are based on principles of gender equality, as fundamentally driving the trafficking of women, as a form of violence against women, and as incompatible with equal social relations between the women and men have taken hold in the policymaking of governments such as Sweden, South Korea, Norway, Iceland, Canada, Lithuania, Ireland and Northern Ireland, and the criminalization of prostitution buyers and pimps is an approach increasingly preferred even in some jurisdictions of the US and UK over imposing penalties on sex industry victims.

The reason this book adopts the language and ideas of feminist abolitionism to discuss the history of the Japanese comfort women is for the purpose of reconciling historical work on military sexual slavery with the large body of empirical research, and testimony of civilian prostitution survivors, that now exists, but which has expanded dramatically since the 1990s when the bulk of scholarship on the comfort station system was produced. This contemporary scholarship empirically and anecdotally documents the reality of civilian prostitution,[36] and the observations it contains of sexual slavery are remarkably similar to those contained in testimony collected since the 1990s on the experiences of wartime comfort station survivors from Korea, the Philippines, Taiwan and China. In spite of this, researchers of the comfort station system continue to adhere to a civilian/military distinction in relation to the system's substantive aspects (e.g. victim harm). I believe, though, they are now doing so on increasingly shaky ground. Testimony from survivors of even contemporary civilian prostitution in Japan, such as the example below, resonate far too well with testimony collected from survivors of the military system to make a civilian/military distinction plausible for much longer. As civilian survivor organizations grow stronger over the next decade, and as even more governments come to adopt a human rights approach to prostitution policymaking like Sweden, the body of survivor testimony, as well as empirical documentation of the harms of civilian prostitution, is likely to balloon, and present a serious challenge to the idea that 'peacetime' prostitution has organized anything but the civilian enslavement of women and girls over the course of world history. Already from descriptions emerging of the experience of Japanese civilian prostitution survivors today we might begin to perceive of this fact:

> Kyouno Marina was a porn star who made a living being used in hardcore films where she was degraded, gang raped, and had men ejaculate inside her. Even if she'd regretted the experience, if the money had been good, or she'd ended up with some savings, that might have been one thing, but the reality was that she finished her career in debt. She carried on doing the films to the point where her body and mind couldn't withstand it anymore; she had already been cutting her wrists to get through the experience. She couldn't go on any further. She announced her retirement, but the film company pursued her over costs for films she was already booked for, but was now refusing to do. She was mentally destroyed in making the films, and now they pressured her further. She had been forcibly dragged along to sets to make the films, and then returned home to her boyfriend who would beat her while she cried. She had nowhere to run and was on the verge of attempting suicide. Her only choice was to disclose to her parents what had been happening, and they borrowed money from relatives to pay off the film company so she could escape …[37]

Some aspects of the description echo interview testimony taken from a Chinese wartime survivor in the early 1990s:

> The parents of a survivor named Li … paid a large ransom but were still unable to obtain her release until such time as she was physically incapable of continuing to service Japanese troops. Japanese soldiers had kidnapped Li from Lizhuang Village when she was fifteen years old. She was raped and beaten daily by a dozen Japanese troops for about five months. Hoping to ransom Li, her parents struggled and eventually managed to borrow about six hundred silver dollars. However, even after accepting all their money, the Japanese troops still held Li

captive. In despair, Li's mother committed suicide. Li's father was driven insane by the death of his wife and the capture of his daughter.[38]

These recorded experiences of women in military and civilian prostitution are not dissimilar enough in their relevant respects, I believe, to make fundamental distinctions drawn between military and civilian prostitution in historical scholarship and elsewhere plausible in either logic or empirical fact. I believe it appropriate now, in the second decade of the twenty-first century, that discussion of the comfort station system begin to take on the language and ideas of feminist abolitionism, given that the matters of sexual slavery at issue (i.e. in wartime and peacetime) are fundamentally the same, and need to be so recognized if effective, coordinated, and just research and advocacy is to be carried out. Komazawa University's Morita Seiya began this task in 1999, and this book is reliant on his early and groundbreaking example. The emergence of civilian prostitution survivor organizations internationally, such as the one in the book's dedication, is an unprecedented development in world history, and an important reason to update discussion of the Japanese military system. While surviving victims of the military system may be dwindling in number as each year passes, there is now a globally organized movement of survivors of civilian sexual slavery who can assume the mantle of their struggle for public recognition and government redress of human right harms, both for prostitution systems operating now and in the past. But for this to become possible, the fundamentally similar experience of survivors of civilian and military prostitution needs to be recognized, and this book is written in hope and encouragement of this recognition.

The language of the book's discussion reflects the viewpoint of contemporary survivors that prostitution is an act of sexual violence inflicted by perpetrators against victims, as is the view of Suki Falconberg quoted at the top of the chapter. Leading Irish survivor Rachel Moran wrote similarly in 2013 that '[i]t hurt like sexual assault. It damaged like sexual assault. It degraded like sexual assault. It *was* sexual assault … prostitution was abuse, it was *paid* sexual abuse'.[39] Accordingly, in the terms of this book, as MacKinnon writes, '[p]rostitute, the noun, is seen to misleadingly and denigratingly equate who these people are with what is being done to them'. In contrast, 'the past participle verb form … highlights the other people and social forces who are acting upon them'.[40] The past participle verb form of 'prostitute' is 'prostituted', and this word is used to describe victims of sexual slavery, regardless of the civilian or military context.

In the feminist abolitionist view, the actions of perpetrators, rather than those of victims, are ultimately defining of prostitution, and this viewpoint generates a language that is respectful of sex industry survivors. The actions of perpetrators are understood to occur irrespective of the will or undertaking of victims, and so the feminist definition of prostitution is not ultimately contingent upon any individual experience of it, in the same way that any individual experience of rape or domestic violence does not ultimately arbitrate the definition of these crimes (e.g. their offence is not lessened by a victim's intoxication or unconsciousness). These crimes are ultimately defined according to the actions of perpetrators. In the feminist understanding of prostitution, too, the individual experiences of victims (e.g. feelings of 'consent' or 'choice') are ultimately a non-relevant consideration to the *definition* of prostitution, because the fact of a perpetrator's actions remains. The individually unique experiences of any prostituted woman or girl are of course important to understand the phenomenon but, regardless of these details, neither blame nor responsibility is attributed to victims because, as MacKinnon writes, in the feminist abolitionist view, people are ultimately

> observed to be prostituted through choices precluded, options restricted, possibilities denied. Although the full scope and prevalence of prostitution's arrangements, with all its varieties of transactional sex, is not known, use of this term reflects an evaluation of considerable information on the sex industry, not an a priori attribution of victim status. Prostitution here is observed to be a product of lack of choice, the resort of those with the fewest choices, or none at all when all else fails. The coercion behind it, physical and otherwise, produces an economic sector of sexual abuse, the lion's share of the profits of which goes to others. In these transactions, the money coerces the sex rather than guaranteeing consent to it, making prostitution a practice of serial rape.[41]

This suggestion that prostitution comprises 'serial rape' is not foreign to feminist theorizing in Japanese; Sugita Satoshi described it in this way in 1999, and made the following point that a woman's consent to sexual engagement cannot be bought, and so the buying of sex ultimately enacts her abuse:

> In the process of buying a 'sexual service', the buyer aims for sexual intercourse with the prostituted person and ejaculation, and to use their body in any way they please. But because the woman's consent does not exist in the first place, intercourse and ejaculation, as well as any other intentional physical contact with her body, are violations of her human rights.[42]

Similarly, Fujino Yutaka in 2001 wrote that

> prostitution might deliver 'sexual comfort' to buyers (mostly men), but it degrades those who are bought (mostly women) … any sexual practice that delivers pleasure to one party and humiliation to the other cannot be described as

anything other than sexual violence ... prostitution has the same characteristics as rape ... prostitution is therefore a practice of sexual violence that suppresses women's human rights.[43]

Sugita and Fujino's understanding is echoed by Korean survivors of civilian prostitution writing today, but an intervening fifteen years of organizing and consciousness raising has been necessary to reach this historical point where clear statements against prostitution are being made collectively by survivors themselves all around the world, as in the following example from a member of Moongchi's Taegu branch (from the organization mentioned in the book's dedication):

> If you think that prostitution is sex, you are so very ignorant. Having sex with your boyfriend 350 out of 365 days a year sounds exhausting, so how could taking several clients each day every day feel like sex? Prostitution is clear exploitation of underprivileged women. It only seems like a fair exchange because johns [i.e. prostitution buyers] pay for the services. And prostitutes are in turn treated like people who deserve to be assaulted and insulted. We are not asking you to see us as victims. We're not asking for your sympathy. We are saying that prostitution is not just our problem. If you continue to think that it is, the problem will never be solved.[44]

This uncompromising view of prostitution as a human rights violation attributable to male perpetrators is obviously many steps removed from the understanding of prostitution that is encapsulated in phrases like 'comfort women', 'comfort station' and 'comfort system' that are used to describe the scheme of military sexual slavery that was created, developed and operated by the Japanese military during the China and Pacific wars with the imprimatur of the Japanese government. There exists a long history of men creating euphemisms for systems of sexual slavery; Dworkin describes Jewish women being kept in venues called 'houses of dolls' for 'prostitution by German soldiers from 2 pm each day', which they called 'enjoyment duty'. They had to file reports on the performance of the 'dolls', and three negative reports meant death.[45]

These kinds of phrases are formulated wholly on a male experience of prostitution as delivering some kind of bodily or psychological reassurance. In other words, women's experience of physical and psychological harm in being prostituted is excluded in definitions that refer to positive experiences like 'comfort' or 'enjoyment' as arising from the practice. (This includes Kurahashi Masanao's irritatingly frequent use of the term 'refreshment' [*rifureshu*] to describe military prostitution, referring to its supposedly positive effect on war weary Japanese troops.)[46] Unfortunately, the word 'comfort' still enjoys popular acceptance and circulation today, and terms alternatively formulated to respect women's experience of harm, such as 'military sexual slavery' and 'rape centre', have not yet fully replaced it. The former word is used regrettably in this book, but it is used for a reason arising uniquely from its argument. Phrases containing the word 'comfort' (*ian*) are extant historically not only in descriptions of the stations set up for officers and troops all over the Asia-Pacific during the war years, but also in reference to the network of *ian shisetsu* (comfort facilities) that serviced factory and mine workers on Japanese soil in the latter years of war (described in Chapter Five). Further, after the war, the Recreation and Amusement Association (RAA; *tokushu ian shisetsu kyoukai*), also referring to the word 'comfort', was set up for occupying troops in Japan. This historio-linguistic trail of connection between the military system and a number of semi-military or civilian systems operating in Japan around the same time period is important to the book's contention that the military system did not emerge in isolation from, or separate to, existing and ongoing systems of prostitution. The linguistic connection casts doubt on the reductionist suggestion, as mentioned above, that the military system emerged uniquely as a product of war and the battlefield.

## What was the comfort station system of military sexual slavery?

The battlefields under consideration in this book are those of the China and Pacific wars, which spanned the period 1937–1945. There is debate over the year the China War began (and also its naming), but Sandra Wilson's 2001 advice is followed.[47] The year 1937 is widely recognized as the official beginning of the comfort station system because from this year the army and navy enjoyed mainland consular support to traffic Japanese women into stations on official papers, as well as consular police support for security details at comfort stations, among other forms of assistance. Even before this immediate wartime period, though, the Russo-Japanese War of 1904–1905 was another significant time of development for military prostitution practices that were carried over into peacetime Japanese society (as described in Chapter Three), and following this the Siberian Intervention of 1918 is also identified as a turning point in the history of the system. Hayashi Hirofumi writes that Japanese consulates in Manchuria prior to the Siberian invasion held meetings with foreign ministry staff to discuss an anticipated trafficking of Japanese women into the region with the influx of troops. Significantly, the army intervened in these talks to insist no bans on the trafficking of Japanese women into the area be enacted, in spite of consular concerns that Japan's image abroad was likely to be tarnished by the traffic. The army successfully argued that the traffic should not be impeded, and undertook to supply military doctors to examine the women for venereal disease so they could be used by troops.[48] While this book does not attempt to re-periodize modern Japanese history to reflect these major turning points in the phenomenon of military prostitution, it does highlight the Taisho era (1912–1926) as a critical fermentation period for the system's development. As discussed in Chapter Two, it was during this era that the sex industry emerged as a significant commercial sector in Japanese society.

Brothels were set up and run by the Japanese military, or by auspiced pimps, brokers and traffickers, for exclusive army or navy use, for joint public and military use, or for use by military personnel together with other men approved by the military (e.g. visiting journalists, local Japanese businessmen, and local guerrilla leaders being wooed for support, or men working in military-related factories) throughout the 1937–1945 wartime period. Military brothels, called 'comfort stations' or 'comfort facilities' (*ianjo* or *ian shisetsu*), were established on Japanese soil, as well as in China, Southeast Asia, on islands in the Pacific, on the Korean Peninsula, in Taiwan, and on Okinawa. Names of specific places where comfort stations existed include: Ambon Island, Palembang, Tarakan, Sulawesi, Surabaya, Kutaraja and Pontianak in Indonesia; Guam; Mong Nai, Ping-jia, Rangoon, Mandalay and Pyin Oo Lwin in Burma; Rabaul; Hengyang, Zhuji, Shanghai, Nanjing, Wuhu, Jiujiang, Xinyang, Changsha, Nanning, Luoyang, Qinzhou, Bengbu and Changzhou in China; Kushiro, Chichi-jima and Kisarazu in Japan; Johor Bahru, Malacca City, Penang Island, Port Dickson, Kuala Lumpur and Seremban in Malaysia; Angeles, Dansalan, Cagayan, Butuan, Iloilo City, Masbate and Tacloban in the Philippines; the Nicobar Islands; Andaman Islands; Hong Kong; Singapore; Truk Islands; Kavieng and Kokopo in PNG; Ie Island, Yomitan and Tamagusuku in Okinawa; and the Kuril Islands.

The system took different forms at different times and locations during the war. Local women were abducted and singly detained in caves for prostitution by troops in China, with low-ranking men autonomously orchestrating these arrangements. Lawyer Kawaguchi Kazuko has historically documented Japanese soldiers stationed in Shanxi prefecture from 1941 setting up their own comfort stations in caves, into which Chinese women were kidnapped and held in total darkness on 'beds made of wooden planks and grass' to be serially raped by soldiers. They were allowed to leave the caves only to go to the toilet, and even this was supervised.[49] One woman was held in this situation for forty days. In the majority of cases, though, comfort stations took the form and operation of Japanese civilian brothels. An ostensible system of payment for military men buying women through the stations was enacted, including ledgers that supposedly apportioned military scrip takings to women. Also similar to civilian prostitution in Japan around the time, some stations incorporated venereal disease checks for interned women. These brothel-like stations were set up by the military directly or by commissioned or collaborating sex industry entrepreneurs, or through military commandeering of existing civilian brothels, public buildings and private houses. In June 1944, Japanese troops commandeered houses on Okinawa to use as comfort stations. They simply hung sheets from the ceilings of the houses to separate the rows of beds they had set out on which women were to be prostituted.[50] A third form of the system comprised already-trafficked comfort women being taken out of stations and re-trafficked in mobile arrangements to locations at the battlefront or distant garrisons. Korean survivor Kim Yonshil recalls being ferried back and forth once a week from her comfort station to a nearby Japanese military barracks that did not have enough women on offer for prostitution.[51] Alternatively, women were taken out of comfort stations in locations where Japanese troops had lost territory and were dragged along with them to be prostituted as the men retreated. Shirota Suzuko recalls soldiers on Truk constructing a comfort station out of lobbed timber in the forest where the men had retreated after US bombing had forced them to withdraw from a military base.[52]

Women of nationality/ethnicity backgrounds including Japanese, Korean, Taiwanese, Chinese, Filipino, Indonesian, Vietnamese, Malay, Thai, Burmese, Indian, Timorese, Chamorro, Dutch and Eurasian were trafficked into the stations. While Korean women are believed to be the majority of victims, Hayashi writes that he is 'sceptical as to whether there is any empirical basis for this assumption … although the number of Korean comfort women was large, the ratio must have been under 50 per cent … it is likely that Chinese outnumbered Koreans.'[53] While controversy still exists about the nationality background of victims, there is agreement that underage girls were in the majority. The average age of comfort station internees in the Philippines was 17.6 years,[54] and girls younger than this were commonly found in stations, including Chinese survivor Wang Aifa who was gang raped upon her arrival at a comfort station in northern China when she was fifteen years old.[55] Women were interned in stations sometimes for years on end. Korean survivor Yi Poknyo, for example, was in a comfort station in northern China for eight years.[56] Hayashi observes three methods by which women were trafficked into stations: through brokers, through requests by the Japanese military to local village heads or through direct abduction by military personnel,[57] but he omits to include the conversion of civilian brothels into military stations, which inherently entailed the spontaneous trafficking of women from civilian into military prostitution.

Hayashi in 1993 attempted to estimate the number of women trafficked into comfort stations worldwide over the years of war through calculating numbers of condoms distributed by the Japanese military to its charges. He estimates that the army gave soldiers nearly twenty condoms per year on average, but he doubts all of these were used in practice. On the other hand, he takes into account the fact soldiers bought condoms from private providers when stationed near large cities like Shanghai. He therefore adopts a conservative set of assumptions to estimate an average number of comfort station visits by troops, to then calculate the likely number of women made available. He estimates that Japanese soldiers made 32.1 million visits to stations in 1942, which meant 88,000 troops were visiting daily. There were 1.7 million Japanese troops dispatched overseas in 1942. On these figures, Hayashi estimates the number of comfort women to have been 'at least in the multiples of tens of thousands, and possibly in the multiples of hundreds of thousands'.[58] Yoshimi Yoshiaki holds the similar view that 'between fifty thousand and two hundred thousand women' were trafficked into the stations during the eight years of war.[59] While this book makes no contributing comment to this discussion about numbers of victims, it does encourage consideration of numbers at the *higher* end of estimates made by historians like the abovementioned Hayashi and Yoshimi. Its argument in this regard is that prostituted victims of the military system have been marginalized and overlooked in historical discussion to date, and the scapegoating of prostituted victims has led to their undercounting among internees of the stations, and their mostly uncomprehended status as military sexual slavery victims has potentially excluded from counting those military stations that operated in close alignment with businesses of the civilian sex industry.

## Why focus on prostituted victims of military sexual slavery?

This book was written at a time of significant transition among countries of the contemporary rich world with regards to how prostitution is understood and addressed. In legislation and policy since the 1980s, prostitution has been conceptualized in countries like Australia, New Zealand, Germany and the Netherlands as a form of work, and the sex industry as a business sector. Before this, prostitution was tackled historically by governments of industrialized countries worldwide as either a public health problem for men (with venereal disease testing of women), or a problem of female sexuality requiring punishment and exclusion (with imprisonment for prostituted women). Following this, the 'harm minimization' approach of the late 1980s was alternatively deemed an enlightened approach to policymaking that was respectful of women's right to enter 'sex work', and men's right to become consumers of 'sexual services'. However, a dramatic shift away from this approach has been occurring since 1999 when the Swedish government declared prostitution a violation of gender equality, and launched a legislative and policy scheme to outlaw the sex industry, penalise and re-educate its customers, lift legal penalties on victims, and create 'exit' programs for the recovery and social reintegration of prostitution survivors. Other countries in the first two decades of the twenty-first century have joined Sweden to institute programs of citizen, bureaucracy, police, judiciary and military education on the human rights harms of prostitution, and to introduce initiatives like 'john schools' for customers of the sex industry to learn of the harms of their behaviour.

This global dissemination of a policy framework in which prostitution is viewed as a gendered human rights violation has, in turn, fostered a nascent intellectual environment in which prostitution in a range of historical contexts has begun to be revisited and re-analysed by researchers as an abusive activity of men (rather than an individual proclivity of women), and a system of sexual violence that has historically served not only the sexual and financial interests of individual men, but also their patriarchal state building ambitions. Japanese-language history writing is ahead of English-language work in this latter field, and includes the work of scholars such as Fujino Yutaka and Shimojuu Kiyoshi. Shimojuu in 2012 published an extraordinary account of pre-war Japanese history that centrally contends the political construction of the Japanese state has relied on the organization of systems of slavery, with prostitution the specific form of slavery maintained in the modern era. He suggests that the male slave labour gangs of the feudal era were abolished in the interests of creating a politically modern form of the Japanese state, but that prostitution was retained in this transition for its politically useful outcomes for the new patriarchal polity.[60] A similarly enlightened shift in historical research on the comfort station system that is newly coloured by principles of feminist abolitionism is beginning to emerge, with feminist historians attached to the Violence Against

Women in War Research Action Center (VAWW-RAC) in Tokyo commencing a groundbreaking programme of inquiry in recent years into the history of the Japanese comfort women, including prostituted women, the comfort station network developed on Japanese soil and the history of stations on Okinawa.

Shifts in policymaking and thinking on prostitution are occurring internationally at the same time the 'justice for comfort women' redress movement is strengthening and expanding, particularly in South Korea, but also in Japan, Taiwan and China. Concurrently, international efforts to propel the Japanese government towards action and reparation for historical crimes of military sexual slavery are escalating. This movement has been active since 1990, but the recent Japanese government swing to the political right and the diplomatic problems this has caused with South Korea and China means the history of the comfort women now, more than any time since the end of the war, generates international attention and tension. For the first time, in 2014, the US congress passed a spending bill that requires the Secretary of State to follow up with the Japanese government matters contained in a 2007 resolution that called for Japan to take responsibility for the history of the comfort women.[61] Also for the first time, in 2014, a US state government building hosted the erection of a statue commemorating the comfort women on its own grounds. Further in 2014, the South Korean Ministry for Gender Equality and Family commenced an application to UNESCO to list historical documents on the comfort station system with the Memory of the World Register, and the Chinese government later joined Korea in this application.[62]

## Contemporary comfort women

These two international developments in the twenty-first century: strengthening ideas about peacetime prostitution as a gendered human rights violation, and escalating foreign government and civil society action against the Japanese government in pursuit of justice for comfort station survivors, particularly in South Korea, have the potential to collide in relation to an issue of civilian sexual slavery that continues to grow in contemporary Japan. Over the past decade, an increasing number of South Korean women have been trafficked into Japan's sex industry, and there are an estimated 50,000 prostituted Korean women in Japan today.[63] Japanese far right extremist groups target these women in their campaigns to encourage an exodus of Koreans from Japan.[64] The history of the comfort station system makes this contemporary traffic an issue of potential diplomatic friction, especially given the efforts of the South Korean government to approach prostitution from a human rights perspective domestically since 2004, which is a policy approach the Japanese government currently resists even considering.

Japan has not yet ratified the United Nations instrument against prostitution, the Palermo Protocol, and the US non-government organization Shared Hope International speculates Japan may be the 'largest market for commercial sex in the world among developed countries'. It estimates that the country's 'sex industry accounts for one ... to three percent of [its] gross national product (GNP), [which is] an amount equal to Japan's defense budget'.[65] The Japanese government has been criticized internationally for its intransigence in taking action on trafficking. The US Department of State in 2004 put Japan on its 'human-trafficking watchlist', and later in 2009 described Japan as a country where '[w]omen and children from East Asia, Southeast Asia, Eastern Europe, Russia, South America, and Latin America are trafficked ... for commercial sexual exploitation'.[66] The Department further criticized Japan in its 2009 *Trafficking in persons report* for having 'conducted periodic police raids of prostitution establishments, including some raids on Internet-based forms of commercial sex', but not having made 'any other efforts to reduce the demand for commercial sex acts' in the previous year. Sex industrialists from South Korea continue to see Japan as a commercially desirable operating environment, and Japan's policy and business environment is a pull-factor for the ongoing trafficking of Korean women across the East Sea by Japanese organized crime groups.

Campaigning has not yet emerged over the issue of Korean sex trafficking, but international policy and legislative developments towards feminist abolitionism, combined with strong South Korean government and civil society efforts towards justice for comfort station survivors, establishes a unique backdrop of ideas and activism that could make such a campaign possible. It is the aim of this book to encourage the combining of these kinds of ideas, so that contemporary forms of civilian sexual slavery might be framed and pursued in the same sympathetic and successful way as has occurred since the 1990s for some groups of military comfort women. Unfortunately, to date, there has been almost no cultivation of an intellectual or activist environment that would allow connections between military and civilian forms of prostitution to be made and acted upon for the purpose of bringing about social change. To date, the historical experiences of comfort station survivors have been all but quarantined from abolitionist organizing against civilian prostitution in both the past and the present, as if these experiences were not those of prostitution. While this approach might well have paved the way for some of the achievements of the justice campaign since the 1990s, we might question the extent of the campaign's success when, in reality, prostituted survivors of comfort stations, as well as contemporary Korean victims of Japan's sex industry, are mostly unable to share its benefits in terms of sympathy or restitution for their mostly identically endured experiences of sexual slavery. The next chapter examines why the 'justice for comfort women' campaign excludes prostituted victims, and what implications this exclusion has for efforts towards redress for military and wartime crimes of sexual slavery against women and girls, in the past, present as well as the future.

# Scapegoat Survivors: Japanese Comfort Women and the Contemporary Justice Movement

There are no exceptions. There are no exceptions for men, who are privileged, to invade. And there are no exceptions for women – which is to say: 'Oh yes, you mustn't do it to *that* woman. But do you see her over there? … Yeah, it's okay. Do it to her. Nobody will miss her'. We miss her! We want her back![1]

Survivors of comfort stations who were prostituted before their internment in the military system are a uniquely identifiable category of victims. They are identifiable not just in terms of being frequently described as having Japanese nationality, but also in the way they feature in contemporary campaigns for and against 'justice for comfort women', and also in the historical literature. Their rhetorical status within this contemporary campaigning and the historical literature in fact places prostituted women outside the category of sexual slavery victim. In this discourse, they are imagined to have experienced wartime military prostitution as something other than sexual slavery, and as having entered comfort stations as something other than victims.

In centrally observing this fact, this chapter offers an explanation for why the rest of the book's history of the Japanese military's sexual slavery system of the China and Pacific wars looks so different from existing scholarship in either English or Japanese. Overall, it composes an argument for why revisiting this scholarship for its sidelining of information about prostituted women and civilian prostitution is important if we are to apprehend a more historically accurate picture of the wartime system. Its contention is that the exclusion of prostituted victims in contemporary campaigning and historical writing has fundamentally skewed analyses developed since the 1990s of the wartime system and its origins. The absence of prostituted women and their unique historical experience has shielded from historical view the sex industry, its infrastructure and entrepreneurs and, most importantly, the Japanese military's reliance on systems of civilian prostitution in developing its wartime scheme. As a result, the chapter contends, analyses of the origins and causes of the system are distorted, and obstruct progress being made towards justice and restitution for *all* survivors.

When prostituted victims are mentioned in contemporary campaigning, they are usually cited by right-wing defenders of the Japanese military in evidence of an argument that comfort stations operated as privately-run venues hosting women working willingly and profitably, and should therefore attract no special attention as historical sites of official wrongdoing. In this vein, high profile political candidate and ex-military man Tamogami Toshio recently claimed that '[c]omfort women are called sex slaves but that's a lie, they were prostitutes and received about the same salary as generals and admirals'.[2] In his view, military prostitution was historically organized using women sourced from the civilian sex industry and therefore amounts to no particular human rights violation. In fact, to the extent it was similar to the civilian prostitution of the time, it is excusable and understandable, given that the prostitution of women in peacetime Japan had already established a standard for socially acceptable male sexual behaviour, and a standard for female 'employment'.

This standard is unimpeachable even when it involves women being trafficked, in historian Hata Ikuhiko's view, which relies upon a belief that prostitution visits upon women no harm greater than that encountered by sportsmen: 'Suppose we categorize young women whose parents sold them to brokers as victims of coercion. Aren't professional baseball players who are paid advances and then traded to another team whether they like it or not also victims of coercion?'[3] Justifications like these for military prostitution on the basis of other existing systems of civilian prostitution and trafficking, however dubious, are popular in right-wing discourse, and the wartime prostitution systems of men of other nationalities are cited in the same rubric. The head of Japan's national broadcaster NHK at his inaugural press conference in 2014 defended the wartime system for the reason that military prostitution is 'common in any country at war'.[4] Most frequently, though, the legalized prostitution system that operated in Japan before the war is the historical standard used to justify the wartime system, as exemplified in Matsumura Masahiro's uncritical claim that 'the women were in fact the wartime version of state-regulated prostitutes ...'.[5] Ultimately, in right-wing terms, the existence of civilian prostituted internees of comfort stations justifies the wartime system as a legitimate extension of Japanese men's peacetime sexual entitlements.

This argument of conservative commentators that women freely chose internment in wartime comfort stations is well known,[6] but less recognized is its shared basis among some arguments advanced by progressive advocates of the contemporary 'justice for comfort women' movement. A liberal idea of freely chosen prostitution pervades and distorts even critical historical accounts of the wartime system, and has continued to do so since the emergence of the movement in the early 1990s. In the understanding of both progressives and conservatives, women were organized for prostitution through comfort stations that operated legitimately as venues where military men could buy women for sex. The system itself is understood by neither camp to comprise the true crime of military sexual slavery; rather, instances of its excesses, such as the military's abduction of underage girls or its tying of women to beds, are seen by progressives as objectionable for their enacting of the sexual enslavement of individuals. To reiterate, these specific instances, *rather than the system itself,* are problematized under the banner of 'military sexual slavery'. Indicating this fact is the near failure of progressives to raise any objection to the military's historical trafficking of women prostituted in the civilian sex industry into comfort stations. This scapegoating of prostituted comfort station victims is exercised even by 'justice for comfort women' activists, particularly in literature produced in the early years of the movement. Yasuhara Keiko, for example, in 1992 wrote that

> [i]n around 1937 the sex industry was a major source of comfort women. Among women in the sex industry, entry into comfort stations was seen as fairly profitable and so there were a lot of takers. These women were able to repay advanced credit in just six months, plus have enough leftover to leave prostitution and start up other businesses. Here I want to highlight the fact that women from the sex industry were able to save an amount of money and get out of the comfort stations quickly. Alternatively, they chose to enter comfort stations in order that they could get out of civilian prostitution more quickly.[7]

Progressives like Yasuhara are unconcerned in equal measure to their conservative foe about prostituted women, and this fact reveals the military scheme itself *not* to be the entity animating their critique of Japanese wartime sexual slavery.

Historian Nishino Rumiko has noted this commonality inhabiting the approaches of progressive and conservative commentators, and lists specifically four ways in which prostituted victims of comfort stations are thereby falsely distinguished from other victims. She sees the following biases as distorting research and advocacy on behalf of Japanese survivors in particular:

1. Most were from the sex industry, and are therefore not seen as victims of the system.
2. Prostituted women are seen as fundamentally different from unmarried virgins in terms of their experience of the system.

3. Japanese women are seen as having been treated better than women of other nationalities in terms of the loans that were advanced to their families or former pimps, the shorter duration of their contracts … their reduced exposure to violence because of exclusive use by officers, their airlifting at the end of war, etc.

4. Japanese women are seen as having enjoyed special personal affinity with soldiers and military men as a result of their shared nationality, and also because of a shared subscription to nationalistic/militaristic concepts like 'sacrifice for the sake of country', and hopes of internment with soldiers at Yasukuni Shrine in the event of death in war.[8]

This chapter describes and critiques these kinds of views of prostituted comfort station victims as serving to falsely construct and denigrate one group of survivors in efforts to plead the case of others. The arguments of conservatives are already well known, but less known is the adherence of some progressive advocates to notions falsely distinguishing prostituted and non-prostituted comfort station victims. The justice campaigning of progressive advocates is seen as a heroic and successful in having secured international sympathy and restitution for survivors, but I see it as having been waged on the basis of an understanding of the military system ultimately identical to that of conservative opponents. This is a fatally flawed approach that renders the justice campaign in need of significant renovation.

## Scapegoating as a methodological framework

Methodologically, I critique this situation as manifesting the 'scapegoating' that Andrea Dworkin wrote about at length in 2000, and which is foreshadowed in her quote from 1991 at the beginning of the chapter. Dworkinian scapegoating involves pleading the deservedness of victims of military violence for sympathy and restitution specifically at the expense of prostituted women. She developed this analysis in a book-length discussion of the experiences of prostituted women, particularly Jewish women, in the second European war, and the significance of their experiences to understanding how despised populations are socially created for the purpose of physical destruction. She observed that

> [p]rostitutes are a big part of the Nazi story: not just because Hitler used them rhetorically as social scapegoats but also because the Nazis both bodily used and punished them … Hitler tried to make Jews as foul and expendable as prostitutes already were, as inhuman as prostitutes were already taken to be …. The brothels they created embodied a sexual fascism in which prostitutes were

lower than Jews; and certainly male Jews agreed. There was no solidarity with Jewish prostitutes before, during or after the Holocaust.[9]

This book is the first attempt to apply Dworkin's thesis to another instance of military prostitution, but it is a thesis not without providence in feminism. It was explored at length by Margaret Baldwin in 1992, if in terms not specifically addressing militarism. Baldwin sought to explain the exclusion of prostituted women from feminist analyses in respect of the fact '[o]ur reform campaigns have little contributed little [*sic*] to the security or visibility of women in prostitution; indeed, they have been hostile to them'.[10] She observed that feminist haste to critique the social construction of women as 'sluts' and 'whores' had resulted in a disavowal of prostitution that not only marginalized and excluded victims, but exploited them in efforts to shield women from other categories of male sexual violence:

> The story that no one is a prostitute, recited with utmost conviction, or with the passion of a final plea for help and justice. And perhaps that is the story that is the prostitution story itself: a woman declaring, with equal parts conviction and resignation, that she is not a prostitute, to please somebody else upon whom her survival depends.[11]

Baldwin sees this 'disengagement tactic' as a 'great mistake' because it involves feminists making a 'profound bargain' on behalf of women. The bargain means that 'possibilities for change afforded some women ... will always be at the price of abandoning prostitutes, of gaining your advantage at her expense'.[12] She condemns it in the bluntest of terms:

> There is a term for women who accept bargains like that. It's called being a pimp's 'bottom woman', the one who treasures his highest regard, and sometimes gets off the street herself, but only if she helps run the less lucky girls. There is also a term for the arrangement which makes this bargain compelling. It's called pimping, period.[13]

Grounded in Dworkin and Baldwin's theoretical insights, the book challenges the 'pimping' of some comfort women so that others might 'gain advantage at her expense' that has characterized discussion of the wartime system to date. Morita Seiya began this task in 1999, and the chapter's analysis builds on his expert assessment more than a decade ago that

> [t]he commonality between conservative and liberal views of the comfort women system does not end with similar rhetorical constructions. They both fundamentally take a perspective that attempts to legitimise the activity of

men who use women for prostitution … it is the means by which the Japanese military conducted the comfort station system, rather than the existence of the system, that is problematised. … 'force' is conceived of very narrowly and, in the absence of this 'force', libertarians … see free will and choice. Right wing conservative commentators … use exactly the same argument. In the absence of a very narrowly defined idea of 'force', conservative commentators see free will and choice, and therefore no harm or problem.[14]

Driving this convergence of liberal and conservative analyses, I argue below, was the coincident emergence of the 'sex worker rights' movement around the time of the building of the justice campaign in the 1990s, which encouraged a view of prostituted victims as having willingly chosen their fate. Since this time, intensifying vilification of comfort station survivors by Japanese right-wing groups on the basis of their assumed prostituted status has caused progressive advocates to rush to respond with arguments emphasizing the non-prostituted status of 'real' victims. These victims were 'Asian' rather than Japanese in historian Yuki Tanaka's view, for example: 'Comfort stations for the exclusive use of officer-class men were often established in large cities. Most of the comfort women in these stations were Japanese. It seems that these Japanese women experienced much better conditions than other Asian comfort women.'[15] This kind of rhetoric, I argue, causes an ongoing purge of prostituted victims from the justice movement, and renders Japanese women mostly invisible as a significant population of comfort station internees.

## The abolitionist history of the 'justice for comfort women' movement

It is perhaps surprising that the contemporary 'justice for comfort women' movement does not appear to have a strong historical connection to abolitionist campaigning, feminist or otherwise. This might seem to be unusual for a movement seeking redress for crimes of military prostitution, especially given that other post-war social movements in Asia have emerged precisely on the basis of opposition to prostitution, and in solidarity with survivors. Katharine Moon describes South Korea's post-war anti-military movement, for example, as initially coalescing around opposition to US army men prostituting local women and girls:

> Although the violence and suffering endured by Korean women who sexually service American servicemen are not the sole causes of the anti-troop movement in Korea, these women's lives and deaths have captured the public's attention

and galvanized collective outrage against both real and perceived U.S. military abuses of power and privilege in their host country.[16]

As Moon describes, the murder of a camptown (i.e. military base) prostituted woman in 1992 sparked the development of an anti-military social movement in the country. This was not the earliest example of social mobilization against prostitution in post-war Korea, moreover. In 1973, feminist and Christian campaigners organized protest action against the corporate sex tourism of Japanese men, known popularly at the time as 'kisaeng' tourism.[17] As Matsui Yayori describes, these campaigners

> demonstrated against Japanese arriving on *kisaeng* tours at Seoul's Kimpo airport … Almost simultaneously, the proceedings of the 'Citizens Committee to Abolish *Kisaeng* Tours' held in Seoul was broadcast on Japanese television.[18]

The cause was then taken up by Japanese campaigners and, as Matsui further describes,

> [i]n December 1973, the 'Women's Group Opposing *Kisaeng* Tourism' was established in Tokyo … Japanese women demonstrated at Tokyo's Haneda airport on Christmas day. About 50 women – students, housewives, and workers of all ages – confronted the Japanese male tourists leaving on *kisaeng* tours with leaflets and with slogans painted on their vests …[19]

This cross-country campaign against the sex tourism of Japanese men was sustained for a number of years on the Korean side, even amidst the violent military dictatorships of the 1970s and 1980s. With the easing of this political environment, and in the lead-up to the summer Olympic Games in Seoul, it culminated in an international conference held on Cheju Island in April 1988 on the topic of 'women and tourism' organized by Korean Church Women United. This group had been involved in anti-*kisaeng* tourism campaigning for a number of years. The conference was attended by around 120 women from Japan, the United States, the UK and other countries, as well members of the important socialist-feminist coalition, Korean Women's Associations United. This step forward in campaigning against *kisaeng* tourism was supported by anti-prostitution activism occurring elsewhere in Asia at the time, and especially in the Philippines and Okinawa. In July 1988, for example, an international conference on the topic of camptown prostitution was held in Naha, after abolitionist campaigning had experienced a resurgence on the island in connection with protest action against US militarism and the de facto military occupation of Okinawa.[20]

The Cheju conference was an important historical moment in the development of the 'justice for comfort women' movement in Korea, and the movement's abolitionist origins might be traced to it, even if they be only weak. According to Bang-Soon Yoon, the conference produced 'limited but somewhat positive political rewards to the comfort women survivors'.[21] These rewards came primarily from the efforts of two women: sociologist Lee Hyun Sook, who declared at the conference that 'Japanese tourists join[ing] with the gisaeng gwangwang [i.e. *kisaeng* tourism] for sex are descendants of the colonial era militarists who hunted for jungshindae [comfort women]',[22] and Ewha University professor Yun Chung-ok, who presented the first ever research report on the comfort women issue in which she described *kisaeng* sex tourism as a form of 'neo-jungshindae'.[23] Yun had been travelling to Thailand, PNG and Japan to interview former Korean internees of comfort stations since the early 1980s. The conference led to the creation of a 'jungshindae research unit' within Korean Church Women United in July 1988, which worked towards the creation of the Korean Council for Women Drafted for Sexual Service by Japan in November 1990 encompassing eighteen social and women's organizations. These groups spearheaded the global 'justice for comfort women' movement thereafter, which was based in Korea, but which spread to Japan, the United States and countries in Southeast Asia. Another direct outcome of the Cheju conference was the launch in 1992 of the Asian Women in Solidarity for 'Comfort Women' group.[24]

While Japanese research and activist groups, including the Japan Resource Centre for War Responsibility and the (formerly named) Violence Against Women in War Network Japan, quickly and diligently took up the cause of comfort station survivors immediately thereafter, the development of the justice movement in Japan might be distinguished from that of South Korea in respect to the movement's mobilization in support of foreign (mostly Korean) victims, and not local women. Illustrative of this fact is comments like the following from Suzuki Hiroko who, as early as 1989, declared that,

> [w]hen the Japanese military began its large-scale manoeuvres in Manchuria, it was the munitions and sex industries that jumped for joy. But the women the sex industrialists offered up to the Japanese military as prostitutes were young Korean women. Japanese women were considered to be flowers of the nation, and associated with the families and relatives of serving men. And so it was thought that conscripting them would reduce the morale of troops, and so the recruitment of Japanese women was limited to women in the sex industry.[25]

By the 1990s, when the justice movement began to develop on the ground in Japan, therefore, a culture of denial and hostility had already developed in the country towards local survivors; this history stretched back to the time of anti-*kisaeng* tourism campaigning.

Perhaps differently from the situation in South Korea, information and public comment about the comfort station system and its victims circulated relatively plentifully in Japan in the 1970s by the time of the *kisaeng* campaign. Some of this discourse was supportive of prostituted victims: in 1973, campaigners like Takahashi Kikue, as the head of the Japan Anti-Prostitution Association, raised the history of the wartime system in critical analogy to *kisaeng* tourism, and edited a comprehensive volume on the topic that included Korean as well as Japanese writers.[26] There was also the publication in 1971 of Shirota Suzuko's biography. However, most of the Japanese-language media reports, academic books, novels and biographies that emerged in the 1970s and 1980s, including Kim Il Myon's history volume of 1976 and numerous memoirs by war veterans, were unsympathetic to (prostituted) Japanese victims. This discourse created an atmosphere that was dismissive of local survivors, and a tendency among advocates to object only to harms additional to prostitution, such as the abduction of women, lost 'virginity', physical violence and infertility. Perhaps even more so than in Korea, therefore, the justice movement developed in Japan with only a weak abolitionist foundation, and a penchant for condemning the wartime comfort station system for reasons additional to its organization of women for prostitution.

Kinoshita Naoko writes that even radical feminists failed to take up the cause of local comfort station survivors in Japan in the 1970s around the time of the anti-*kisaeng* tourism campaign, even if they did respond to information about the history of the wartime system in a 'highly sympathetic way'. According to Kinoshita, they 'expressed no apparent awareness or sympathy about Japanese victims of the system', and instead 'identified victims solely as Korean wives and daughters'. Feminists appear to have believed Japanese comfort women had thought themselves superior to Korean comfort women during the war, and that Japanese victims had known what they were signing up for (and were therefore undeserving victims).[27] Its misogyny notwithstanding, Kinoshita concedes that this response is likely to have been heavily influenced by media reporting of the comfort women issue in the early 1970s, which was significantly biased towards the view that 'Japanese women were agents of their own prostitution through the comfort stations, rather than victims of sexual violence'.[28] Popular media in the early 1970s differentiated sharply between Japanese 'prostitutes' and Korean 'virgins', and described Japanese women as having been 'riddled with venereal disease'.[29] Pornographic accounts of the experiences of Japanese survivors also emerged in the late 1970s.[30] Kinoshita makes the point that even Japanese survivors themselves at this time might have been inhibited in coming forward because of the salaciousness of these accounts, and also because of the (mis)perception that, compared to the heinous treatment meted out to Korean victims, their experience had been relatively non-traumatic, and so publicly declaring themselves survivors would have been an act of disrespect.[31]

While 1970s anti-*kisaeng* tourism campaigning eventually contributed to the development of a justice movement in Korea after the 1988 Cheju conference, therefore, the movement that developed in Japan in the 1990s emerged in an environment of hostility towards Japanese survivors created by popular media reporting over a number of prior decades. Prominent historians, such as Nishino Rumiko, Fujino Yutaka, Ikeda Eriko and Onozawa Akane, today question how the current situation came to arise in Japan whereby prostituted victims, especially Japanese victims, are largely excluded from justice campaigning efforts.[32] Nishino writes, for example:

> For a long time, Japanese comfort women have skirted the edges of people's concern over the issue. We can say this represents the denial of harm inflicted on Japanese victims of the comfort women system, and we might question why this has been the case.[33]

Further, Onozawa Akane questions why this state of affairs appears to have worsened in recent times:

> Now, more than ever, the claim that Japanese women were 'prostitutes' who chose to become comfort women, and so do not warrant concern, is trumpeted loudly and defiantly. We might wonder why this is occurring, and question the underlying cause of such evident low-level comprehension of human rights in Japan.[34]

We might point to the weak abolitionist origins of the justice movement in Japan in possible answer to these questions. The near absence of an anti-prostitution perspective in the historical development of the movement rendered progressive advocates in Japan ill-equipped in the twenty-first century to respond to the escalating claims of right-wing opponents that comfort station survivors were 'merely' prostitutes and therefore unwarranted objects of concern. Responses to claims of this kind have unfortunately demonstrated hallmarks of Dworkin's scapegoat thesis, and Hirai Kazuko has remarked upon one outcome of this: 'The reason we have now a fixed model of a "comfort woman" is precisely because we haven't properly taken the time to listen to the experiences of Japanese survivors of the system'.[35] Examples of arguments from progressive historians and activists adhering to falsely drawn distinctions between prostituted and non-prostituted victims are recounted further below, and shown to be similar to typical right-wing articulations of the wartime system.

## Prostituted victims in the rhetoric of right-wing defenders of the Japanese military

Among right-wing views of the comfort station system, the most well known at the time of writing are those of the mayor of Osaka and co-leader of the Japan Restoration Party, Hashimoto Toru. He claimed in 2013 that, '[w]hen soldiers are risking their lives by running through storms of bullets, and you want to give these emotionally charged soldiers a rest somewhere, it's clear that you need a comfort women system'.[36] In this comment Hashimoto appears to subscribe to a notion of environmental stress as causing men to require 'rest' in the form of organized sexual access to women, and this access as achieving some kind of institutional benefit, given the alleged fact that '[a]ll militaries have needed to establish mechanisms to relieve the sexual energy of troops'.[37] Accordingly, Hashimoto recommends that US troops stationed on Okinawa in the present day avail themselves of the local sex industry, because this would 'reduce the incidence of sexual crimes against local women'.[38] He made this remark after visiting Futenma air base on Okinawa where US troops are stationed, where he criticized the US military command for inadequately controlling the 'sexual energy' of its marines. In a face-to-face meeting with a commanding officer, he urged the United States to drop its 'political correctness' (*kenzenron*) on prostitution, and loosen up about its troops frequenting the sex industry: 'No problems will be solved in this world if everyone hides behind political correctness'.[39] The 'political correctness' Hashimoto refers to is likely to be the official policy of the US military from November 2005 to bar its troops from buying women for prostitution wherever they are in the world, even if the sex industry in the location they are visiting or stationed is legalized. Through internet-based social media Hashimoto followed up his visit to Okinawa with the opinion that the US ban 'discriminated against women who exercised free choice in being in the sex industry'.[40] The view Hashimoto promotes of prostitution is therefore wholly positive – he sees benefits accruing to both perpetrators and victims of sexual exploitation, and particularly in the case of camptown prostitution. At the base of his views is a notion of sexual access to women as a male human right, including in situations like war where groups of men live largely segregated from female populations. While Hashimoto couches his comments in rhetoric about male 'sexual energy', at the core of his argument is a belief that institutions like the military have a responsibility to men to organize women for sexual access, whether through direct means like military-established comfort stations during war, or indirect means like permitting troop patronage of civilian sex industry venues during base deployment or occupation.

Hashimoto's comments are generally representative of right-wing defences of the wartime prostitution system in their reliance on ideas about women's inherent suitability and enthusiasm for sexual servitude.[41] His views are unusual only to the extent they link the wartime system with contemporary civilian prostitution (albeit the sex industry catering to the military), which is a slant perhaps arising from Hashimoto's background as a lawyer formerly representing the Osaka adult entertainment industry association, which possibly makes him unusually alert to an understanding of military prostitution as an extension of the peacetime sex industry.[42] While most right-wing comment on the history of the wartime prostitution system draws less direct connection to contemporary civilian prostitution, Hashimoto's views are typical of those of conservative commentators who attribute the wartime system to the commercial enterprise of private entrepreneurs, and the profit-seeking motivations of their prostituted internees. The view of right-leaning public figures, as well as conservative historians, is one of prostitution as an entitlement of men. This view is characterized as a 'perpetrator' perspective of the wartime slavery system by Nishino Rumiko who writes that

> [t]o judge individual victimhood according to whether or not a woman had been formerly prostituted or whether money was a consideration in her entry into a comfort station is to adopt a perpetrator perspective, and to employ a criteria that suits the interests of those responsible for the comfort women system.[43]

Right-wing defences of the Japanese military and its historical comfort station system exert significant influence on contemporary Japanese society and the campaigning of justice advocates. In recent years, advocates have been forced to repeatedly respond to right-wing activism, including events like the following in 2012 described by Tessa Morris-Suzuki:

> In response to mayor Hashimoto's Twitter comments on the 'comfort women' issue, Osaka citizens invited an 86-year-old Korean former 'comfort woman', Kim Bok-Dong, to speak to a public meeting about her experiences. The

meeting took place without incident, despite (in the words of a friend of mine who attended) the presence of 'quite a few "nasty" looking men … standing near the main door of the building making dreadful stares at people who attempted to enter'. A small number of police were also in attendance outside the meeting hall.

It was not until more than four months after the gathering (and almost two months after Japan's general election) that a member of the Zaitokukai filed a complaint with the police, claiming that he had been 'assaulted' by supporters of the 'comfort women' … who had denied him access to the September 2012 meeting. Despite the delay, police took up the case with alacrity, descending on the houses and offices of 'comfort women' supporters to search their premises for incriminating evidence, and even conducting a search of a cafe where the support group holds informal meetings.[44]

Advocates have had their time and energy taken up not just by these kinds of activities by right-wing agitators, but also by the contrivances of the currently conservative Japanese state, such as a report released in 2014 by the Study Team on the Details Leading to the Drafting of the Kono Statement etc., which was convened by the Abe Shinzou-led government to 'review … the process in which the Kono statement was issued by the administration of Prime Minister Kiichi Miyazawa'.[45] This 'study team' published a 'review' of the diplomatic negotiations that preceded the release of the Kono statement in 1993, which expressed apology and a degree of official culpability for the history of wartime military prostitution. The study team included Hata Ikuhiko, and rhetorically aimed to chastise the South Korean government, which had begun to escalate its international activism in criticism of the Japanese government's inadequate response to the history of the comfort women. It did this by publishing details of the negotiations between the two governments that preceded the release of the Kono statement because, as the study team asserts in the report introduction, 'the good intentions of the Government of Japan at that time are not being recognized'.[46] It had been mutually agreed between the two governments at the time of the statement's release that these negotiations would be kept secret.

These two examples of right-wing advocacy are just a couple among many of recent years, and represent some of the organized backlash currently taking place against modest gains made on behalf of comfort station victims over the past twenty-five years. They are obscene in their disregard for survivors in their dwindling years of life, and their harmfulness to victims and their advocates worldwide cannot be overstated. However, as the next section contends, a political environment permissive of this kind of anti-survivor propaganda and activism has been allowed to grow in Japan as a result of progressive advocates disavowing prostituted victims, in my view. Nishino observes this problematical political situation in her comment that right-wing defenders of the comfort station system

> have continually used the argument to evade responsibility for the system that the women used were prostitutes who commercially benefited from arrangements. We [i.e. progressive advocates] have responded to this rhetoric rigidly with the argument that the women were forced, and were not commercially involved. But this argument has its limits. It begs questions as to whether the payment of money to women in comfort stations made it a commercial activity, and whether the internment of formerly prostituted women in comfort stations made their operation unproblematic.[47]

The next section describes an example of the left-wing 'rigid rhetoric' that Nishino critiques, and notes features making it identical to the scapegoating tactics of opponents.

## Progressive scapegoating of prostituted victims of the wartime system

Most contemporary advocates of the justice movement fail to adopt an abolitionist stance in their defence of comfort station survivors, even when this means their arguments take on the rhetorical hues of those of right-wing proponents. Progressive advocates insist on the slavery of the wartime system through highlighting features of the system that supposedly differentiate it from civilian prostitution. As Morita notes, they critique the wartime system only to the extent it did not follow standards set down by civilian prostitution. In his words, 'the arguments of the sexual liberals leave no basis for fundamentally challenging the basis of the comfort women system. They only leave room for challenging the way the system was operated'.[48] Chunghee Sarah Soh's writing perhaps most clearly and frequently exhibits this tendency, and her work is recited here as representative of the types of arguments progressive advocates use to distinguish deserving from undeserving victims, both in Japan and elsewhere. Her opinions are notable because of the abundance of her writing on the topic, and her stature as a major academic contributor to the field. She describes herself as an 'expatriate anthropologist affiliated with an academic institution in the United States'[49] originally from South Korea. Soh has published a 350-page book on the issue, plus over a dozen journal articles and book chapters. Her writing exerts great influence over the academic field in English, Japanese and Korean, and is cited widely and frequently as authoritative opinion on the topic. Her views as described below, however, are significantly marked by Dworkinian scapegoating in my opinion.

In her work since the 1990s, Soh has repeatedly articulated the view that prostituted women are lesser victims of the wartime system, and she refers to Japanese prostituted women specifically. Soh coins the phrase 'concessionary types of *ianjo* [comfort station]' to articulate a belief in the graduated nature of the harms experienced by women according to the 'type' of station in which they were interned. Further, she claims that 'the degree of sexual violence and abuse the comfort women suffered varied with geographical and chronological factors as well as with the ethnicity of individual women'. In Soh's analysis, it is the 'lack of autonomy' experienced by non-prostituted 'comfort women', and the 'certain amount of choice' exercised by prostituted women, that establishes a 'fundamental difference between "comfort women" as sexual slaves and prostitutes as sex workers'.[50] As such, she asserts, 'the lives of the "military comfort women" should be conceived of as sexual slavery ... not as prostitution'.[51] The prostituted women she refers to are mostly understood as having Japanese nationality, as indicated in her remark that '... Japanese women enjoyed greater earning power and better living conditions than the other women'. The receipt of money is deemed to further distinguish the two categories of victims in respect of the alleged fact that 'comfort women did not receive payment for soldiers' use of their bodies, [and so] their experience is different from those of 'prostitutes [who in contrast are] engaged in "business"'. In sum, therefore, according to Soh, '... the experiences of these women [comfort women] varied greatly and cannot simply be reduced to victimization and exploitation in total'.[52]

Soh has a view of prostitution that prior experience can obviate victimization and exploitation, as illustrated in her comment that 'women's experience of the comfort stations as being either good or bad would have been heavily influenced by the individual woman's past experiences and her personal sensitivity'.[53] We might understand the phrase 'past experiences' to mean a woman's past experience of being prostituted; in other words, as having been trafficked into a comfort station from a brothel. Soh offers no explanation as to how a woman's experience of prostitution in a comfort station might have been less intolerable as a result of prior prostitution in a brothel, and contemporary social science research suggests that women in fact endure prostitution as an experience of *cumulative* harm, with ever-worsening social, mental and health outcomes.[54] Soh's contention throughout her body of work is nonetheless that we can condemn the military system only in relative terms, and judgements as to the human rights violation of the system must first account for a victim's prior prostituted status or 'personal sensitivity'.

Soh seeks to differentiate not just the experiences of comfort station internees, moreover, but also those of the military men who prostituted them. She states her 'purpose' in writing her 2008 monograph was to

> complicate the prevailing simplistic images by contrasting specific individual cases, which add glimpses of shared humanity between Korean comfort women and Japanese soldiers, and confounding the stereotyped portrayal of violent military hypermasculine sexuality in the dominant story.[55]

The 'dominant story' Soh seeks to challenge is that of Japanese military men being unqualifiedly criminal in their prostitution of women through comfort stations. In other words, as not necessarily individually culpable for supporting and perpetuating a system of wartime sexual slavery. She offers the usual historical apologia for Japanese troops that they were bullied by comrades into prostituting women, but goes further than most historians in additionally proposing a humanitarian basis to their sexual use of women in comfort stations:

> Some young soldiers apparently adopted a more positive outlook on their officially approved access to public sex at comfort stations. They seem to have tried to uphold their personal dignity by self-consciously engaging in sexual relations with comfort women as fellow human beings ...[56]

Soh concerns herself with the 'personal dignity' not of comfort station internees but the men who prostituted them, but does not explain how these men might have been able to prostitute women while 'self-consciously' engaging with them as human beings. In constructing this narrative, Soh appears not to see prostitution as inimical to the treatment of women as valuable individual persons. Her understanding of prostitution's harm is apparently relative, and dependant on the kind of 'outlook' men bring to the situation. Morita critiques this kind of analysis in the following terms:

> No matter how oppressive the Japanese military was compared to other militaries in the world at the time, and no matter how debased soldiers became within the violence of the military machine, the extremity of the sexual violence inflicted on women in the warzone, and on comfort women, and the fact these crimes were accepted with such tolerance at the time, is testament only to the nature of the surrounding environment that gave rise to them.[57]

Soh's assertion that soldiers treated women in comfort stations as erstwhile girlfriends is found in right-wing comment on the wartime system, as are many of her arguments, in my view. In particular, her reflection that she can 'imagine how individual soldiers might have relied on comfort women to fulfil their needs and desires for the customary kind of care work – sexual and otherwise – that women provided and of which men were deprived during long military campaigns far from home'[58] echoes sentiments expressed by right-wing advocates like Hashimoto Toru that the organization of women in comfort stations was necessary to the wellbeing of troops in battle. That sexual access to women is a right, of which men might be 'deprived' (i.e. wrongfully have taken away), is a view further revealing of Soh's fundamentally similar take on sexual politics to her conservative opponents. Her apparent belief in male sexual entitlement is exactly the frame of mind that disallows men like Hashimoto comprehending objections to the military prostitution of women. Soh introduces no critical perspective on these kinds of beliefs in sexual access to women as a necessary component of male health and vitality, despite this idea being premised on an essentialistic notion of male sexuality as needing female outlet. We might expect progressive historians like Soh who purportedly adopt a feminist stance in their work to alternatively advance a socially constructivist view of human sexuality as relational and contextualized, rather than hydraulic and indiscriminate.

Soh's opinions about the comfort station system appear to have received no critical attention before now, despite their exceeding similarity to arguments made by another scholar who attracts significant criticism from both Korean as well as Japanese academics and activists, including in the form of calls for her book to be pulped. Yuha Park's 2013 Korean-language monograph published in Japanese in 2014 advances almost exactly the same thesis as pursued by Soh: that there existed different 'types' of comfort stations, the experience of victims was not uniform, and so the wartime prostitution scheme cannot be universally condemned. Continuing the non sequitur, Park further argues that women's internment in comfort stations did not necessarily enact their sexual slavery, and because Korean women harboured individual identities as 'women of the Japanese empire' their status as victims is questionable. This questionability arises, in Park's view, from their sometimes failure during the war to consider themselves victimized. In other words, a lack of victim consciousness on the part of individual Korean women who were interned in comfort stations should cause us to think twice about designating them victims.[59] Ultimately, these kinds of arguments advanced by Park are largely indistinguishable from those of Soh in their insistence that the actions of Japanese men in sexually enslaving women in wartime might not be universally and absolutely condemned.

While Park and Soh's analyses frequently replicate the prostitution-endorsing views of right-wing advocates, they are certainly not articulated in the same rhetorical terms; Soh especially uses the language and ideas of a totally different sphere of political ideology. This sphere is occupied by ideas that developed in the late 1980s in the United States, and spread to other parts of the world in the 1990s, which are generally categorized as belonging to the 'sex worker rights' movement. Soh uses the term 'public-sex work' throughout her writing to refer to prostitution, which is similar to the way Kamala Kempadoo refers to women in comfort stations as 'historical proponents of transnational sex work'.[60] York University's Kempadoo is one of the earliest and the best-known English-language theorists of the 'sex worker rights' perspective. This perspective adopts a liberal approach to prostitution as a form of work 'chosen' by women in constrained circumstances, but as nonetheless representing their exercise of individual human 'agency', and so requiring endorsement as a form of employment with labour rights and protections. It is a perspective generally silent on the question of whether men should have a right to female sexual access organized through commercial systems of prostitution, and so stands in direct contrast to the abolitionist view of prostitution as a form of male violence against women.

The next section briefly canvasses some ideas circulating in academic discourse in Japan in the 1990s that markedly reflect the US-generated 'sex worker rights' ideology of the time. This discussion aims to convey a sense of the left-wing rhetorical environment within which the justice movement developed in Japan. Ideas about prostitution as 'choice' and 'work' circulated strongly around this time, and it is my contention that these ideas formed a barrier to the justice movement challenging the bias reigning in Japan since the 1970s that prostituted women, including those of Japanese nationality, were unequal victims of comfort stations.

## 'Sex worker rights' discourse in Japan in the 1990s

It is well known that post-war Japanese society right up to the current day has been highly tolerant of prostitution and the sex industry.[61] The economically booming 1980s in particular is known as the decade when the business and culture of the sex industry gained a foothold in the country.[62] So, by the 1990s, I suggest, Japanese society was already highly suggestible to the ideas of the American 'sex worker rights' movement, given the normalization of prostitution that had already occurred in the country. The beginning of the movement in Japan might be traced to 1993 when *Sex work: writings by women in the sex industry* was published in Japanese translation. This book claimed moral authority in presenting an 'authentic' (and favourable) assessment of prostitution by 'sex workers', but since has been revealed to have been written mostly by people without experience of being prostituted.[63] The year after, in 1994, Japan's most well-known liberal feminist, Ueno Chizuko, published a book supporting the 'sex work' position titled *The work of sex* and, following that, a plethora of similar publications emerged in Japanese, including a 1997 edited volume titled *Uru shintai kau shintai* (Saleable body, buyable body).

This latter volume contains a chapter by Tsukuba University's Chimoto Hideki that advances arguments for the recognition of prostitution as 'work'. While its writing is perhaps more blunt and unsophisticated than most examples of its kind, his discussion is described here for its clear articulation of the kinds of views that circulated in Japan on 'sex worker rights' during the 1990s, precisely at the time the 'justice for comfort women movement' was developing in the country. It is my contention that these liberal ideas influenced the justice movement's view of the historical experience of prostituted victims of comfort stations.

In typical terms, Chimoto begins his chapter by suggesting that prostitution should be deemed a service profession in a similar vein as 'doctors, nurses, medical personnel, in-home assistants, and teachers[,] ... female clerks in large companies, female airline stewards, department store elevator girls, coffee shop waitresses, [and] barmaids ...' because these categories of employment 'similarly do not involve the production of commodities but, rather, require the involvement of the individual self in their performance'. Further, '[i]n all of these professions, men demand interpersonal communication and a woman's presence in the form of their individual identity'. Prostitution is equivalent to other forms of women's work, therefore, in its primary function to service men: 'There is absolutely no difference between a female clerk receiving a wage for office tea-making on the basis it brings happiness to her colleagues, and a sex industry worker earning money through their "technique" in pleasing customers'. Chimoto's claims of equivalence in this regard notably require understanding prostitution from a male perpetrator point of view. From a woman's perspective, we might see every difference in the world between being prostituted by a man and serving him tea, as evidenced by the tireless efforts of feminists in implementing workplace sexual harassment laws all over the rich world, including in Japan.

Chimoto suggests that, while structural impediments to 'free choice' might exist in relation to prostitution, such as poverty, hardly anyone enjoys total free choice in respect of their working lives anyway, not even men. This observation is offered in support of his view that coercive forces at the social level should be ignored in making judgements about the labour status of prostitution, because these structural elements are uniformly present in relation to all forms of employment. Chimoto offers a peculiarly lateral analogy in illustration of this argument:

> Even taking the example of a law faculty graduate from the University of Tokyo who gets a position in the finance ministry or a major company … it would have taken just a small diversion in their prior life history, or something to have occurred within their family, for this outcome to have been changed, and their future opportunities severely constrained. Given this level of constraint for people even in these kinds of top-level positions, we can't use criteria like 'choice' or 'coercion' for judging prostitution.[64]

But we might notice that any degree of free-choice denied a man as a result of life or professional circumstance is rarely likely to render him vulnerable to victimization in the sex industry. Women, on the other hand, especially working class and racially despised women,[65] face prostitution as a continual threat arising from individual failure to sustain employment in low-paying and low-status jobs, which are the main types of work available to them. Chimoto's unlikely choice of an elite male worker to illustrate his argument perhaps inadvertently reveals the fact that a man's failure to sustain employment usually results in his relegation to a lower status or lower paid job, but for women already at the bottom of the employment heap, this failure has the entirely different consequence of prostitution in the sex industry, with all the lifetime harms of physical and psychological injury that entails.

Arguments like these in support of a view of prostitution as work, and not sexual slavery, were dominant in academic discussions of prostitution in the 1990s throughout the Western world, and continue to be so today in countries like Germany, Japan and Australia. These arguments at the time had a significant effect on the policymaking of many governments, and legislation defining prostitution as a form of work emerged internationally during the decade. A number of agencies of the United Nations, as well as global organizations such as the International Labour Organization, adopted a view of prostitution as work, and made policy recommendations accordingly. Even major international feminist treaties, such as the Beijing Declaration of 1995, condemned prostitution only in its 'forced' form. The sex industries of a number of Western countries achieved high levels of integration into the mainstream economy through vehicles like trade shows, stock market listings and business partnerships around this time. In this atmosphere it is perhaps unsurprising that the nascent 'justice for comfort women' movement developing in Japan in the 1990s raised little objection to the longstanding conservative view that prostituted victims of comfort stations had willingly submitted themselves to military sexual exploitation as an income generating form of 'work'. This view of prostituted victims had existed since the 1970s in popular discourse on the issue, and in the 1990s it was reinforced through the ideas of the 'sex worker rights' movement that proliferated in the Japanese academy.

## Myths about Japanese comfort station survivors

As mentioned at the beginning of the chapter, Nishino identifies four ways in which prostituted Japanese women are distinguished from other victims of comfort stations, and thereby viewed as willing participants rather than victims of military sexual slavery. Nishino does not attribute their differential treatment to any ideological influence of the 1990s 'sex worker rights' movement, but when progressive proponents discuss prostituted victims their rhetoric takes on its language and ideas, I suggest. The following ways in which Japanese victims of comfort stations are described as experiencing a lesser form of harm are notable for their incorporation of ideas about prostitution as 'work' and a practice not necessarily injuring of women. These ideas form the ideological basis of the 'sex worker rights' position and, I suggest, lie also at the base of the scapegoating of prostituted comfort station victims that has marked progressive advocacy on behalf of 'real' sexual slavery survivors in Japan since the 1990s.

A common suggestion of even the critical historical literature is that Japanese women were interned in stations designated for use by military officers, rather than for use by multitudes of troops, and therefore experienced a lesser form of harm than women of other nationalities. Typical of its articulation is Kim Il Myon's 1992 claim that 'Japanese comfort women were high class, so they mostly did not serve non-commissioned officers or troops. They were able to pick and choose who they served, and their working conditions',[66] and US historian Laura Hein's 1999 assertion that '[o]fficers ... reserved Japanese women for themselves and allotted the women they considered racially less desirable to their subordinates'.[67] These accounts of the historical experience of Japanese women rely on an understanding of prostitution as inflicting harm only in relative terms, with factors like 'working conditions' making a difference to the nature and extent of its violation. Dworkin is critical of the assumption underlying this idea: that women experience men's prostitution of them as less physically and psychologically harmful in direct proportion to the amount of money they receive for it, or other surrounding material factors. She counters that, 'from the perspective of a woman in prostitution or a woman who has been in prostitution[,] the distinctions other people make about whether the event took place in the Plaza Hotel or somewhere more inelegant are not the distinctions that matter'. The only thing that matters, in Dworkin's view, is the fact that a man pays to use the 'mouth, the vagina, and the rectum' of a woman for sexual gratification. 'The circumstances don't mitigate or modify what prostitution is'.[68]

The historical accuracy of the claim that Japanese women were prostituted exclusively in 'officers clubs' is empirically questionable, and evidence of Japanese victims being prostituted alongside women of other nationalities in brothels designated for troops is presented in Chapter Five. In the meantime, we might consider testimony included in Takasaki Ryuuji's 1994 collection from a *Yomiuri Shinbun* newspaper reporter who visited a Japanese military base town located thirteen kilometres north of the Manchurian city of Hankou in July 1939. He came across a district of ten military comfort stations which were 'unusually' filled almost entirely with Japanese women. These women, according to the reporter, were being prostituted by troops during the day and officers in the evening and night.[69] While, certainly, the existence of comfort stations interning Japanese women exclusively might have been unusual on the Chinese mainland by 1939, the testimony of Japanese survivors unfortunately more than amply shows their prostitution by rank-and-file troops alongside women of other nationalities. In fact, it is a claim not supported even in the testimony of Korean survivors, such as one account included in Radhika Coomsawary's 1996 United Nations report that suggests women of all nationalities were used by officers upon their initial trafficking into comfort stations, and then passed on to troops. In the words of a Korean survivor, 'I realized that during the first year I, like all the other Korean girls with me, was ordered to service high-ranking officials, and as time passed, and as we were more and more "used", we served lower-ranking officers'.[70]

Furthermore, and inexplicably, there is pervasive denial in the historical literature that the victimization of Japanese women in comfort stations took place at all. In many cases, historians simply forget to mention Japanese women when they list nationalities of victims, or else they suggest their numbers were insignificantly few: 'An extremely small number of Japanese prostituted women were recruited as comfort women'.[71] In other cases, historians actively deny that Japanese women were targeted for trafficking on the basis of their 'value' to pimps in the civilian sex industry. Alice Yun Chai suggests that,

> [b]ecause of the reluctance of procurers to release Japanese prostitutes in large numbers, and the rapid spread of venereal disease among Japanese prostitutes and soldiers, young Korean women were drafted as military sex workers. Korean women were known to be socially secluded and strictly indoctrinated with the Confucian ideals of virginity and feminine chastity.[72]

When historians do recognize prostituted Japanese women as having been trafficked into comfort stations, they often exclude them from the category of 'Japanese woman', and so cast prostituted women as a species separate from the Japanese female population (perhaps that species called 'sex worker'?).

Alternatively, when 'Japanese women' are recognized as having been comfort station victims, this is often for the purpose of placing them in opposition to Korean women in order to explain the latter's disproportionate vulnerability to trafficking. Seungsook Moon, for example, suggests that

> the military turned its attention to seventeen- to twenty-year-old Korean women as substitutes for Japanese sex workers. Aware that women in Korea's Confucian society were instilled with an education that valued rigid chastity, the military replaced Japanese sex workers with young Korean women who were chaste enough to be free of venereal disease and young enough to endure disease if it developed.[73]

This explanation rests critically on the idea that Japanese 'sex workers' were, as Nishino has noted, riddled with sexually transmitted disease, and therefore unsuitable for military purpose. Rarely do historians evoking this argument pause to comment on its nonsensical basis: even if Korean victims did really enter comfort stations free of disease, their prostitution by the same men who had prostituted Japanese women would have inevitably and unfortunately rendered them infected in no time. Nonetheless, the following excerpt from Yun Chung-ok is typical of arguments in the historical literature:

> The Japanese military originally recruited Japanese women for comfort stations, but venereal disease gradually spread within the forces, and because troops then raped and gang raped local Chinese women in occupied areas, it spread further

to local populations. Also, there were suspicions that some Chinese women were spies [and therefore a potential risk as comfort station internees]. But this didn't lead the military to think they should therefore traffic non-prostituted Japanese women into comfort stations on the mainland. Rather, the military decided to traffic unmarried young Korean women who were brought up in a Confucian culture and an environment of chastity.[74]

This kind of explanation comes close to blaming prostituted Japanese women for the trafficking of their Korean sisters, who are assumed not to have been trafficked from the sex industry (an assumption questioned in Chapter Five). It is often followed up with the argument that non-prostituted Japanese women enjoyed some degree of ethnicity-based protection and privilege at the specific expense of Korean women. Yumiko Mikanagi, for example, writes that

> Japanese women's bodies and their reproductive capabilities were protected by the state policy as mothers of future soldiers. It is true that this itself shows lack of respect for Japanese women as individuals but the fact that their bodies were protected by the state must not be neglected. In contrast, Korean women (and Taiwanese women, too) were only seen as sex objects and as a result large numbers of Korean women were forced to serve as sex slaves for the Japanese military and suffered extensive psychological and physical damage throughout their lives.[75]

In this mess of arguments, explanations for why Korean women were disproportionately targeted for trafficking into comfort stations are beset by contradiction and paradox. On the one hand, Japanese women are imagined to have been too refined, or too maternal, or too useful to the sex industry, to have experienced the true horror of comfort stations as it is documented in the historical literature but, on the other hand, they are suggested to have been too greedy in their profit-seeking as 'sex workers', or riddled with sexually transmitted disease, to be suitable for military purpose. On the flip side, Korean women are argued to have been targeted on the basis of their chastity and purity, but nonetheless observed to be prostituted en masse by men in squalid stations at cheap rates.

Irrespective of the particular combination of ideas used to distinguish Japanese and Korean victims, we might see racially typecast views of women as significantly driving this body of academic work that focuses myopically on the nationality background of comfort station victims. Its confused rhetorical terms pit Japanese against Korean victims, and Ueno Chizuko has critiqued it on the basis that 'the distinction between forced and voluntary is equivalent to matching Korean comfort women against Japanese comfort women, with the result that a division is brought into play on the basis of nationality'.[76] It is important to note that this division, as shown in the arguments hitherto described, is established not just by right-wing critics but also by progressive advocates. Moreover, I argue, it is established along lines not fundamentally defined by victim nationality, as Ueno contends, but, rather, prostituted status. It is my view that critical historical accounts deploy a strategy of Dworkinian scapegoating under a cloak of liberal concern that the dynamics of racism be prioritized in analyses of the military system. Certainly, we might foreground dynamics of racism in analysing aspects of the history of the comfort station system, but the examples of cited above, I suggest, offer no useful guiding tool of analysis for doing so. In fact, worse still, their scapegoating of prostituted victims is cloaked in a guise of concern about racism.

## Radical historical critique

There is a nascent but growing alternative mode of critique being developed by Japan's most authoritative historians that might be seen as truly radical in its analysis of military prostitution as sexual slavery regardless of the origins of victims and means by which they were trafficked into stations. The fundamentally different perspective that commentators now bring to their assessment of the history of the comfort station system is perhaps most clearly demonstrated in an example of analysis that addresses the same question Mikanagi comments on above with regard to state protection supposedly awarded non-prostituted Japanese women who were spared trafficking into comfort stations on the basis of their purported reproductive value to the wartime state. As described above, Mikanagi's interpretation of this historical phenomenon contains the tacit assertion that wartime benefits accrued to Japanese women at the specific expense of Korean and Taiwanese women. An alternative analysis offered by Hirai Kazuko is that the Japanese state had already long marked out a population of its female citizens for sexual objectification and sexual slavery through its creation of an extensive civilian prostitution system before the war, and this arrangement in which a population of Japanese women was quarantined for 'sexual enjoyment' was sustained in wartime, and resulted in their trafficking into comfort stations abroad. This approach did indeed preserve non-prostituted Japanese women for their reproductive use value, but importantly did so at the expense of a population of *Japanese* women and girls, in addition to Korean and Taiwanese victims. Hirai explains that

> we must recognise the structural violence inherent to the civilian prostitution system that trafficked and exploited impoverished girls [before the war]. The comfort women system was an extension of the civilian legalised prostitution system. The military and Japanese state divided women into two categories – those for reproduction and those for sexual enjoyment – and then targeted women in the latter category for trafficking into comfort stations.[77]

Hirai importantly connects the historical plight of Korean and Taiwanese comfort station victims with that of Japanese women who were prostituted both in civilian and military systems. Her analysis, I believe, manifests a fundamentally different understanding of the nature of the military sexual slavery system that centrally accounts for the experience of its prostituted victims.

In a similarly radical fashion, Nishino and Yoshimi have recently critiqued the extent to which progressive advocates fail to incorporate an understanding of social structures that historically operated to channel large numbers of women into the military system, even when traffickers did not deploy measures like abduction or physical coercion against individual victims. Nishino urges reconsideration of the justice movement's understanding of 'force' so that prostituted victims might no longer be excluded from campaigning. She writes that '[w]e have to employ a social understanding of "force" in order to re-examine the construction of "comfort women" that is based in a rhetorical framework of either "trafficking victim" or "willing participant".[78] Similarly, Yoshimi urges progressive historians to reconsider their drawing of distinctions between victims for its unhelpful effect of lightening the weight of historical responsibility on the Japanese military and its state backers, given the opportunity this mode of argument offers for opponents to suggest some women were willing victims. He explains:

> The comfort women system of the Japanese military has been defined as problematic only to the extent any individual woman might have been forced into a comfort station. Regardless of the means by which women entered; for example, whether they sailed on a luxury liner and then boarded a limousine to arrive at a comfort station, and all the while fully consenting to this travel, the military cannot evade culpability if it forced a woman to enter into sexual relations with military men in a comfort station ... and if we say that the comfort women system was a system of sexual slavery then we cannot concurrently say

that women could have been exercising any choice in entering in sexual relations with the military men.[79]

This kind of analysis by Japan's leading historians has emerged only recently, but its authority and rigour is likely to exert great influence over the direction of the justice movement from now on. It is a mode of analysis that centrally incorporates the perspective of feminist abolitionism and, in rejecting considerations like choice in accounting for the experience of victims of military prostitution, it is a perspective that fundamentally challenges the viewpoint of the 'sex worker rights' movement that was influential internationally in the 1990s, including in respect to Japan's justice for comfort women movement, in my view. This recently developed approach represents a major shift in the political positioning of progressive advocates because it newly and centrally accounts for prostituted victims of military sexual slavery as equal victims of the actions of the Japanese military, and owed equal sympathy and restitution. The analysis is currently being developed by contemporary Japan-based scholars including Morita Seiya, Nishino Rumiko, Onozawa Akane, Ikeda Eriko, Kim Puja and Yoshimi Yoshiaki, and guides the discussion of the rest of this book.

# The Taisho Democratization of Prostitution

Liberty for men is often construed in sexual terms and includes liberal access to women, including prostituted ones. So while, for men, liberty entails that women be prostituted, for women, prostitution entails loss of all that liberty means.[1]

… the liberty of wolfs entails the death of the lambs. To tolerate pimps and prostitutional clients and to let them have their liberty means the horrible slavery and rape of the prostitute. We should not tolerate that; we should not be liberal with these oppressors.[2]

The 1920s is conventionally described as a period of liberal democratization for Japanese society. Social gains made during the decade are seen to include the growth of popular, labour and student movements; the achievement of universal male suffrage; the introduction of the *Factory Act* regulating wages and working hours; and the proliferation of new cultural and media products. Historians like Charles Schencking describe the emergence of public welfare facilities after the 1923 Great Kanto Earthquake, and also a stronger role for bureaucrats in social policy making and urban planning.[3] The emergence of 'established' political parties and the development of parliamentary government during the period prompts historians to use the phrase 'Taisho *demokurashii*' to describe the years between 1912 and 1926 that are imperially named the 'Taisho' era. This fourteen-year 'democratic' turn in Japanese history was, according to the late William Beasley, underwritten by money flowing in from Asia with retreating European business interests during the First World War, and was supported by human capital moving into Japan's cities at a time of accelerating urbanization and industrialization. Beasley conveys a sense of the modern trappings urban society took on as a result:

City centres acquired paved roads, street lighting, and Western-style buildings for banks, office blocks and department stores … Modern transport meant a better supply of goods, including items for the home, like kerosene lamps, and a wider selection of foodstuffs. It also made it easier for Japanese in most parts of the country to indulge an apparently insatiable taste for travel.[4]

Even if consumer and capitalistic artefacts did proliferate in Japanese society in the 1920s, historians, including Beasley himself, nonetheless raise doubts about the extent to which democratic institutions and processes really did take hold. Beasley writes in critical terms that 'businessmen [got] a voice in matters of national economic policy' during this time, and they 'constituted a political pressure group – hostile to socialism and the trade unions, opposed to large budgets, committed to private property and the rule of law'.[5] As a result, according to Andrew Gordon, Japan's economy 'sputtered from crisis to crisis' throughout the 1920s as 'European competitors returned to Asia after the war'.[6] As the years progressed, 'institutions in pre-war Japan became dysfunctional to all but the military ... and pre-war civil servants were less autonomous and less influential than is routinely assumed'.[7] Tetsuo Najita's round-up of the era is equally pessimistic:

> Society was severely strained as the population doubled, the industrial revolution advanced, unabated, and industry decisively outstripped agriculture (leading to a steady decline of the regions in demographic and cultural power as against the cities), mass culture and modern forms of hedonism spread with conspicuous vigor through much of urban society, and parliamentary politics appeared to intellectual leaders in the country to be hopelessly mired in corruption.[8]

This debate over the extent of progressive change occurring in the Taisho years is well known among historians, and Janet Hunter highlights its main point of contention when she writes that 'the so-called "democracy" of the Taisho period is often contrasted with the "fascism" of the Showa [1926–1989] period, and the nature of the relationship between these two phenomena remains a matter of historical controversy'.[9] Indeed, it might seem perverse to insist on liberal elements of a decade that was immediately succeeded by years of militarism and total war mobilization. Rather than scratching around for signs of democracy, an alternative approach is indicated (but not pursued) by Elise Tipton when she suggests that the pop-cultural "'erotic, grotesque nonsense" fad of the time seems to represent the "dark valley" into which Japan was descending' in the late years of Taisho.[10]

Historians regularly find evidence of Japan's impending 'dark valley' in social, economic and political aspects of the 1920s, including the financial and labour markets, international terms of trade, technology, political institutions, party politics, cultural products, education and rural life. Origins of 1930s fascism are routinely and widely sought in the Taisho years, even in spite of Carol Gluck's criticism that such 'invertibilism makes poor history-writing'.[11] Gluck suggests that pursuing the causes of 1930s fascism in Taisho society produces historical analyses that are circular in construction – intellectual self-fulfilling prophecies. Nonetheless, there exists barely an inch of Taisho era history that has not been mined in service of 'invertibilist' scholarship, and it is a body of work that broadly aligns with the perspective of this book. Looking to peacetime society for the origins of wartime institutions and practices is simply to recognize, I believe, that the culture and conduct of militaries do not develop spontaneously with war but are rather generated and supported by prior-existing civilian systems.

Methodological differences aside, Gluck might be nonetheless pleased to know there remains one facet of 1920s Japanese society almost untouched by invertabilist scholars, even after decades of research on the Taisho era. It not only remains free of historical 'dark valley' attributions, but is actively spotlighted by historians as a key indicator of Taisho *demokurashii* in all its progressive glory. Historians find very few antecedents of wartime fascism in Japan's sex industry of the 1920s. On the contrary, as described next, they manage to find signs even of women's liberation in the prostitution of the Taisho years. This chapter critiques accounts of Taisho-era Japanese society that, it argues, overlook or minimize the expansion of the sex industry and the escalating male demand for the prostitution of women that occurred during the period. It undertakes this critique to suggest that analyses of the origins and causes of the comfort station system have been ill-informed by an understanding of pre-war Japanese society as a time of progressive improvement in sexual politics. The chapter details expansion and proliferation of the sex industry during the era, and describes the conditions of Japanese women's lives in civilian systems of prostitution around the time. These conditions are noted for their similarity to recorded accounts of women's experience of later military comfort stations.

## The Japanese 'New Woman'

Historians rarely look for signs of fascistic sexual politics in the society, economy or polity of 1920s Japan; in fact, gender relations of the era are celebrated under a banner of relaxed 'sexual mores'. This relaxation is purported to have been beneficial for women and reflective of female social progress.[12] Barbara Sato's 2003 book chapter, with its title 'The emergence of agency' presumably referring to women, promotes this view of the 1920s as a period of social progress. She makes the argument that a historically distinguishable female social category – 'the New Japanese Woman' – emerged during the decade as a product of struggle between female consumerist and sexual individualism, against a repressive state. The New Woman was 'constantly undercut by conventional forces working within the state', but her struggle against them led to 'gender awareness', and a 'new subject position for women'.[13] This appears to have been achieved in the absence of any female collective organizing and political resistance, let alone any significant decline in barriers to paid work. Hunter notes that, 'whereas the male [labour market] participation rate declined only slightly [between 1920 and 1930 in Japan], women's participation fell by over three times as much'.[14] Muta Kazue is equally categorical that 'the New Woman phenomenon in Japan did not appear in connection with the suffrage movement and related activities … the Japanese New Woman came to the scene without political leverage'.[15]

Sato's description exhibits a typically liberal tendency to posit the state, rather than the discrimination and violence of a diffuse male citizenry,[16] as women's main obstruction to progress, and so sees withdrawal of the state from women's lives as invariably enhancing their 'agency' and therefore comprising ipso facto evidence of social gains. Certainly, Japanese *men* won victories *vis-a-vis* the state in the Taisho era (e.g. voting rights), but it might be a leap to suggest this produced trickle-down effects for female equality. Feminist historians critique the idea that social gains achieved by men automatically translate to greater equality for women: Joan Kelly notes that 'liberal history suggests that women enjoyed the same historical advances as men', but 'feminist history uncovers the fact that significant declines in the status of women occurred in precisely the periods that male history has suggested that historical gains were made'.[17] An example of this is found in Sheila Jeffreys's discussion of Britain in the 'liberal' interwar years, which records that

> [t]he pre-war feminist critique which had been building up momentum throughout the last quarter of the nineteenth century, threatened to deprive men of the use of prostitutes without providing them with a substitute in the form of wifely enthusiasm. The decline in prostitution required compensation. The 1920s [therefore] witnessed a concerted onslaught on the problem of the 'resisting' woman …[18]

Threats to male sexual entitlement prevailed similarly in interwar Japan. Iwata Shigenori notes that women attempted, but did not succeed, in getting a law passed in 1920 that would have placed marriage restrictions on men detected as infected with venereal disease. Infection rates in Japan at this time were close to that of tuberculosis, and women's groups sought to protect wives from the reproductive and health effects of marrying an infected partner.[19] In so doing they challenged a core tenet of male sexual culture: Iwata describes anthropological fieldwork done in 1935 that recorded men in a Nagasaki village believing that contracting a venereal disease was a mark of manhood, and represented social independence (*ichininmae no ningen*). Women's groups also pursued restrictions on prostitution, alcohol, concubine possession, and arranged marriage in the 1920s.[20] Despite the boldness of this campaigning, these women aren't the female agents commentators like Sato exalt; when they describe Japan's 'new woman' achieving 'empowerment' in the Taisho era they tend to, as Vanessa Ward observes, describe this group of women in oppositional terms as 'conservative', 'Christian', or loyal to a repressive state.

## The dark valley of prostitution

This favoured liberal version of Taisho era history in which sexually adventurous 'new' women achieved 'agency' finds its way into studies examining even the most deprived and sexually violent spheres of Japanese society. On the premise women achieved a more assertive economic and social status in the Taisho era, historians describe even the sex industry as a site of female opportunity. Mark Ramseyer at Harvard University, for example, examines contracts of women indentured to legal brothels in the 1920s. He uses rational choice theory to analyse the contracts, and generates remarkably upbeat observations of the benefits of indentured servitude. He suggests that women became indentured to brothels not necessarily as a result of predation and manipulation by pimps, traffickers or fathers, but as a result of having weighed up their options and made a rational decision in their own best financial interests. He explains that,

> [g]iven the substantial stigma women incurred in entering the [sex] industry, many women hesitated to take jobs at brothels (and many parents hesitated to send their daughters to brothels) without some assurance that they would earn much higher wages than they could earn elsewhere ... [and] indentured contracts offered that assurance.[21]

In addition to advance payments, Ramseyer assures readers 'the prostitutes [also] earned reasonably high incomes, and many women were poor. Some women independently chose the job simply because it paid so much'.[22] Even further, through becoming indentured women were able to stop pimps firing them because, 'when a brothel paid a prostitute several years' wages in advance, it put itself in a position where she could force it to keep its part of the bargain'.[23] Topping this off, 'most women apparently received room and board free'.[24]

Sheldon Garon at Princeton University, likewise examines legalized or 'licensed' brothel prostitution in 1920s Japan, and is equally effusive about its prospects for women. He declares that there are 'grounds to question the representation of the licensed prostitute as necessarily the passive victim of family poverty' because 'relatively few of the newly registered prostitutes in Tokyo during the mid-1920s were novices, freshly separated from their families'. In fact, '[m]ost had worked previously as barmaids, geisha or licensed prostitutes in other brothels'.[25] Further weakening their claim to victim status is the fact that, '[c]ompared to ordinary prostitutes in many other societies, licensed prostitutes in Japan apparently spent more time eating, drinking and flirting with clients'.[26] But Garon does register one concern: that prostituted women were not fully able to realize their individual agency because the Taisho era state sought to 'regulate people's sexuality' through the legalized system, and 'restrict[ed] the liberties of the prostitute in the interests of effective regulation'.[27] Like Sato, Garon worries about state intervention as an impediment to female equality, and so writes favourably of the growth of a non-brothel, unregulated sex industry sector in the 1920s. A purported lack of government regulation and their 'erotic atmosphere' leads him to link these businesses with better outcomes for women: 'Many of the Ginza-type cafes ... promoted an atmosphere of eroticism' and so 'the sexuality of waitresses could not be easily managed'. Even if, he admits, 'waitresses were encouraged to entice male passers-by, sell kisses, and sleep with clientele after hours'.[28] Elise Tipton echoes this account in even more euphemistic terms when she writes that *kafes* gave women 'a degree of financial independence' and, at the same time, 'allowed, and encouraged, them to display and express their sexuality'.[29] So, even with acknowledged pressure from pimps to acquiesce to prostitution, historians still see progressive gains for women in the burgeoning unregulated sex industry of the Taisho era.

The late Miriam Silverberg at UCLA even more strongly insists on a view of *kafes* as a form of business brought into being by women newly exercising their sexuality in defiance of a repressive state – namely, a masochistic form of sexuality. She contends that '[t]he *jokyuu* [i.e. *kafe* waitress] participated in erotic relationships inside and outside the cafe', and this involved 'desires for dominating the clearly gendered other or for being dominated by that other'.[30] An example perhaps illustrating Silverberg's observation of sexual domination mediated through *kafes* is Tipton's description of practices known as the 'organ' and the 'subway' that were popular in the venues. In the 'organ', a waitress would 'lie across patrons' laps like a keyboard and sing notes when they touched different parts of her body'. In the case of the 'subway', a buyer would be allowed to 'feel a waitress's body by inserting his hand through slits in her skirt'.[31] Nonetheless, Silverberg describes *kafes* in a way that elides any commercial basis to their operation, let alone involvement in mediating the prostitution of women. She appears to see the venues as having operated as erstwhile clearinghouses for heterosexual coupling: 'In the cafes of modern Japan, seduction moved both ways between men and women in an era when women's articulation of erotic desire was explicit … The cultural consequence for both male and female during the modern years was an awareness of the power of the erotic'.[32]

This romantic characterization is difficult to reconcile with accounts of *kafes* sourced from women with actual experience of the venues. Tanikawa Mitsue in the early 1980s interviewed a 71-year-old woman who had been employed in a *kafe* between the years 1929 and 1933 from ages 16 to 20. The woman's experience is almost indistinguishable from that of accounts of women in brothels around the time, which are described at the end of this chapter. There were twenty-seven to thirty women in her venue which was located near a brothel district and had a second floor of rooms where women would be prostituted by *kafe* customers. Just like venues in the brothel district, women were not allowed to freely come and go from the *kafe*, and every one of them had been trafficked into the venue through loans advanced by the proprietor.[33] The suggestion that *kafes* were qualitatively different from brothels is also difficult to reconcile with their status in law at the time. Hayakawa Noriyo in 1997 found no substantive difference in government regulation of prostitution venues inside or outside Japan's legal brothel districts in the Taisho era. He writes that, while *kafes* weren't legally defined the same way as brothels, prefectural ordinances nonetheless still mandated their official registration, as well as required venereal disease testing of women.[34] Fujino Yutaka adds that a law requiring testing of women in 'registered' venues (i.e. geisha venues and *kafes*) was passed in 1927 and, from 1928, government-subsidized testing commenced under the oversight of the Home Ministry.[35] The indistinguishably of *kafes* from brothels and the other businesses of the Taisho era sex industry is further indicated in a 2010 discussion by Rikkyo University's Onozawa Akane. She writes in succinct terms that 'the emergence of *kafes* simply reflected a [business] transition by brothel owners … the decline in brothel prostitution in the late 1920s and early 1930s was exactly paralleled by the rise in *kafe* prostitution'.[36] Onozawa points to renovation in the sex industry's business model away from legalized brothels and towards *kafe* and restaurant-like venues during the period. She cites evidence of brothel owners proactively turning their businesses into *kafes* and other venues that could be registered as 'food and alcohol' establishments.[37] She suggests that they did this from the time of the Showa-era depression of 1927, but government researcher Fukumi Takao, who carried out a large-scale survey of Tokyo's sex industry in 1926, writes that *kafes* mediating prostitution emerged noticeably after the Great Kanto Earthquake of 1923, in Tokyo at least.[38] Regardless of the precise historical moment of their emergence, Onozawa emphasizes the fact *kafes* emerged as an alternative operating venue for brothel operators whose business model came under pressure on varying fronts in the 1920s.[39] Sources of pressure included the (limited) success of anti-prostitution abolitionists in getting the government to take action against the sex industry, and active intervention by a committee of the League of Nations in lobbying Japanese diplomatic officials to dismantle the legalized prostitution system and suppress the international sex trafficking of Japanese women. In transitioning to *kafes*, brothels owners were able to somewhat protect their business interests from these negative developments, and also evade the regulations of the legalized brothel system; including its taxes, and restrictions on harbouring underage girls.[40]

## Ideological resistance to a prostitution 'dark valley'

If historical evidence weighs against the utility of drawing any meaningful distinctions between different sectors of Japan's sex industry in the Taisho era, then what accounts for the lengthily described charms of *kafes* populating the literature? This question is significant if we consider, as does the next chapter, that *kafes* and similar venues made up the bulk of Japan's pre-war sex industry, and that this industry might have had connections with the later development of the wartime comfort station system. Failing to account for the full scope of Japan's pre-war sex industry potentially places limits on connections that might be uncovered between civilian prostitution and wartime sexual slavery, and also may inhibit understanding of the experience of victims prostituted and trafficked between the two systems, especially in the case of Japanese women prostituted in *kafes* and then trafficked into comfort stations, for which there is historical evidence.[41] A further risk is that ideologically-driven analyses of 'peacetime' prostitution as perpetrated by freedom-loving Japanese 'New Women' – and other analyses likely influenced by distorted ideas about female sexuality – generate frameworks that are unhelpfully mapped onto analyses of wartime prostitution. We might recognize this as occurring in the examples cited in the previous chapter where historians describe Japanese women as having been less sexually enslaved in comfort stations than women of other nationalities. Perhaps these historians are simply unable to reconcile their deeply held belief in the existence of the Taisho-era 'New Woman' with the possibility that Japanese women could have subsequently undergone sexual slavery in military brothels.

It is perhaps not a coincidence that all four of the above-cited historians are US university-educated, and came of age at a time when, as Kate Millet noted in 1970, prostitution was being 'confused through a thoughtless equation of sexual freedom with sexual exploitation'.[42] Millet identifies this 'confusion' as politically motivated in that '… the older patriarchy [had] used the now faintly embarrassing methods of open slavery and thereby failed to coerce a sufficiently resigned subservience in women: one who is forced is not really abject, only compelled'.[43] Andrea Dworkin in 1981 observed the success of 'left-wing ideology' in overcoming this deficiency. With its emergence in the 1960s, the ideology of 'sexual freedom' became the 'unrestrained use of women, the use of women as a collective natural resource, not privatized, not owned by one man but instead used by many'.[44] This unrestrained use was attributed to the will of women on the assumption that 'the sexuality of the woman actualized is the sexuality of the whore',[45] and was posed as benefiting all women to the extent that prostitution is 'her political will as well as her sexual will; it is liberation'.[46] In other words, a set of ideas grew out of the 'sexual revolution' of the 1960s that equated female sexual freedom with sexual exploitation, and these ideas worked to promote a 'sufficiently resigned subservience in women' that was more effective than the 'compelled' subjugation of the past.

While these ideas might have had only weak currency in the 1920s,[47] the authors above nonetheless retrospectively apply them to the Taisho era, I suggest, and specifically to the example of *kafes*, in their tacit assertion that female sexuality was authentically exercised through these venues in the form of prostitution, and this exercise set the Japanese 'new woman' free. Women's 'desire' to be prostituted is suggested in the way historians describe *kafes* as harbouring an 'erotic' atmosphere, and as comprising businesses brought into existence by women 'actualizing' a newfound sexuality, such that the 'erotic air' of the venues developed specially tuned to a free and abundant sexual servicing of men. This kind of understanding of Japanese Taisho era history is not conducive, I argue, to considering connections between pre-war civilian prostitution and the development of the military sexual slavery system of the immediately succeeding Showa years. In other words, the existing English-language historiography of the Taisho era poses an obstacle to productive inquiry into peacetime conditions inhering in 1920s Japan that might have contributed to the emergence of large-scale systems of female sexual slavery in the 1930s and 1940s.

Another body of literature posing an obstacle to an analysis of the 1920s as a period fermenting of conditions conducive to the development of military sexual slavery is historical and anthropological work on prostitution in Japan in the pre-modern era (i.e. before federation in 1868), which in English includes volumes that frequently have 'Yoshiwara', 'geisha' or 'courtesan' in their titles.[48] This scholarship rightly emphasizes the pervasiveness and longevity of organized prostitution in Japan since the fifteenth century. Indeed, semi-regulated systems of prostitution have operated in Japan for historically longer than perhaps anywhere else in the world.[49] Systems of taxation, and regulation in the form of restrictions on women's mobility and testing of venereal disease, have been implemented at regional and higher levels in Japan from feudal times, and the heinousness of this history is expertly documented by historians such as Sone Hiromi and Shimojuu Kiyoshi.[50] However, this large body of work on pre-Meiji era prostitution mostly fails to distinguish the era's relatively contained, family-orchestrated, and elite male-focused prostitution of the feudal period from the democratized and industrialized prostitution industry that developed in Japan after 1868, with its systemized trafficking, commercial practices and profits, and diversified forms. In other words, the prominence of scholarship describing Edo-era prostitution in Japan has served, perhaps inadvertently, to naturalize developments in the Taisho period, as if the fact of a burgeoning prostitution industry was an historical inevitability. But the large, industrialized and diversified sex industry of the modern era was new and unprecedented, even if the groundwork for its development had been laid in the Meiji period and before.

## The sex industry boom of the Taisho era

The volume of men and money moving into Japan's cities in the Taisho era meant sex entrepreneurs sat ready to financially capitalize on an expanding consumer base, but tapping into this market required more flexible forms of business operation and the integration of prostitution into the commercial mainstream (*rokotsu na baibaishun no hatten*).[51] The old brothel model of prostitution business was no longer as popular as the new *kafes*, mainly because *kafes* were cheaper to run and patronize.[52] Fujino also notes the absence of age restrictions on *kafe* employees, which meant proprietors could potentially mediate the profitable prostitution of girls (although prefectural governments passed ordinances against this as the decade progressed).[53] For these reasons and more, Japan's sex industry diversified in a wide range of business forms in the Taisho era, including into geisha venues, *kafes*, restaurants and drinking houses (*inshokuten*), traditional inns (*ryokan*) especially around hot springs resorts, and billiard and dance halls.[54]

Inexplicably, historians take this sex industry diversification to indicate improvement in the conditions in which women were prostituted, or some kind of less harmful form of prostitution as developing in the Taisho era. This analysis might be understood as reflecting a liberal bias towards understanding the harm of prostitution as deriving from its surrounding circumstances, rather than its actual practice itself, which is found throughout the world to induce rates of post traumatic stress in women greater than that of war veterans, even when prior childhood sexual abuse is discounted as a correlating variable.[55] Rather than improvement or beautification, it is perhaps more accurate to understand the diversification of the sex industry in the Taisho years as simply representing the expansion of the prostitution sector, as well as indicating escalating rates of male demand for the sexual buying of women. Historians generally do not discuss the fact of significant sex industry expansion in the Taisho era, perhaps because of a prior held view of *kafes* and other 'diversified' forms of the sex industry as not mediating the prostitution of women.

In fact, a streamlining of operations to meet escalating rates of male demand for the prostitution of women was achieved by Japan's sex industry during this time, which was already well organized and resourced by the 1920s. The business of prostitution was well established in the country by the beginning of the twentieth century: brothels were legalized in federal legislation in 1900; networks were established to traffic Japanese women into brothels throughout Asia and the Pacific by the mid-nineteenth century (see Chapter Four); and prostitution was an accepted and socially entrenched practice of elite men in their business, political and military dealings already by the turn of the century. Nonetheless, historian Nakamura Zaburou reflects on the fact that Japan in its history had still never experienced an era quite as 'tawdry' as the years of Taisho.[56] By this decade, the number of non-brothel sex industry districts in the country exceeded 700 sites,[57] and in Tokyo alone there were 24,589 *kafe* and other similar venues operating by 1924, even after most venues had been burnt down in the Great Kanto Earthquake the year before.[58] Just three years later, by 1927, there were 50,056 women in legal brothels, 80,086 women in geisha venues, and 101,032 women being prostituted through *kafes*, restaurants and other similar venues nationwide.[59] This totalled around 230,000 women out of a total Japanese population of around 59 million in 1925, of which 49 per cent were female. There was therefore, according to Fukumi, one prostituted woman for every 599 men in Japan by 1924, which equates to one woman prostituted per 593 women in the country.[60]

This phenomenon of 'diversification' and the proliferation of sex industry venues in Taisho-era Japan means that Garon is not incorrect when he suggests that women in legal brothels during this time had often been prostituted in other types of sex industry venues beforehand, and so were not necessarily 'novices, freshly separated from their families', as he pithily asserts. Indeed, Kusama Yasoo cites research carried out between 1921 and 1922 in which 91 out of 681 women sold into the legalized Yoshiwara brothel district had come from geisha venues. Another 301 had come from *kafes* and similar venues, and 131 from 'illegal' venues.[61] Overall, more than 76 per cent of women surveyed in the district had been prostituted in *kafes* or geisha venues beforehand. While Garon divines female empowerment and agency in these numbers, Kusama notes that debt accumulated in other venues had mostly forced the women into the brothels.[62] The identical way in which geisha venues, *kafes* and brothels entrapped women through debt is confirmed in his comment that 'women in [non-brothel venues] are stuck in the same old-fashioned [*furui-gata*] system as compared to the debt that is found in the geisha system ... and the legalized brothel sector remains impervious to improvement [in terms of allowing women to leave through paying off debt]'.[63] Entrapping women through devices like debt was crucial to sustaining an industry that was rapidly expanding in the Taisho era; without sufficient numbers of women stably organized in systems of prostitution the industry risked not fully capitalizing on the demand burgeoning among Japanese men at the time. Even before this, though, the development of infrastructure and logistics facilitating the trafficking of women and girls into the industry had been crucial to securing a base for its operations.

## Trafficking: The sex industry supply chain of the Taisho era

The transport and organization of such large numbers of women and girls in venues arranging their sexual buying and selling in Taisho-era Japan is likely to reflect the existence of well-developed trafficking networks in the country, if we consider Jeffreys's observation that trafficking is the essential 'supply chain for prostitution'.[64] The trafficking activity that organized women's prostitution of the time reflects, I argue, a solidly industrial base having had been developed for the purpose of channelling women and girls into *kafes* and other venues in the period. The strength of this base, I contend, casts doubt on the suggestion that individual female sexuality drove the trade, which is the tacit suggestion of much of the historical literature. In fact, 'intermediary' businesses arranging the trafficking of women into geisha venues were legalized by some prefectural governments in the Taisho years, and Kusama Yasoo notes that 3,000 such legal brokers were operating in Japan by 1930. As a result, he writes, no less than 40,000 women were being brokered into the sex industry each year by legal operators.[65] Even this level of supply was inadequate, though, because Kusama adds there were more than 70,000 requests made by pimps (*hankagai no shihonka*) to the brokers to source women each year.[66] He warns, moreover, that this figure accounts only for legal brokering, and excludes the activity of illegal operators.[67] Fujino writes that, by the year 1930, the global depression affecting Japan had led to high rates of trafficking of young women out of northern prefectures, most of whom were destined for geisha venues, drinking venues and other businesses outside the legalized brothel sector. While Japan's home ministry was aware of the traffic, and the fact prostitution brokers were recruiting in impoverished farming areas, it believed local organizations were taking the problem in hand and so did not need to act.[68]

The activity of illegal brokers is described in an account by a former national police superintendent published in 1999. He writes that there were around 1,000 rickshaw drivers in Tokyo in the 1920s who would lure girls into illegal brothels after they had arrived in the city from the countryside. Drivers would congregate especially around Ueno train station, and would target girls who looked like they had come from the countryside, talking them into accompanying them to cheap accommodation. They would then manipulate the girls into taking on debt through selling them kimonos, or encourage them to enter a brothel out of filial duty to send money back to their parents.[69] Other brokers would travel to countryside areas with offers of 'factory work', and bring girls back to Tokyo where they would be passed onto another broker who would on-sell them to illegal brothels. Yoshida writes specifically that most of the prostituted women in the sex industry districts of Tamanoi and Kameido in the Taisho era had been manipulated in this way. He quotes a letter to a Tokyo newspaper from 1923 in which an Ueno station employee writes that 'every day' there are groups of 'two to three men' who alight trains accompanying groups of girls aged between 15 and 20, and there are between 15 and 16 of the girls. The employee laments these men were 'customers' of the railway company, so he could not do much about them, but he 'does think they are up to no good'.[70] Kim Il Myon explains that brokers travelled to country areas pretending to be watch or medicine sellers, dressed up with fob watches hanging off their coats.[71] By the time the economic depression hit in 1929 and mass crop failure engulfed Japan's northern prefectures in 1934, the vulnerability of women and girls to the manipulations of traffickers and brokers had escalated. Rural rights activist Aoki Keiichirou recalls visiting a mountain village in Akita prefecture around this time where, out of 370 households, there had already been 200 girls sold to brokers, some as young as ten years old.[72]

Offering loans to families in return for the indenturing of daughters was the device that successfully facilitated the large-scale procurement of women and girls in the later years of Taisho, especially in the years of economic depression at the end of the era. Ramseyer sees this servitude as productively arranged by legal contract, but he fails to mention that parents were frequently offered top-up loans on these contracts to extend the time their daughters would remain in prostitution, and there were also instances of parents fully selling off their daughters to pimps.[73] Others would actively seek out pimps to issue additional loans when their daughters' contract expiry dates were nearing.[74] A former Taisho-era brothel pimp interviewed by Tanikawa in the early 1980s recalled a 25-year-old woman committing suicide after her father had visited the brothel to take out a further loan against her indenture, which he promptly used to buy a woman for prostitution at a nearby brothel.[75] As mentioned, debt functioned as a critical tool of retention for women and girls in the Taisho-era sex industry, and centrally underpinned the systems of trafficking that circulated a significant portion of Japan's female population among brothels, *kafes*, and other venues that made up the system of civilian prostitution.

Hayakawa Noriyo explains that interest on debt, as well as various fees and fines, were levied by pimps to such an extent that women often found their debts to be higher at the end of the contract term than the beginning.[76] There were fines for all manner of transgressions (such as falling asleep with a buyer), and costs and fees for everything under the sun (such as changes in clothing style for each of the four seasons).[77] Kusama lists examples of costs that would be added to existing debt, including for clothes, makeup, fees for taking time off, hospital expenses, stationery, furniture and bedding.[78] Another significant cost is highlighted in Tanikawa's interview with a former brothel district pawn shop owner who noted women would often borrow money from him to buy morphine: 'There were a lot of addicts', he recalls.[79] Fukumi Takeo in the late 1920s surveyed more than 5,000 women in all sectors of Japan's sex industry, and found that the majority were bonded to pimps through debt.[80] In relation to this finding, and contradicting Ramseyer's analysis, he expresses the view that debt was a major factor making exit from the sex industry difficult for women, and notes sceptically that, even if indenture contracts were drawn up for specified durations, time limits were not adhered to because pimps 'employed means to slow down repayment'.[81] An example of this is written about by Kusama who describes a woman in a brothel in the Yoshiwara district who entered in 1915 and spent three years and ten months in the brothel. By the end of this period, she had paid off only 14 per cent of the debt owing when she entered. Another woman in a Yoshiwara brothel entered in 1916 and had paid off only 28 per cent of her debt after three years and one month.[82]

## The prostitution of girls

Indentured servitude was a procurement strategy that led to the trafficking of, notably, a high proportion of underage girls into Japan's Taisho-era sex industry, especially into *kafes*, geisha venues, and other non-brothel venues that were comparatively unregulated. By 1926, 53 per cent of victims being prostituted through 'restaurants' in Tokyo prefecture were under 18 years of age, and 5 per cent were under the age of 14.[83] Kusama cites a 1927 home ministry survey of Tokyo geisha venue internees that found 17 per cent as between the ages of 14 and 17.[84] *Kafes* interned young women at similar rates. A 1926 survey of 2,585 waitresses in *kafes* in Osaka and Tokyo showed that 13 per cent were aged 18, 8 per cent were aged 17, 3 per cent aged 16 and 4 per cent aged 14.[85] Kusama nominates two reasons for this high proportion of underage girls in Japan's sex industry: regional governments were allowing girls from age 16 to work at *kafe* venues, and underage girls could be legally sold into geisha venues under the guise of receiving artistic 'training'.[86]

Historical evidence of Japan's pre-war civilian sex industry relying on the trafficking of underage girls for its business operations is a fact possibly not irrelevant to the later development of the comfort station system. Chapter Four notes that, while the majority of Japanese women trafficked into comfort stations had already reached adulthood, they had almost always been prostituted before this in the civilian sex industry *since childhood*. This was particularly the case for women trafficked into comfort stations from 'geisha' venues. The use of adoption contracts by geisha venue proprietors as a central plank of their procurement activity made the prostitution of underage girls a particularly notable feature of these businesses, and geisha venues were a common site of origin for Japanese women trafficked into comfort stations.

Geisha venues (and also occasionally *kafes* and brothels)[87] used adoption contracts to encourage parents to transfer young daughters to brokers on the ruse these children would receive years of artistic and cultural training. Kanzaki explains that girls were trafficked (*jinshin baibai*) into geisha houses through house managers buying the right to 'adopt' them through payments to parents or brokers. At around age 14, a girl, who had often been working as a servant in the house up until this time, was prostituted in outcall escort-type arrangements to places like 'geisha restaurants' or *ryoutei*. Kanzaki describes a *ryoutei* as a 'prostitution hotel with banquet facilities'.[88] Women and girls lived in geisha houses under the control of a 'proprietor' (*ookami*), and there are numerous accounts of the brutal enforcer role performed by these women. Adoption contracts allowed these proprietors to source girls even younger than those recruited for brothels or *kafes* while evading laws prohibiting trafficking and debt servitude. Kanzaki describes the procurement tool of adoption contracts as 'exacting an unimaginable toll on the human rights of girls who [are] entirely under the control of their "parental" masters' in geisha venues.[89]

It was these girls who later became part of the population of adult Japanese women who filled comfort stations during the war, and we might see their particular vulnerability and malleability after years of sexual abuse (prostitution) from childhood as having been possibly useful to the military in developing its wartime scheme. These women had already sustained the harms the contemporary medical literature describes for child victims of prostitution, including 'broken bones, bruises, reproductive complications, hepatitis and STIs … [and] psychological hardships including depression, PTSD, suicidal thoughts, self-mutilation and strong feelings of guilt and shame'.[90] They were frequently trafficked into comfort stations on the contrivance they would be relieved of debts accumulated in the civilian industry after one year of service;[91] the implication was that time spent in a military brothel would forevermore free them from the world they had entered as children. Nishino Rumiko notes the central role of the Japanese military in arranging this contrivance in her following comment:

> A trick of perpetrators to evade responsibility is to suggest that prostituted women chose to become comfort women so there is nothing to problematise with regard to their internment in comfort stations. But given the fact the Japanese military supplied funds for the buying out of debt bondage contracts,

or advanced funds for the offering of loans, its role in trafficking women out of the sex industry into comfort stations is clear.[92]

Occasionally, prostitution in military venues did indeed allow Japanese women to escape the civilian sex industry,[93] and so there are a couple of Japanese survivors who describe their experience in military brothels in relatively positive terms; Shirota Suzuko in an interview in the 1980s commented that her experience of wartime military prostitution had not been too bad, for example.[94] But, as Hirai Kazuko notes, we might pause to reflect on what this might say about their prior experience in Japan's civilian sex industry:

> Some women attributed positive experiences to their time in comfort stations due to the fact this was the first time in their lives they had been offered any 'special' treatment over others, such as being reserved for officers when other women had to service troops. It also reflects the heinousness of their lives in civilian prostitution before the war.[95]

If military comfort stations represented any type of refuge for Japanese women, what do we imagine conditions were like in the world from which they fled? Nishino further suggests we might focus on the harms done to women in comfort stations irrespective of where they were trafficked from:

> Due to poverty, patriarchy and the state-endorsed legalised prostitution system these victims had been robbed of their ability of free choice, and the comfort women system became an extension of the civilian prostitution system, and so we should not seek to assess the 'victimhood' of women used in the system, but instead seek to interrogate the violence, human rights violations, and contempt for women that the comfort women system enacted.[96]

## Geisha sector prostitution

A number of socialist and Christian social campaigners in the Taisho era had a good understanding of the world in which women and girls were prostituted in Japan, and their understanding was solid even in relation to geisha businesses, which they saw as enjoying unwarranted ideological protection on the basis of an association with the elite arts. Masutomi Masasuke in 1915 criticized commentators who 'euphemized the current situation of women in the geisha system by suggesting that they were the successors of *shirabyoushi* [Japanese medieval female dancers]'.[97] He criticized these *sanbiron* (romantic theories) promoted by people he called *geigi hitsuyou ronsha* (pro-geisha theorists) on the basis they promoted *sanbiron* arguments merely to protect geisha businesses as a prostitution system for elite men.[98] Masutomi claimed that while some women in the system might practice the arts, 'the geisha of today are generally just converted licensed prostitutes' and, '[b]efore the beginning of the Meiji period [1868–1912], they were in the brothels of the red light districts'.[99] He argued that elite men had driven the movement of these women into geisha venues because these men had recently 'come to be embarrassed by the [red light] districts'.[100] We might understand Masutomi's comment about 'embarrassment' as referring to the heavier scrutiny Japanese men came to attract in the Taisho era in relation to their patronage of brothels, which were criticized as enslaving women by a committee of the League of Nations. Geisha businesses, on the other hand, were notorious for their discretion and efforts to protect customer privacy.

A graphic account of the prostitution of a 17-year-old girl in a geisha house in 1938 is contained in the 1971 biography of the Japanese comfort station survivor described in the book's introduction. Shirota Suzuko recalls the first night she was prostituted by a male buyer who had paid extra to Shirota's geisha house owner because she had not yet been sexually penetrated by a man (i.e. because she was a 'virgin'). The buyer, a 60-year-old CEO of a medical supplies manufacturer, prostituted her in the back room of a geisha restaurant where Shirota had been in attendance at a banquet held for the man and his associates earlier in the evening. Shirota did not understand that she had been bought for prostitution, and appears not to have understood what the man was going to do to her. When the man eventually told her to take her clothes off, she resisted and told him that she wanted to leave. She attempted to leave, but found that the room's door was locked. The man went ahead and raped her, apparently violently. Shirota writes that her kimono was 'torn to shreds'. She bled so much from her vagina that the man had to eventually call the geisha restaurant proprietor to come and clean up the room. When the proprietor came, Shirota remembers the proprietor criticizing her for the fact the man had been excessively violent. As a result of the rape, Shirota was infected with venereal disease, and was subsequently bedridden for a number of months. As soon as she recovered, her geisha house proprietor sold her off to a brothel.[101]

A similar account of the trafficking of a girl into a geisha house before the Second World War is contained in a book translated under the English title *Autobiography of a geisha*. In it, Sayo Masuda recounts having been sold into a geisha house before the war at age 12, and then prostituted inside and outside geisha venues until her mid-twenties.[102] Masuda's experience included being both prostituted and seriously injured. She witnessed first-hand the death from illness of a woman in her own geisha house, as well as the death of another from suicide. Anger at the male customer who was behind her friend's suicide causes Masuda at one point in her autobiography to remark: 'Cut a geisha and she hurts; red blood comes out. We're not cold-blooded creatures. Does he think we're geisha because we want to be? That we just love doing it?'[103] She recalls men's sexual violence against women and girls in geisha venues in a number of places in the book, including the following description of a typical situation facing women when dispatched to geisha restaurants:

> [A] group of, say, three young men hire a geisha and tell her, 'It's exhibition day!' or 'We're going to play gynaecologist!' They strike up a rhythm and start to undo her obi. All three of them gang up on her and hold her down; then one of them tries something utterly shameful. The geisha screams for help.[104]

These kinds of accounts of sexual violence endured by women prostituted through the geisha sector of Japan's sex industry in the Taisho era are difficult to come by, perhaps because of the romanticized place the 'Japanese geisha' occupies in particularly the English-language historical literature. Although limited, the accounts nonetheless allow glimpses into the horror of the world Japanese prostituted victims of comfort stations inhabited before their trafficking into the military system. A more fulsome account of this world as having been almost indistinguishable in its atrocity compared to the later military sexual slavery of the wartime period is contained in an account of legalized brothel prostitution in Japan's pre-war civilian sex industry.

## Women's experience of brothels in the Taisho era

The most comprehensive account of conditions in Japan's immediate pre-war sex industry is contained in a monograph published by historian Tanikawa Mitsue who began researching women prostituted in Sapporo's legalized brothel district in 1980 after interviewing a hairdresser who had formerly worked with women in the district. Tanikawa came across her initial information about the district only incidentally; she had interviewed the woman for the purpose of researching Hokkaido's pre-war traditional hairsetting industry. Tanikawa recalls feeling so distressed by the respondent's account that she was moved to research the issue. She then spent four years interviewing twenty-five people connected to the pre-war brothel district, including former prostituted women, pimps and customers. The interviews published verbatim in Tanikawa's book published in

1984 document in extraordinary detail the nature of the treatment sustained by women in Japan's Taisho-era brothels. The brothels were part of a legalized district that opened up in 1869 to cater to new settler Hokkaido migrants who were mostly male. The district boomed for fifty years. There were 916 people in Sapporo in 1872, with thirty brothels selling 300 women, and the number of brothels remained the same up until the 1940s. Most women in the brothels came from poor farming and fishing villages in the northern prefectures. As with all legalized prostitution in Japan at this time, women were not able to freely leave the district.[105]

The remaining paragraphs of this chapter describe in detail aspects of women's lives in the brothels, as recounted to Tanikawa by individuals connected in different ways to the Sapporo district in the Taisho era. The accounts are only a few of those contained in Tanikawa's collection, but are selected on the basis they specifically describe the sex industry as it operated sometime during the fourteen years of the Taisho period. The accounts are herein summarized without much editorial; their mode of reading might therefore be encouraged to replicate that exercised for accounts of military comfort station life, such as for those contained in collections like *The true stories of the comfort women* or *Chinese comfort women: Testimonies from imperial Japan's sex slaves*.[106] Accounts of civilian prostitution past or present are not often afforded the respectful forms of reading that have developed for testimony collected from comfort station survivors, despite individuals like Tanikawa and this book's author experiencing 'distress' in encountering and recording them. But, as was originally the case for Tanikawa, it was these accounts that originally prompted the current project, and their weight and significance will hopefully similarly move readers now in English. Tanikawa is unusual for having documented evidence of women's lives in civilian prostitution; there exist few similar collections for periods reaching as far back as the 1920s in either Japanese or English. Her work perhaps sets a good precedent for a field of future research centring on survivor testimony that examines the lives of women in systems of civilian sexual slavery all over the world in a similar way to the work done to date in pursuit of justice for comfort station survivors.

## Accounts of Taisho-era civilian sexual slavery

There was a police station located immediately next to the entrance gate of the brothel district, and women had to receive permission from police to exit through it, as well as have prior permission from their individual pimps.

Attempts at escape were punished by severe beating, and police would retrieve escapees on behalf of brothel owners.[107] A woman who lived near the brothel district told Tanikawa of an incident that she could 'never forget' in 1931 or 1932 where she saw a woman aged 24 or 25 running in bare feet along a public street, holding sandals in her hand, constantly looking over her shoulder in broad daylight. Her hair and kimono were dishevelled. There was a man aged in his fifties following her wearing a male kimono, 'walking slowly'. It looked like he was her pimp. It was like 'he was a cat preying on a mouse', the woman recalled. 'I was so scared I couldn't take a step further'. 'The woman was running north out of the town, but I wonder what happened to her after that … She came from the direction of the brothel district, so I assume she was a prostitute'.[108] In a similar story recounted by another of Tanikawa's respondents, a woman who lived in the brothel district neighbourhood for fifty years saw two bare-footed women running down the laneway at the back of her house when she was in first-year primary school in 1940. She remembers one of them being caught by a brothel owner and screaming for help.[109]

A former constable interviewed by Tanikawa who was stationed at the brothel district police station for three years described pimps to her as 'horrible' (*hidoimono*), and noted that some underage girls in the brothels had been 'adopted' by pimps.[110] He remembered that very few of the girls came from Sapporo, and most were from the northern prefecture fishing villages where the *nishishi* catch had ran out.[111] The constable was occasionally responsible for being present at weekly venereal disease tests (this was not his job, but the sanitation department sometimes ordered him to attend). There was no nurse present during testing; just the doctor, himself, and a person charged with writing down results.[112] He described to Tanikawa in sympathetic terms the dire state of health he saw many women in at the hospital: 'Some women's genital regions were "purple" and "oozing" because of the number of men they had to service'. 'There was one woman who saw thirty men a night, and she couldn't walk the next day'. 'The doctor asked her whether she would be all right [from thereon in], and she replied that she just wanted to pay off her debt'. The women squirted manganese dioxide liquid into their vaginas after being used by customers in an attempt to prevent infection and pregnancy.[113] There was no requirement for men to use condoms in legal brothels at this time in Japan.[114] The constable remembered one woman becoming mentally ill with syphilis of the brain. She was admitted to hospital but was likely to have died there because penicillin was not in use in Japan at that time.[115] Women in the brothel district frequently developed advanced symptoms of venereal disease because they went to great lengths to hide infection, because mandatory hospital admission and time off would add to their debts. The constable described to Tanikawa his being 'disgusted' at the sight of a row of women sitting on a hospital bench waiting to be tested and wiping each other's genitals with cloths in the hope it would improve their chances of hiding infection. He told Tanikawa he felt sorry for the women in having to face the dilemma of enduring venereal disease or else accumulating debt through hospital admission.[116] During his three years in the district he saw ten women commit suicide.[117]

An administrator with the district brothel association interviewed by Tanikawa was able to recount details of prostituted women's lives learnt through having to submit paperwork to police about them when they applied to register in the district (i.e. when they were first trafficked into a brothel in the district). He recalled the fact that 'most of the women had graduated only as far as primary school, and were not really able to write. Writing their name was about as much as they could do'. 'There was not one woman who entered the industry without debt'. 'There was not one instance in which a woman was employed directly by a brothel owner – they were all brought in by brokers [*shuusenya*]'.[118] He told Tanikawa that all the women had been sold by parents, but not directly to the brothels – they had previously passed through *kafes* and other venues where their debts had escalated to the point where they had to enter a brothel. According to the administrator, there were 300–340 women in the district in the Taisho period, with only seven of these women originally from Sapporo. But even women born in Sapporo (i.e. the location of the brothel district) had previously been in prostitution venues in Tokyo or Osaka.[119]

A survivor of the district spoke to Tanikawa about her entry into one of the district brothels at age 18 in 1937. Both of her parents had died. She recalls this had been the time military men had began to pour into Sapporo. From her story recorded by Tanikawa it appears that she was prostituted for the first time in the brothel, but this would make her account an extremely unusual case. She told Tanikawa that her first time being prostituted was by a pimp from another brothel.[120] After this, she was 'taught' by other women in the brothel how to service customers, but this teaching was simply to do whatever the customer wanted ('*kyaku no iu ga mama*').[121] In discussing her experience with Tanikawa, she emphasized her abhorrence at having no ability to refuse any individual customer because of the punishment that would result.[122] Even though she was not one of the brothel's 'top-ranking' earners, she nonetheless remembered having to service seventeen to eighteen men on busy Saturdays.[123] This went on for nine years. During this time she became sick, infertile and was hospitalized three times with gonorrhoea, once for a stretch of one-and-a-half months.

A woman who ran a bathhouse in the brothel district from 1936 told Tanikawa that she saw a number of women die from venereal disease, and she speculated that their deaths were aggravated by the fact that they received inadequate food in the brothels.[124] Indeed, a number of Tanikawa's respondents recall knowing about the practice of brothel managers withholding of food from women who failed to attract enough customers. A former pimp similarly spoke to Tanikawa about his strategy of denying heating to women who failed to attract customers,[125] which must have posed a significant health risk, given Hokkaido's extremely low temperatures. A cafeteria waitress who worked in the district from 1949 when there were still fifteen to sixteen brothels in operation recounted to Tanikawa her memory of women coming into the cafeteria to eat because they had not attracted any customers the night before. They paid for the food on credit, but invariably had difficulty paying off their debts to the cafeteria.[126]

## Conclusion

The political, economic and cultural 'liberalism' of the Taisho era is widely framed as a democratizing force that generated progressive trends in pre-war Japanese society, including in relation to the condition of women. Historian Fredrick Dickenson describes a 'robust culture of peace' prevailing in this interwar period.[127] Historians are enthusiastic about the emergence of the Japanese 'new woman' during the Taisho era who was sexually liberal and active in her attempts at 'erotic' engagement with men, and in profiting from this engagement. Rarely mentioned, however, are escalating rates of prostitution buying among Japanese men and accumulating sex industry profits around the time. When acknowledged, moreover, these facts are rarely cited in evidence of any developing 'dark valley' in the sexual politics of Japanese men and women; on the contrary, they are attributed to female sexual liberation, or things like 'urban culture'. Prostitution is attributed to women as their will and freedom, and not to any consolidating sexual fascism among Japanese men during the Taisho years. If Japanese men did harbour a will towards peace in the Taisho era, this peace does not appear to have extended to their relationships with women and children; extensive networks of traffickers, brokers, pimps and proprietors developed to meet demand from men for the prostitution of women and girls. The industrialization of prostitution in the 'tawdry' years of Taisho reflects, I argue, a decidedly peace-less historical time for women, and an environment of escalating male hostility and violence towards women and children that had unfortunately predictable consequences for the Showa years.

Clarifying the sexual politics of the Taisho era in this way allows for more light to be shed on the historical development of the comfort station system from the 1930s. Rather than the empowerment of women, the Taisho era might be better understood as a period in which Japanese men made unfortunately large gains in sexual rights and entitlements. Access to women for prostitution might be recognized as having been 'democratized' in this era, and this suggestion has been made by Miho Matsugu who writes that, 'to be able to buy the services of a geisha for an evening was a symbolic act of democratization and modernization' in the view of middle class men during the era,[128] with '"[m]ass-produced" geisha', who are 'products of social inequality and patriarchal sexism', 'provid[ing] the illusion of equality for men'. The next chapter suggests that this democratizing trend continued into the 1930s as the military became involved in mobilizing Japanese women for prostitution and in collaboration with the civilian sex industry. Rather than the repression historians see Japanese men as enduring in the war years, the next chapter highlights the consolidation and expansion of Taisho-era male sexual rights in the form of military prostitution that was achieved during the early Showa years through the vehicles of war and militarism.

3

# The 1930s Militarization of Civilian Prostitution

Today was Sunday, so I was busy receiving soldiers from early on in the morning. We were so busy last night I didn't get a wink of sleep. And then today it has been busy again. In other words, I haven't slept in 24 hours. I am so worn out. The number of soldiers is starting to drop off now, so I have to clean my room and fix my makeup. When I look in the mirror I see a ghost staring back at me. I constantly feel sick. But I have to go back out into the shop [i.e. brothel reception]. I have no choice. So it won't be until noon tomorrow that I'll be able to go to bed and sleep. By then I will have worked for 40 hours straight. (Diary entry of a prostituted woman in a civilian brothel in Japan in the 1930s.)[1]

The gradual encroachment of military ideas and practices on Japanese society in the 1920s and 1930s is well documented. While the full extent of total war mobilization in Japan is seen as having taken place not until the early 1940s, historians nonetheless identify many ways in which the military exercised influence over Japan's society and economy before this. Much of this description is broad and abstract – such as trends in school education towards the teaching of nationalistic ideas – but there are also concrete examples of ways in which the institutions, organizations, and cultural practices of Japanese society were directly co-opted by the military towards its own ends. Some of these examples are noted in the first part of the chapter.

There are, however, few accounts of military co-optation of Japan's civilian sex industry in the 1920s and 1930s, in either English or Japanese. This is despite brothels in the 1930s advertising discounted rates for military personnel on their weekly Sundays off,[2] and being popularly frequented by troops as the opening quote shows. When on leave from duty, soldiers lined up to prostitute women in civilian brothels in a similar fashion to their later patronage of comfort stations, which one soldier recalled was like 'waiting in line to use a public toilet.'[3] Suzuki Yuuko thinks the 'policy and organization' of the 'comfort women' system capitalized 'one hundred per cent' on 'know-how' generated by Japan's long-running legalized prostitution industry. She adds that private prostitution entrepreneurs were made 'full use of' by the military.[4] Onozawa Akane writes that recruiters for navy comfort stations in Shanghai at the beginning of 1938 were active in Gunma, Yamagata, Kouchi, Wakayama, Ibaragi and Miyagi prefectures attempting to lure women out of sex industry venues to comfort stations abroad. The navy had issued a request for 3,000 women to be recruited in this way.[5] As the war years progressed and demand for prostitution grew, the military commandeered existing civilian brothels within Japan, directed the creation of private-run comfort stations in the country, and ordered the conversion of geisha venues into exclusive military-use establishments. The second part of the chapter describes these ways in which Japan's homeland sex industry was co-opted by the military before and during the operation of the wartime comfort station system.

The discussion of the chapter highlights the contribution of civilian prostitution and Japan's 'peacetime' homeland sex industry to the creation of the military system. This role was not limited to fostering permissive attitudes towards prostitution among men who went on to become soldiers, even if this was also a significant outcome of the proliferation and normalization of the pre-war sex industry, and is described later in the chapter. Further, this role was not limited to fashioning the manner in which comfort stations were set up, run, and patronized, as Yoshimi Yoshiaki has noted as a significant influence of the civilian sex industry in relation to the military system:

> Soldiers using military comfort stations usually paid a fee. Therefore, to soldiers, going to a military comfort station was not much different from purchasing the services of a prostitute at a civilian brothel in Japan or the colonies.[6]

Even more concretely, I argue, the civilian sex industry formed an infrastructural and logistical base from which the military was able to establish its comfort station system, first within Japan and then abroad. This direct connection between civilian and wartime prostitution is left mostly uncommented upon in accounts of the comfort station system, and this lacuna, I argue, has inhibited full comprehension of the peacetime origins of military sexual slavery, as well as understanding of the extent of human rights violation perpetrated against Japanese women in civilian, and later, military prostitution. The argument of the chapter is that the scale and sophistication of Japan's sex industry by the 1930s was an important aid to the creation of the wartime sexual slavery system, and so the prostitution of the Taisho-era should be recognized not just in ideological but also practical and concrete terms as facilitating its creation.

## Military co-optation of Japan's civilian economy and society

The military mobilization of Japan's industry and commerce began from the time of the Russo-Japanese War (1904–1905), but Michael Barnhart nominates the Diet's 1926 approval of the army's request to create a Cabinet Resources Bureau – 'Japan's first agency charged with overseeing a total mobilization effort' – as a watershed moment in the progress of domestic military takeover.[7] Barnhart writes that the Bureau established 'supervisory and control organs for all important industries', and that '[t]hese organs in turn would fall under the jurisdiction of the Imperial Army'. While there was nationalization of the electric power industry and other developments in the late 1930s, including an active-duty requirement for parliamentary ministers in 1936 and a 33 per cent increase in the army budget in the same year, Kerry Smith writes that military mobilization 'had been quietly underway since early in the 1930s, as military and civilian planners laid the foundations for closer ties between the state and industry through legislation, regulation, and the promotion of companies friendly to the military's needs'.[8] Historians are mostly in agreement that tangible indicators of military mobilization emerged in the early 1930s, but Orihara and Clancey make the striking observation that the 1923 Great Kanto Earthquake was an earlier historical marker of progress in the military's ascendancy. Following the earthquake,

> a state of *hijouji* [emergency] was stressed to emphasize the role of the Japanese military, but more importantly, to show that these soldiers, who had only recently been criticized as elitist and even redundant in the Taisho press, were in fact on the people's side ... The military now emphasized its role of providing safety and security for the population at home rather than just expanding and defending the Empire abroad.[9]

Richard Smethurst's work from 1974 describing military co-optation of rural civic organizations in the 1930s gives support to this view of military efforts to leverage civilian social institutions in the name of domestic 'safety and security'. He writes that the 'army quickly supported and encouraged ... martial societies [in rural areas], and, a few years later, reservist groups (*zaigou gunjindan*)' as well, which 'performed patriotic, relief, military, and community service duties'. These all-male, proto-military groups engaged in a wide range of social activities, including 'ceremonies to show respect for the imperial family, to remember the war dead, and to honour the families whose sons fought in the two wars during 1890 to 1910 ... [and] they also contributed money and labour to the families of war casualties, helped the families of those on active duty both during the wars and in peacetime, and even gave patriotic education to women'. Even more directly towards military ends, the men 'carried out military training for youth group members to emphasize martial ideas, especially discipline and obedience, and performed all manner of local construction and repair projects and disaster relief'.[10] Iwata Shigenori suggests the groups concurrently functioned as a vehicle for men's patronage of the sex industry in pre-war Japan; older group members would accompany younger members to brothels, or the men would engage in prostitution in groups while away together on overnight trips to hot springs resorts.[11]

The military's hijacking of Japan's economy and society in service of its warmaking in the 1920s and 1930s is easily identifiable in these examples of mobilization of private industry and civil society organizations. The mobilization of public institutions, too, is well documented in accounts of the army's use of school facilities and curricula in the 1930s. While examples of educational pre-war military co-optation are often described in terms of ideological influences, such as the gradual infiltration of imperialistic teachings into classrooms, Mangan and Komagome write more concretely that, '[i]n 1925[,] all middle and higher schools were ordered to include military training in their curriculum'. Even before this, moreover, 'non-commissioned reserve officers instructed the pupils in elementary drill'. And then, from 1925, 'serving officers were assigned to schools as military training instructors … [and] [t]he training included battlefield command, shooting practice with live ammunition, lectures on modern weapons and military tactics'.[12] Yoshimitsu Khan adds that, from 1938, '[s]chools were … required to conduct routine physical examinations for military preparedness'.[13] The logistical base that schools appear to have become in the 1930s for the implementation of military training and recruitment preparations is a clear example of the army co-opting a social institution towards operational ends in pre-war Japan.

While cultural products and practices were more likely marshalled in support of the military's ideological agenda, rather than for any operational function in the 1930s, some fairly specific accounts of military leveraging of culture are nonetheless available. Jeremy Phillipps, for example, writes that an 'imperialistic tendency of expositions [i.e. "trade expos"] became … clear in the 1930s, when they were used as military propaganda devices to justify the invasion of China'.[14] He cites the example of a Kanazawa prefecture political party going 'so far as to petition directly the city government to change the name of [a scheduled] exposition from "Industry and Tourism" to "Industry and Military"'. While this request was ultimately rejected, Phillipps notes that 'the media adopted militarism as an unofficial third theme of the exposition, and the bulk of its reporting was focused on the militaristic and imperialistic themes of the exposition'.[15] Cultural consumer items were similarly used by the military around this time as a means of promoting its interests within civilian society. Emily Horner writes that '*[k]amishibai* came into existence in 1930, just as Japan was modernizing, militarizing and preparing for imperialistic wars with nearby Asian nations'.[16] For the military, these children's paper picture plays were '[f]ar cheaper to produce than movies, with greater accessibility than radio broadcasts, and targeted at young children', and so '*kamishibai* became a primary form of propaganda and indoctrination'. She notes the plays frequently featured teachings about Japan's 'warrior code'.[17]

## Civilian prostitution and the shaping of male sexuality

While historians thereby identify concrete and specific examples of Japanese industry, civic organizations, social institutions, and even cultural products being targeted by the army and put towards military ends in the 1930s, this analysis rarely extends to the sex industry, in spite of its size, prominence and pervasiveness before the war, as described in the previous chapter. Venues, trafficking networks, sexually transmitted disease testing schemes, and other structural features of the industry are only occasionally noted as furnishing the military with an infrastructural base in creating its comfort station system. When the pre-war civilian sex industry is described as an institution prefacing the development of the military system, historians like Suzuki Yuuko generally limit this attribution to the sexual values and practices it fostered among men in the pre-war period.[18] In other words, civilian prostitution is mostly described as ideologically acculturating Japanese men to the sexual attitudes, ethics, and practices that characterized the wartime comfort station system, rather than as furnishing the military with the facilities, business know-how, procurers, brokers, and supply-chain networks (i.e. trafficking systems), as well as the practices of violence and intimidation that are invariably required for the task of rounding up large numbers of women for prostitution, whether in peacetime or in war.[19]

Ideological and behavioural links between Japan's pre-war civilian sex industry and the emergent wartime prostitution system are of course important to understanding peacetime antecedents of military sexual slavery, and so are considered next. The anthropologist who has written most comprehensively about behavioural links is Chuo University's Iwata Shigenori. Inexplicably, his work is almost nowhere cited in discussions of the comfort station system, either in English or Japanese, despite his fairly substantial writing on the topic in two articles in 1991 and 1998. I recite Iwata's research at length below for the clarity it brings to understanding the ideological and behavioural groundwork that was laid by Japan's civilian sex industry in advance of the military system. I return to civilian infrastructural bases of the military system later in the chapter.

## Behavioural antecedents of military sexual slavery

Iwata is concerned with the prostitution behaviour of Japanese men in the 1910s and 1920s: when it emerged, and why. He aims to understand what kinds of sexual values and practices drove them to participate in military prostitution with apparently little compunction. (Indeed, Kano Mikiyo writes that, '[a]fter reading more than 20 books written by former Japanese soldiers, and dating from 1951 to as recently as August, 1991, I've come to this conclusion. Most of the authors were extremely nonchalant in their recounting of stories of rapes or of forced prostitution'.)[20] Iwata begins his examination on the assumption that

> the sexuality of Japanese men in the military and on the battlefield cannot be totally divorced from that fostered within their daily lives carried out in civilian Japanese society ... while the military bears responsibility for the destruction of the human rights of the comfort women and the tacitly accepted rapes of the battlefield, we might wonder why Japanese men failed to feel any sense of abhorrence or guilt in relation to these practices.[21]

He explicates this assumption with the claim that 'the prostitution sexuality [*kaishun no sei o sonaeta*] of Japanese men, both married men and young male youth, was behind their acceptance of the large scale organization of "comfort women" that took place after the Nanjing Incident'.[22] The term 'prostitution sexuality' is defined as 'an impoverished male sexuality in which women are seen as lesser, and as nothing more than objects for the satisfaction of sexual desire', but in practice, Iwata uses the phrase more concretely to denote a sexuality cultivated through patronage of the sex industry.[23] He investigates how and why this sexuality historically developed among Japanese men in the pre-war era through looking at traditional cultural practices taking place in Japan's rural areas where most of the population lived up until the 1930s.

Iwata answers his research question in controversial terms, and his view that traditional rural cultural practices gave rise to a habituated practice of prostitution among Japanese men at the turn of the twentieth century attracted criticism from Japan's top-ranking anthropologists when it was published in the late 1990s. Iwata found that the system of organized male youth group-based sexual control of girls in rural villages (which is well known among Japanese anthropologists and referred to as '*yobai*') formed a historical base to the emergence of normalized and widespread prostitution behaviour by Japanese male youth from the 1910s.[24] In Iwata's words,

> the sexuality of *yobai* practised by male youth in villages in [sexually] controlling girls expanded into the public sphere [from the turn of the century], and transformed into the shape of the prostitution sexuality that became characteristic of the modern Japanese state. The decline in [the cultural practice of] *yobai* did not represent any fundamental change in the nature of the sexuality practiced among youth, but simply spelt its transition into the broader sphere of prostitution. The traditional cultural basis of *yobai* established a foundation for this transition in male sexual control over women, which simply found a new form in the prostitution of the commercial world ... money merely became the new medium by which this [sexual] control was organised.[25]

In coming up with this finding, Iwata analysed oral testimony from a range of men speaking about their youthful sexual practices of the pre-war period. A man born in 1925 in Shizuoka prefecture, for example, recalls how young men in his town formed a 'club' where they would 'talk endlessly' about which girls in the town would acquiesce to sex and where these girls lived. In addition to attempting to arrange assignations with these girls, the club members would walk together for an hour outside of the town to visit brothels using money sourced through stealing and selling rice from their family storehouses. To pay for prostitution they also appropriated funds awarded by the local government office to their youth group for monitoring house fire outbreaks at night-time.[26] A second example of historical overlap between practices of female sexual control exercised by groups of male youth in the tradition of *yobai* and the buying of women for prostitution is noted in Iwata's recorded testimony from another man from Shizuoka prefecture. This man in his youth had lived with other young men in a 'house' (*yado*), which was a traditional living arrangement in some parts of rural Japan in the pre-war period. According to the man's testimony, the male youth living in the *yado* would use money received on festival days to buy women for prostitution. Members of the group would also go out in twos or threes at night time to facilitate one of the group members entering a village house to engage in sexual activity with a local girl.[27] A third man born in a Shizuoka village in 1911 recounted to Iwata the fact male youth ten years' older than him were visiting the houses of local girls for the purpose of sexual access, but by the time he was old enough to join the group (*seinendan*), this practice had died out in favour of visiting local prostitution venues. The man recalls going on an overnight trip with his *seinendan* in 1934 during which time members of the group visited a tourist brothel district.[28]

On the basis of these and other examples, Iwata nominates an historically specific time period over which the sexuality of *yobai* became the widespread and socially accepted male prostitution behaviour that characterized the Taisho era, and so explains why, by the 1930s, Japanese married men were habitually frequenting legalized brothels and geisha venues in the cities, and younger men *kafes* and other cheaper venues. This historical period of transition where the traditional practice of *yobai* was succeeded by the practice of buying women for prostitution forms the basis of Iwata's view that there exists an anthropological foundation to the prevalence of prostitution in modern Japanese society. (This view is notably different from the popular view that there exists a 'cultural' foundation to the prevalence of prostitution in modern Japanese society.)

It is not difficult to comprehend Iwata's suggestion that the 1930s was the decade in which male patronage of the sex industry came to be normalized in Japan, and traditional practices of sexual exploitation of young women in villages died out in favour of prostitution as the main sexual practice of Japanese male youth. He notes that the emergence of day-labouring and working away from home that came with industrialization and urbanization meant male youth individually began to have money to spend on prostitution,[29] and there exists empirical evidence to support this observation. By 1932, Japanese men were conducting nearly 23 million prostitution transactions per year.[30] They had carried out over 61,000 transactions each day in 1928 (by way of comparison, this roughly equals the *weekly* figure for prostitution visits in the Australian state of Victoria in contemporary times),[31] and per year, this amounted to 22,273,849 visits. This meant that women were servicing 470 men per year, but Kusama Yasoo notes that 'ten per cent' of these women would have likely taken time off or been in hospital due to venereal disease or other ailments, some women would have taken time off for 'accidents', and others would have been 'on the run'.[32] Taking this into consideration, Kusama estimates that women nationally were being bought by 498 men per year, and by 844 men per year in Tokyo.[33] He notes that there was an increase in the rate at which men prostituted women in Tokyo after the Great Kanto Earthquake in 1923, and speculates this was because of an influx of builders and engineers into the city in the reconstruction taking place after the disaster.[34]

Iwata then explores how this 'prostitution sexuality' manifested among men going off to war in the late 1930s.[35] He emphasizes the extreme sense of sexual entitlement that Japanese men apparently harboured upon arriving at battlefields.[36] Citing an example from 1938, he writes that a Japanese-run Shanghai military field hospital had a separate wing set up for comfort women suffering venereal disease. According to the account, a group of soldiers who had just landed at the port visited this wing and were told by staff they could not have sex with the women interned there, because they might become sick. To this, the troops replied they did not mind, and asked to be given access to the women regardless. In another example, Iwata cites an entry in a Japanese military doctor's diary from 1939 that describes Chinese locals jokingly asking him whether Japanese troops had come to China to fight or to prostitute women. Apparently, the troops were so brazen and prolific in their patronage of prostitution venues that their behaviour had become a running joke among the local population. Iwata sees these two examples as indicating the sexually debased (*asamashii*) nature of Japanese male sexuality by this stage of Japanese history.[37]

Other illustrations can be cited in support of his understanding. One historian has noted, for example, that, in the late 1930s, Japanese navy men would literally run the one kilometre that separated the Korean port where they docked on Wednesdays, Fridays, and Sundays and the local comfort station.[38] Another writer has described a soldier stepping off a warship in Okinawa in 1944 that had just sailed in from Manchuria and exclaiming with glee, 'so we get to make love to Okinawan women this time?'.[39] The Japanese military went to great lengths to make sure women were ready and waiting for troops to prostitute as soon as they arrived at new barracks, and so comfort stations were set up in advance of troop arrival. Yuki Tanaka writes that the Japanese military trafficked women even to front line battlefields, and even as late as November 1944. He recounts the fact that, in this month, seven Korean women were 'sent to [a] comfort station on Tokashiki Island, a small isolated island of Okinawa'.[40] This was less than one year before the end of the Pacific War, and a time when the Japanese military barely had any ships left for troop transport, let alone supplies to fight the war. Fujino Yutaka notes that comfort stations within Japan were kept running even during the American bombings towards the end of the war, and a domestic comfort station was approved for opening in Tokyo to cater to military police on as late as 15 May 1945.[41] Kanzaki Kiyoshi recounts the fact that 300 prostituted women died in the Yoshiwara brothel district in the March 1945 US bombings of Tokyo, which was one-third of the women housed there at the time.[42] Regardless, the district reopened three months later with twenty women in seven brothels.[43] The military assisted with this reconstruction through promising to supply free building materials on 10 August 1945, only days before the end of the war.[44] The conclusion of the war on 15 August invalidated all contracts made by the military, but Kanzaki writes that, astoundingly, the military followed through on this particular contract and transported across town building materials harvested from the ruined remains of Tokyo houses. In a truly absurdist ending to the story, Kanzaki notes that the Tokyo city government also donated 300 mattresses to the reconstructed brothels.[45] In aggregate, these examples paint a picture of Japanese men in war that is almost farcical in its preoccupation with maintaining ongoing access to women for prostitution.

## Pornography consumption among military men

Contemporary feminist social scientists find pornography consumption to be positively correlated with men's buying of women for prostitution,[46] and feminist theorists understand pornography to comprise a form of prostitution by virtue of its documented recording of prostitution acts.[47] Melissa Farley describes pornography as 'a form of cultural propaganda which reifies the notion that women are prostitutes'.[48] Pornography is further understood to both reflect and fuel social conditions conducive to men's prostitution of women.[49] Catharine MacKinnon suggests pornography consumption has specifically measurable outcomes in war: 'The saturation of what was Yugoslavia with pornography upon the dissolution of communism ... has created a population of men prepared to experience sexual pleasure in torturing and killing women'.[50] The same phenomenon, if in less widespread terms, might be observed for Japanese men in the China and Pacific wars. Mark Driscoll describes the beginnings of a pornographic magazine market developing in Japan in the 1930s, which he sees as a 'crucial mass cultural precedent for the eroticized violence that characterized Japanese militarism in Asia'.[51] I agree with Driscoll's assessment of pornography as representing a cultural indication in the pre-war period of the nature of the sexual behaviour practised by Japanese men, and therefore a bellwether of the sexuality that would be exercised in war. The following paragraphs therefore briefly describe the state of pornography production and consumption that reigned in Japan before the onset of Showa era fascism.

While Mark McLelland has written about pornography consumption among Japanese male civilians (many of whom who were recently demobilized) in the immediate post-war period,[52] pre-war accounts describing pornography usage are mostly limited to military contexts. Stewart Lone, for example, notes a 'wartime rise in illicit erotic photographs' around the time of the 1904 Russo-Japanese War, and cites evidence that '[t]here were repeated arrests of those making and trading such material' around this time within Japan. Nonetheless, according to Lone, 'erotic images continued to be made and, as in the case of one Gifu city photographer, the intended clientele was clearly the army in Manchuria'.[53] These photographs were apparently made out of women prostituted in the sex industry. Lone writes that, '[a]ccording to one of Gifu city's photographers, when finally uncovered and questioned by police, there was … a market for illicit nude portraits of Gifu's brothel workers among soldiers at the front'.[54] Naoko Shimazu's research on Japanese society during the Russo-Japanese War supports this observation of pornography consumption by soldiers. She quotes a military surgeon who wrote that,

> [s]eeing that at first postcards of beauties became all the rage, and in seeing the lustful bodies it was possible to satisfy some desire, this method [of supplying pictures of 'beauties'] was simply not enough, and in the end, there was a boom of pornographic prints (*shunga*) as well as naked photographs of beauties, people … competed to obtain these … Some of the more popular ones depicted prostitutes or nude models dressed as Red Cross nurses, who became the iconic image of the war for both the Japanese and Russian soldiers.[55]

Japan's photography industry was well set up to organize prostituted women for pornography production by the end of the twentieth century. Maki Fukuoka writes that photography businesses came to be historically concentrated in an area of Tokyo close to the Yoshiwara brothel district. These businesses in Asakusa 'could count on those who visited the theatre district and pleasure quarter as potential clients … [and so] photographic studios in Asakusa … began to sell portraits of famous kabuki actors and courtesans' in the nineteenth century.[56] Demand for pornography products expanded with the advent of the Russo-Japanese War, and by the time of the Pacific War Japanese men were apparently combining pornography consumption with prostitution: Korean survivor Yun Turi testified to the Korean Council for Women Drafted for Military Sexual Slavery by Japan that Japanese soldiers had brought a pornographic book titled *48 Rules* into the comfort station room where she was held and demanded she simulate its pictures.[57] According to an account taken from a Japanese survivor, pimps used pornography to 'teach' newly interned comfort women how to 'open their legs and position their hips' in order to that their vaginas be easily accessible for penile penetration by troops.[58] By the end of the war, Japanese military men appear to have prostituted women in comfort stations for the purpose of pornography production. Bang-Soon Yoon writes that,

> in the Spring of 1945, the U.S. military captured large quantities of pornographic photos of Japanese soldiers and young 'oriental' women who must have been 'comfort girls' abandoned by the defeated Japanese forces stationed at the headquarters of the Japanese Army at Shuri Castle near Naha.[59]

While evidence of pornography production and consumption by Japanese military men is scant, I think the role of these materials in promoting the prostitution activity of troops during wartime cannot be overlooked if we seek to identify cultural antecedents of military sexual slavery, and especially those circulating in peacetime.

## Civilian sex industry response to military demand

Whether for debt-bonded labourers, troops, or military factory workers, Japan's civilian prostitution industry stood ready and waiting in the 1930s to respond to male demand for sexual access to women, as well as the military's logistical needs in organizing this access, both at home and abroad. The militarization of the homeland sex industry occurred in a myriad of ways in the 1930s, and this history points to a significant role for the business of 'peacetime' prostitution and its entrepreneurs in developing wartime sexual slavery. As mentioned, this role was not merely ideological. Logistical and infrastructural support provided by the civilian sex industry in catering to military needs has a long history in Japan. As in many places around the world, the industry has a history of setting up businesses in areas around where troops are stationed,[60] but the scale and early historical development of these 'camptown' prostitution areas in Japan perhaps indicates a uniquely long and close relationship between the country's sex industry and its military, and an especially high level of cooperation in securing male sexual access to women. This cooperation has historically included negotiating 'discounted' prostitution rates for military men, as mentioned above, as well as the locating of sex industry businesses conveniently for military requirements. In 1981, physician Saga Jun'ichi spoke with a survivor of the geisha system, Yamamura Tsuya, who recounted the fact that high-ranking officers from Japan's naval air squadron would patronize geisha restaurants while their underlings visited brothels in the years immediately before the war. In the small town where Yamamura lived, the geisha restaurants were conveniently located directly across the road from the brothels.[61]

Fujime Yuuki cites a number of nineteenth-century examples from different parts of Japan showing the responsiveness of the civilian sex industry to shifts in the regional stationing of troops. She highlights the fact that '[n]ew red-light districts were built, old ones expanded, and declining ones resurrected' according to shifts in troop positioning within the country.[62]

> In Fukuchiyama, motivated by the transfers of the Sixteenth Battalion Army of Engineers in 1897 and of the Twentieth Infantry Regiment the following year, people in the [prostitution] trade, expecting large profits, bought up vacant lots to expand the red-light district. The Dokicho Red-Light District in Fushimi, Kyoto, which had declined after the Meiji Restoration, was rebuilt for the Sixteenth Division. When the Seventeenth Division arrived in Okayama after the Russo-Japanese War, the number of brothel employees and prostitutes increased dramatically.[63]

Imanaka Yasuko describes the development of prostitution districts around army and navy bases in Hiroshima prefecture from the late 1800s, and writes that, by the mid-1920s, there were around 460 prostitution entrepreneurs operating in the prefecture selling between 2,200 and 2,700 women. She notes that the majority of these were in Kure and other districts patronized primarily by the military, and their numbers rose with the onset of war.[64] An account from Naoko Shimazu suggests that demand for the prostitution of women in Hiroshima was fierce. An incident arose during the Russo-Japanese War in which 'some several hundred soldiers waiting to embark on their journey to the front caused a major disturbance in the red light district [in Hiroshima], when one brothel was destroyed and many sustained injuries'.[65] By the 1920s, Hiroshima was host to Japan's sixth largest sex industry, in spite of ranking eighth largest city by population in Japan that year.[66] Imanaka describes Hiroshima's economy as reliant on military bases and armament factories, and notes the especial centrality of the sex industry to the city's economy and regional society. By way of example, she describes the city holding a welcoming party in 1935 for the navy's second fleet arriving into port. The city *kafe* association, brothel association and other industry associations joined together with the local newspaper company, government officials, and youth association to put on a banquet for the arrival. In the four days the fleet was stationed in Hiroshima more than 1,500 military men patronized brothels.[67]

Lone describes pre-war competition among Japanese towns to attract military bases to their areas on the basis of the economic inflows they expected to result. Part of this was anticipation of sex industry profits. He cites a case in which the Japanese army had announced after the Russo-Japanese War it would establish a base in the Gifu prefectural town of Kanazu. Among business leaders in the town, 'the common assumption ... had been that the real profits of military consumption would go to the brothels of Kanazu'. In anticipation of this surge in business, 'several new brothels had opened in mid-1907 and around 60–70 extra women were brought into the city; this raised the total number of licensed prostitutes at that point to around 350 (up from about 290 in mid-1906)'. Lone offers the analysis that '[m]ost of these new women were housed in the cheaper brothels, suggesting that their intended market was the ordinary soldier'.[68] Apparently, the anticipated level of patronage by soldiers did not eventuate, but another historical account shows no similar demand shortfall among counterparts in the navy. Shimokawa Koushi writes that, '[i]n 1918[,] sailors stationed near the Ryuuguu brothel district in Kyoto prefecture staged a boycott over the prices they were being charged in the brothels, and blocked entry to other customers outside the brothel district gate. The picket went on from November 1918 to February 1919, and finally resulted in the introduction of a "military discount system" in brothel districts'.[69]

From this example, it appears cost was still a barrier to Japanese men exercising the full extent of their demand for the prostitution of women in the 1920s, even though the military appears to have cooperated with civilian pimps in an effort to keep these costs as low as possible. Kanzaki writes that '[t]he navy ... approached pimps for help, specifically in relation to its Shibaura conscript training camp. In response the pimps agreed to give the conscripts a reduced voucher for 20 yen per 2-hour block, which was usually priced at 30 yen'. He comments that 'nationalist fervour' probably led the pimps to agree to this deal,[70] but it is also likely that historically friendly ties between the sex industry and the military played a part. The closeness of this relationship is further suggested in a memoir written in 1966 by Fukuda Toshiko, who was a woman prostituted through a Yoshiwara district geisha venue since childhood. She recalls that one room of the Yoshiwara brothel association headquarters was given over to military police in the 1930s so they could keep check of troops frequenting the brothels.[71]

The sex industry had a financial interest in cooperating with the military in these ways because, as the war progressed, an expanding proportion of its customer base comprised military men. Kanzaki in the early 1970s interviewed six women prostituted through the Yoshiwara brothel district during and after the war, and was told by one of them that the majority of her customers during the war had been soldiers.[72] Another woman who had left home (a fishing village) at age 17 because of her father's violence had travelled to a port town where the navy was stationed. She confided in Kanzaki that all women in the town during the war were being bought for prostitution by navy men.[73] Fukuda recalls the fact that, by 1938, soldiers were frequenting brothels on a regular basis on Sundays.[74] Around this same time, fathers were bringing sons to brothels after having received call-up notices, and military superiors were bringing along subordinates, including underage youth.[75] A former 25th infantry division soldier in the early 1980s told researcher Tanikawa Mitsue that he first visited a brothel at age 21 when he received his call-up notice and an older colleague took him along. The visits became regular after entering the military; each Sunday he and his fellow troops would walk five kilometres to the brothel from the base.[76] This weekly activity appears to have been sanctioned by the military, because another 25th division conscript active during the years 1928–1929 told Tanikawa that soldiers could leave the barracks on Sundays only if they had a condom in hand.[77]

Kanzaki writes that soldiers paid 1.5 yen to use prostituted women in Japan's civilian sex industry during the daytime and notes the military directly approached licensed brothel owners to turn their facilities into comfort stations for troops as the war years progressed. This was done not merely on an ad hoc basis. In November 1944, an army ministry *onshouka* (rewards department) representative met the head of the brothel owners' association and told him the military wanted to start directly overseeing prostitution venues for use by troops in battlefield areas, and would like the 'experienced' pimps of the Yoshiwara brothel district to undertake the task nationally from their base in Tokyo. The navy insisted these pimps needed to initially supply 30–40 women to a hotel in Beijing the Japanese military had commandeered. While the state of the war subsequently worsened and so this plan did not eventuate, Kanzaki notes another example of the Japanese military going through local police to request Yoshiwara pimps set up comfort stations on islands off the Japanese coast where the navy was in battle with US troops. The pimps complied with this in February 1945 and sent thirty women with futons to the islands on the basis the military would pay for their food and lodgings, and the pimps would receive station profits tax-free. Because the women were deemed to be in significant danger in being dispatched to a battleground, it was decided they would receive 40 per cent of earnings, which Kanzaki writes would have probably been the largest proportion of earnings they had ever been allocated from their own prostitution.[78] The reason why women might have nonetheless accepted inducements from pimps and traffickers to move into comfort stations is indicated in Yoshida's observation that

> [m]ost women were bonded to comfort stations with debts of between only 200 to 300 yen, and so they could repay, and even save, money in a number of months, unlike the situation in the civilian sex industry within Japan where most women would be exploited in brothels for years on end.[79]

As the war years progressed, a declining population of Japanese military men were left stationed in Japan, and most of their prostitution activity shifted to sex industries abroad, and eventually to the military-created comfort stations. This shift is described in Chapter Four. Similarly, the number of women in Japan's civilian sex industry declined as they were transitioned wholesale into the military system. Hirai Kazuko explains that 'the military, pimps and traffickers collaborated to target women in the sex industry for trafficking into comfort stations. They did this through offering large advance loans, and an opportunity to escape the civilian sex industry after the end of the debt contract'.[80] Similarly, Onozawa writes that, 'from the time of the China War, the Japanese military used the system of debt bondage practiced conventionally within the civilian sex industry for its own purposes in "buying" women to intern in comfort stations, and government agencies cooperated with this activity'.[81]

Nonetheless, even men who were left in Japan, as well as men brought into Japan as labourers and factory workers, continued to be afforded sexual access to women within the country via an officially-endorsed 'comfort facility' network. Historian Ogino Fujio offers an example that vividly exemplifies the military state's apparent belief in the political usefulness of prostitution. He suggests it was the 'common sense' (*tsuujou ishiki*) understanding of the Japanese government before and during the war that securing male sexual access to women was useful to the war effort. He describes a high level government agency supplying 'comfort women' to a station catering to Chinese forced mine labourers in Toyama prefecture in 1943. Women were trafficked to boost the productivity of debt bonded labourers held in terrible conditions, and the Japanese government thought supplying women for prostitution would bolster worker output.[82] The comfort station ran only for a short length of time as a 'pilot project' at one mine in Toyama but, nonetheless, Ogino sees the example as illustrating just how strongly the Japanese military state believed in the utility of prostitution.[83]

In the 1940s, comfort stations were established around industrial districts throughout Japan. The next section describes Japan's home ministry setting up these homeland comfort facilities in close cooperation with private prostitution entrepreneurs. In fact, as described next, homeland civilian sex industry integration with military prostitution became so comprehensive in Japan in the 1940s that any line dividing peacetime prostitution and wartime sexual slavery might be seen as having all but disappeared.

## Total war mobilization and Japan's civilian sex industry

The close relationship that existed between Japan's military, wartime government and civilian sex industry in the 1940s is described in detail by Onozawa Akane in a 2010 monograph. Her book describes efforts by Japan's home ministry to liaise with the military, the police, as well as civilian prostitution entrepreneurs to set up 'comfort stations' in industrial areas within the country. This programme for the creation of a homeland 'comfort women' network took place from 1944, and resulted in the establishment of nearly 5,000 comfort stations around Japan. Onozawa's research is notable for the view it offers of the wartime comfort women system as coming full circle in terms of developing as military prostitution within the homeland civilian sex industry, and then returning to Japan in the form of 'comfort facilities' at the end of the war to operate in service of all men mobilized for military purposes, and not just troops. This remarkable view of the comfort women system is important to understanding military prostitution as operating as an institution of sexual slavery regardless of the location and context of the venues, the men who patronized them, or the women who were interned in them.

While Kanzaki and Fujino suggest the impetus to developing comfort stations in industrial areas in Japan was to sexually placate exploited male factory workers, Onozawa alternatively cites a sex industry association survey from the 1940s that found growth in prostitution businesses around industrial areas was being driven by factory owners using the venues for 'corporate entertaining' to make sure owners of sub-contracting businesses did not move out of the area, and were enticed to be loyal to their factories. The survey suggested factory owners and executive managers were the main customers of prostitution venues in Japan's industrial areas.[84] Onozawa contends that a male 'nouveau riche' made money out of Japan's war economy, and these men drove ongoing demand for prostitution. They also brought their factory employees along to the venues. As before the war, there was a class gap between the types of venues Japanese men used for prostitution. Rich men used geisha venues, and working class men used *kafes*, brothels, and drinking venues. In industrial districts, this meant that women running alcohol-related venues, and women in industrial areas generally, came under pressure from male workers for demands for prostitution. This was especially the case from 1942 when alcohol-related 'entertainment' venues began to be converted into boarding houses for factory workers as harsher anti-decadence restrictions were applied for the sake of the mobilization of the wartime economy. The number of prostitution venues and prostituted women declined in Japan from this time.[85] Authorities had also placed restrictions on advertising and opening hours for entertainment venues between the years 1939 and 1941.[86] On top of this, wartime decadence policies meant no more permits were given for geisha venues after 1942.[87] The home ministry had also instructed local authorities to limit the number of women entering sex industry venues due to requirements for the wartime mobilization of factory workers.

However, as the war years progressed, Onozawa detects a change in the approach adopted by authorities in relation to sex industry venues in industrial areas. While the government continued to enforce shut-downs of 'high class' geisha venues, it concurrently proposed that 'lower class' hostess venues that had closed down should be revived to offer the 'comfort' that was considered necessary for men in work. Onozawa comments in only vague terms as to why this shift occurred: she suggests it was out of concern for disruption around industrial districts. She cites a March 1944 home ministry report directing local authorities to encourage the development of lower-class prostitution businesses called '*ian shisetsu*' ('comfort facilities') that would 'comfort' workers according to the 'industrial circumstances' of the particular area, and its 'social requirements'.[88] As a result, according to a January 1945 police agency report, by February 1944, a total of 177,001 female workers had either resumed or moved into prostitution businesses such as *kafes* and geisha venues, and this figure included 42,568 formerly prostituted women, of which 7,131 were in officially designated 'comfort facilities'. Of these 4,842 official comfort facilities, geisha boarding houses (*okiya*) were the most common type of venue that had been officially converted, followed by geisha restaurants (*machiai*) and hostess-serving restaurants.[89] Onozawa writes that the home ministry envisaged these 'comfort facilities' would retain the 'entertainment' element of their former venues (such as geisha houses), but that this would be heavily simplified (*kansoka no tettei*). The ministry deemed the comfort facilities would offer 'Japanese-style food and drink, friendly communication, and sexual relations' (*kokumin inshoku ishi sotsuu oyobi seiteki ian*).[90] However, setting up the facilities was difficult because of a lack of necessary provisions, insufficient numbers of women, and the fact proprietors were still wedded to their past business models of profit seeking. More than 40,000 women in geisha venues had left the sex industry during the closure of high-class venues from 1941, and 16,000 had moved into different industries altogether or resigned from the sex industry.[91] This difficulty was compounded by the fact civilians became no longer able to choose their employment from 1944.[92] As a result, businesses that did open as official 'comfort facilities' were fewer than 'required', and were overwhelmed with customers.[93]

Accordingly, Onozawa cites urgent and repeated reference to the need for 'comfort facilities' littering government reports, and reflects on the level of demand for prostitution that continued to circulate among Japanese men even in the late war years. She notes that some areas continued to organize women in large numbers to meet this demand. In Gunma prefecture, for example, twenty new sex industry venues opened up *each year* between the years 1937 and 1940, with thirty extra women on offer between 1937 and 1938 alone.[94] Looking at Gunma specifically, Onozawa finds that while there was a shift within the sex industry in terms of the types of venues that operated during the war mobilization years, there was a contraction in the size of the industry and the number of women prostituted was not that large overall. In Gunma, there was a shift towards the establishment of drinking venues catering to factory workers.[95] She suggests that demand for prostitution rose in Gunma with the influx of workers into industrial areas.[96]

Nonetheless, a 'shortage' of women entering officially endorsed comfort facilities constrained their establishment in most parts of Japan, and Onozawa reflects on the hardship this must have imposed on women in the venues in terms of being prostituted by so many men, but also the degree of pressure that women, both formerly in the sex industry as well those who had not been, must have faced in terms of procurement activity by brokers and pimps to enter the venues, especially given the shortage of food in Japan in the 1940s, as well as the increasing number of men with money in industrial areas who were able to solicit women. Economic breakdown in the country in the 1940s, as well as a breakdown in public order, would have made women highly vulnerable to such demands.[97] Furthermore, Onozawa writes that the home ministry noted that business owners (mainly geisha venue proprietors) were shutting down their businesses and then immediately starting up new enterprises, which meant they were probably pursuing women formerly in working in their venues over debts owed, and were thereby attempting to trap the women into continuing prostitution. They were able to do this, Onozawa writes, because debt bondage had not been banned, and so former prostitution business owners were legally allowed to pursue women over debts in their attempt to establish comfort facilities. She expresses the view that this loophole was crucial to the ability of former geisha business proprietors in being able to procure sufficient numbers of women so that they could legally open their new businesses under the auspices of the home ministry.[98]

An example of an officially endorsed comfort facility operating within Japan is described by Yun Chung-ok in a 2003 publication on the basis of an interview she conducted with the former owner of a large-scale comfort station that operated near the Matsushiro Underground Imperial Headquarters in Nagano prefecture. Construction on the headquarters began in November 1944 using Korean labourers. The 'comfort facility' that was located near the construction site was built to a size of 200-tsubo (more than 660 square metres), and interned only Korean women. The owner, who was aged 83 by the time of the interview, described conditions within the station, which was patronized mostly by Japanese military men (but also Korean labourers), as '*donchan sawagi*' (riotous). He had been ordered to set up the brothel by Japanese civilian police. The manager was Korean, and he trafficked four Korean women in their early twenties out of Korea into the station. The women did not once leave the station once they arrived, and they had arrived wearing farm clothes and scarves.[99]

## Conclusion

The wartime mobilization of Japan's homeland sex industry from the 1930s relied on existing close historical relationships between pimps and the military. These relationships were developed over the course of Japanese history from the time of the Russo-Japanese War with the development of 'camptown' prostitution districts, patronage of civilian venues by *seinendan* male youth groups, pornography production for distribution to soldiers, and brothel visits by conscripts on their days off. In later years, the military cooperated with pimp associations in overseeing troop patronage of civilian brothels, negotiating price discounts, and in requisitioning civilian facilities for the creation of 'comfort facilities' for male factory workers at home. In aggregate, the civilian industry provided important logistical, infrastructural, and business know-how to the military as the military transitioned its operations from out-sourcing the business of organizing male sexual access to women (i.e. to the civilian industry) in the early years of the Showa era, towards creating and operating its own 'comfort station' network as the war years progressed. There was, throughout the war, ongoing cooperation between civilian and military actors in organizing this prostitution, and the 1940s history of homeland 'comfort facilities' operating in Japan clearly shows this. Chapter Six describes ongoing cooperation between the military and the civilian sex industry on Okinawa till the end of the war. There was also cooperation in regards to trafficking. The next chapter describes in greater detail the military's relationship with traffickers in arranging the transport of Japanese women out of the civilian sex industry and into comfort stations, both at home and abroad. Only with the expertise of civilian pimps and traffickers did the military have any chance of sourcing a population of women large enough to stock its rapidly multiplying battlefield brothels, I argue, which proliferated with the surge of Japanese men spilling out into Asia and the Pacific in the 1930s and 1940s.

# The Military Democratization of Prostitution

Do you really think a woman enjoys going out into a warzone and having sweaty, beast-like men torment her body to its limits? All of us were poor and couldn't get enough to eat; we needed the money. Don't you think that's why we gritted our teeth and put up with it? ... Women's bodies are real flesh and blood. They're not machines. Think about what happens to those real bodies when fifty or hundred men get on top in succession. They swell up bright red, and get injured all over. You can't close your legs; you walk around like a crab. Even in that state you still have to see men the next day. So all I could do was pour as much cold water on myself as possible, and cry my eyes out. (A Japanese survivor prostituted on Rabaul.)[1]

[A total of] 35 ... soldiers and I packed two lunches each and departed ... There were seven huts with straw mats instead of floors. We ate lunch, and then all the soldiers lined up by platoon in front of the drapes. It took an average of five minutes per soldier. It looked as if we were waiting in line for a public toilet, but all the soldiers were satisfied upon returning to base.[2]

One day I was told by my battalion chief to set up a comfort station. I talked with the military doctor attached to the medical unit stationed with us, and then started work. The location was decided quickly: the Dutch had left behind a hotel that was used by tourists. There were seven individual rooms decorated in western-style; it was almost too good to use as a comfort station. Next I needed to round up some women. That wasn't a problem; the Dutch troops had left behind a few women of the night in the nearby town. But it would be a problem if they had VD, so the military doctor examined a bunch of them, and the four who passed were installed in the hotel as comfort women. (Account from a Japanese veteran stationed in west Sumatra in 1942 published in 1978.)[3]

The trafficking of women out of Japan and into brothels in China and elsewhere in the Asia-Pacific has a history going back to the mid-nineteenth century. This traffic was organized primarily to meet the prostitution demands of Japanese men,[4] and was arranged mostly by Japanese pimps and brokers.[5] These men included troops, but also business, bureaucrat and working men in Japanese colonial settlement areas and on construction projects like dams and railways in north-eastern China, as well as in areas where Japanese venture capitalists were trying to get footholds, including British Malaya and the Netherlands Indies. Demand for prostitution was met also through the trafficking of Japanese women into legalized brothel districts on Japan's colonies of Korea and Taiwan, but this is discussed separately in the next chapter. Disentangling the overseas adventurism of Japanese men in the pre-war years from their prostitution and pimping of female nationals is a historically difficult task. When Salvation Army abolitionist Masutomi Masasuke travelled to north-eastern China in 1907, he reported back that Chinese locals were under the mistaken impression that the Japanese flag was a commercial symbol of prostitution, because brothels in the area all flew it out front.[6] By the turn of the twentieth century, Japanese men abroad had given the world little reason to associate their national origins with anything other than prostitution, perhaps apart from slave labour, drug smuggling and war.

The pre-war trafficking of Japanese women and girls throughout the Asia-Pacific is well discussed by historians using the fetishized term 'karayuki-san' to describe its victims, and is estimated to have targeted a total of 100,000 women.[7] This is a significant number if we consider Kurahashi Masanao's observation that the nineteenth century traffic was organized using fishing boats that could carry around only ten women, accompanied by crews of four to five men, that would take more than seventy days to travel from the port of Nagasaki to Vladivostok.[8] Nonetheless, pimps, brokers and traffickers managed to transport Japanese women to most destinations where their countrymen disembarked abroad, and this led, as Kurahashi describes, to demographic skewing of the expatriate population. In Harbin, in 1902, for example, 74 per cent of the female Japanese population was prostituted,[9] and this figure rose to 77 per cent for Port Arthur in 1903.[10] The equivalent figure for Mukden in 1907 was 59 per cent.[11] By 1916, there were close to 10,500 prostituted Japanese women in the Asia-Pacific region, but Kurahashi warns that this figure is likely to be significantly underestimated due to reluctance among individual women to disclose, and difficulties encountered by consulates in collecting accurate data.[12] While many Korean and Chinese women were also prostituted in invaded areas, it is notable that, in the nineteenth century at least, they were not yet targeted in the numbers of Japanese women, who were commercially organized for sexual servitude to their countrymen at both home and abroad.

The Japanese government attracted international condemnation over this traffic in the twentieth century, including from the League of Nations, and this led to its banning in Japanese law in 1920. Although, as Stephanie Limoncelli intimates, even after the trade was wound down, demand for prostitution among Japanese men abroad continued to be met by Japanese women. She writes uncritically that '[b]eginning in 1921, Japan began bringing these women back to Japan, leaving them only in enclaves where they would be needed to service Japanese men'.[13] These men were increasingly deployed by the military and stationed in invaded areas, such as the puppet state of 'Manchuria' in north-eastern China. Kurahashi suggests that Japanese women prostituted in Siberia were moved to these military-occupied areas after 1932,[14] and discussion further down supports this observation that women trafficked out of Japan to the mainland before the war became early victims of sexual slavery organized through military stations. Japanese men had already prostituted these women on home soil before their trafficking abroad and, in some cases, prostituted them again once they were repatriated home at the end of the Pacific War.

Popular books like *Sandakan brothel no. 8* and films like *Karayuki-san, the making of a prostitute* describe the procurement of girls by brokers operating in Nagasaki and Kumamoto prefectures through credit offered to indigent parents as the means by which the pre-war traffic was organized. The indenturing of daughters directly from parents was a timeworn strategy of Japanese traffickers, and one they used for the domestic trade as well, as described in Chapter Two. Less attention has been paid, however, to the pre-war trafficking of women and girls out of Japan's civilian sex industry into brothels abroad. Similar to the history of the 'comfort women', this pre-war history of trafficked Japanese women and girls mostly leaves out its prostituted victims. This is in spite of accounts, as in the following two excerpts, showing specifically the trafficking of *prostituted* women and girls out of Japan in the pre-war years:

> In one trafficking case uncovered by port authorities and reported in newspapers in 1911, two women and one girl (ages 24, 21, and 16) were trafficked from the port of Yokohama, all with debts owing to their trafficker, and all of whom had been indentured to him for two to three years after being bought from venues in a prostitution district in Gifu prefecture.[15]

> In 1932, a broker came into his [i.e. the interviewee's] shoemaking shop with around twenty-seven to twenty-eight women in tow to buy shoes for them, and his boss asked the broker how he had harvested so many women. He said the women already each had around 20,000 yen of prostitution debt, so they were going to Manchuria. The shoemaker himself later went to Manchuria for six years, and met a lot of prostituted Japanese women. They said to him they were seeing around twenty-five Japanese troops each day from 8 in the morning till 4 in the afternoon. This was in 1941.[16]

The trafficking of prostituted women is discussed in this chapter as an important pre-war context to the development of the military sexual slavery system of the late 1930s. This context is argued to be one in which Japanese men travelling abroad in the twentieth century, whether for military or business activity, exercised demand not just for the prostitution of women, but the prostitution of *Japanese* women specifically,[17] and in settings replicating the practices and conditions of Japan's domestic sex industry. Large-scale trafficking networks were organized by Japanese pimps to meet this demand, and these networks became subsequently useful to the military. There were of course prostituted Korean women trafficked out of Japanese coal mining towns,[18] non-prostituted women trafficked out of Japan,[19] as well as unspeakably large numbers of Korean, Chinese and women of other nationalities trafficked within Asia to be prostituted by Japanese men from the 1930s onwards. While these women and girls are not the focus of the chapter, their prolonged victimization in numbers exceeding even those of Japanese women is understood in the discussion to be a grossly predictable outcome of demand cultivated for the prostitution of local women in the crucible of 'peacetime' Japan.

A second observation of the chapter pertaining to the pre-war context of the comfort station system relates to demand for prostitution generated and promulgated by elite Japanese men. I understand elite military men, both within Japan and abroad, as having played a critical role in the historical development of the sexual slavery system. This role is discussed according to a framework that I dub the 'military democratization of prostitution'. Its suggestion is that elite men 'democratize' civilian prostitution when they embark upon war and military activity. This understanding is captured in a remark by Suki Falconberg, a contemporary US survivor of military prostitution, that '[m]en gain by war. They have the pleasure of rape: they mount starving women, "cheap whores", and take their pleasure …'.[20] Falconberg's perspective that warmaking furthers the sexual aims of its proponents is echoed in this chapter, which suggests that military activity is a vehicle for expanding and consolidating prostitution rights among a broad base of male nationals, and the rights thusly consolidated are fundamentally those of *civilian* prostitution. Driving the development of prostitution systems in wartime, I argue, are the considerations of men in peacetime. These considerations are specifically those of ruling-class men who take advantage of military activity to inculcate their prostitution ideas and behaviours among a broad section of the male citizenry, and reap the rewards of this dissemination once 'peacetime' society resumes. The rewards they reap are discussed only briefly in the chapter as taking the form of sexual bribery to ensure pliant acquiescence to exploitation in 'peacetime' society, but the preceding process of military democratization of prostitution is explained in detail in the second half of the chapter.

## The pre-war trafficking of prostituted women out of Japan

Contemporary researchers note that 'male demand for sex services is a hard market to saturate,'[21] and this point finds vivid historical illustration in the actions of Japanese men in the pre-war years. Their demand drove even the trafficking of women out of Japan as they moved abroad. Historians record a police crackdown on prostitution drinking venues (*tokushu inshoku ten*) within Japan from 1933, and a sharp decline in the number of these venues from 1935, but Song Youn-ok explains that half of their internees were actually trafficked out to Manchuria (with the other half being moved into local geisha venues).[22] Kurahashi Masanao and Mark Driscoll discuss the pre-war fundraising methods of Japanese entrepreneurs who, they suggest, established brothels abroad using trafficked Japanese women to raise capital needed to start other businesses. Kurahashi writes that, 'excluding brothels, the Japanese businesses created in Siberia and northern China in the early twentieth century included laundries, photography shops and cafeterias, but even these businesses were launched using capital raised through the prostitution of women, and so Japanese overseas development has prostitution as its "chilling back-story" (*osamui hanashi*)'.[23] Driscoll writes similarly that 'two-thirds of the bosses of large Japanese enterprises in the Asia-Pacific began their business careers as low-level human traffickers'.[24] However, even in these critical accounts of the pre-war trafficking of Japanese women and girls, little mention is made of the Japanese men abroad who must have generated demand for the prostitution of women as consumers, and not just as pimps. In other words, Japanese pimps were able to so successfully raise capital through setting up brothels aboard only because of the prostitution demand of their countrymen who had moved abroad as soldiers, labourers or fishermen. After all, as Kurahashi notes, there is little evidence that overseas Japanese brothels were patronized by locals.[25] As the years of the twentieth century progressed, this custom came increasingly from Japanese military men, and Kim Il Myon writes that the Kwantung army from the time of the Manchurian incident in 1931 encouraged Japanese prostitution business entrepreneurs, whom he suggests had already established substantial operations in Japan, Korea, Taiwan, Singapore and Shanghai by this time, to further set up brothels and geisha restaurants (i.e. brothels for officers) in Manchuria.[26]

The trafficking practices and networks developed in the pre-war years to cater to this overseas demand were useful in the military's later creation of comfort stations. Onozawa Akane writes that the 'large number of women organized for entry into comfort stations was made possible by the unmonitored trafficking activity that took place of women out of Japan's civilian industry', and cites evidence of brothel owners from both Osaka and Kobe being ordered by the military to traffic women to Manchuria to set up comfort stations, which were then run by the pimps under the direction and monitoring of the military. She importantly observes that 'the conventions of trafficking used within the domestic sex industry were exercised for the purpose of trafficking women abroad into comfort stations – the military paid off the women's debts to local geisha venue owners'.[27] Nishino Rumiko writes that the majority of Japanese women recruited for trafficking into comfort stations abroad were from the sex industries of Onkagawa in Kyushu, the Matsushima and Tobita sex industry districts in Osaka, and the Fukuhara sex industry district in Kobe.[28] An audit taken of Korean survivor testimony reveals that 40 per cent of them entered comfort stations between the years 1938 and 1940, but a larger proportion (45 per cent) entered between the years 1941 and 1943;[29] it is likely that women trafficked out of Japan filled the intervening chronological gap. Hata notes that numbers in Japan's sex industry dropped by more than 40,000 in the four years after 1937 when the military began to organize the system in earnest.[30] Nonetheless, their trafficking continued throughout the war; civilian industry survivor Fukuda Toshiko recalls a number of women she knew from the Yoshiwara brothel district going off in 1941 after the military made a direct request to the brothel owners association for their procurement.[31] Fukuda, who is no longer alive, was a Yoshiwara geisha restaurant proprietor (i.e. a pimp) until 1958, after taking over the business from her adoptive mother. She had been adopted as a 3-year-old in 1923. She wrote about her life in prostitution in 1966, and the memoir was published in 1986.

Women in invaded territories did increasingly fall victim to trafficking into comfort stations as the years of war went on, and particularly prostituted women,[32] but it is nonetheless significant that the military never gave up on attempts throughout the war to traffic women out of Japan. Japanese women (both prostituted and non-prostituted) continued to be targeted victims of military prostitution, even while women of other nationalities were being procured in comparatively larger numbers. Evidence of the military's sustained efforts to traffic of women out of Japan is described in an extraordinary piece of research undertaken by a women's organization in Fukuoka that surveyed local newspapers published between 1937 and 1945 for information about the trafficking of women into comfort stations abroad (given that ports in this area were the major routes used by Japan's wartime traffickers). The group found a great deal of evidence of the trafficking of women out of the region throughout the years of war. For example, one newspaper report from 1938 noted that Moji port authorities were receiving on average five to six watch-list notifications *per day* of women likely to have been trafficked by brokers.[33] Another article from 1939 estimated that half of all people embarking on the regular Nagasaki-Dairen passenger ship were 'camp-following' women accompanying the military to the mainland.[34] The researchers comment that this assessment is likely to have been accurate, given their discovery of large number of classified ads placed by untraceable individuals using addresses of local motels seeking women to travel to the mainland under various guises. Sometimes these guises were very thin. An advertisement in a Fukuoka newspaper in 1940 sought women 'between the ages of 21 and 40' who were 'pretty' and 'healthy' and had guardianship permission to work in a military 'facility' (*kaikan*) in China. Around the same time, the researchers note, there was a broker working as a 'military recreation unit' representative over a number of months in 1941 who made contact with a Fukuoka-based sex industry entrepreneur to recruit women out of *kafes* and other local prostitution venues to transport to the mainland.[35]

Nevertheless, military prostitution did not universally deliver Japanese men sexual access to their countrywomen. Low-ranked military men had to make do with Korean, Chinese and other women forced to dress in kimonos, don Japanese female names, sing the Japanese national anthem and eschew speaking in their own languages.[36] Korean women had to 'sing, dance and play the violin' for these men in a projected vision of the Japanese 'geisha', as described by Joshua Piltzer. In the case of Korean survivor Mun Okju who was, according to Piltzer, 'abducted by Japanese military personnel in 1940, sent to Manchuria, and forced to provide sexual services for between twenty and thirty soldiers a day … was often called to sing at officers' banquets and farewell parties, often alongside Japanese geishas'.[37] Even if the model and blueprint for the military system was Japan's civilian sex industry and its female internees, compromises nonetheless had to be made in the face of real-world exigencies. These exigencies included, in Yoshimi Yoshiaki's view, logistical and infrastructural barriers to the trafficking of women into comfort stations in the latter war years. He writes that 'the army wanted comfort women to be Japanese subjects (Japanese, Koreans or

Taiwanese). But there were not sufficient numbers, and importing women from Japan, Korea and Taiwan required time and effort. So the army quickly turned to rounding up comfort women locally'.[38]

Japan's homeland sex industry and its victims nonetheless remained the aspirational model for the development and operation of the comfort station system throughout the war, even if practical barriers to its full expression abroad were ever-present. The system took on the trappings of the Japanese civilian sex industry, and adhered to many of its conventions. In comfort stations, for example, men paid more money to prostitute their countrywomen over women of other nationalities, and in some cases Japanese women were sequestered for exclusive use by military officers. Officers paid for the privilege of prostituting these women in venues that mimicked the format of homeland geisha venues and *kafes* (i.e. 'officers' clubs').[39] They were afforded the further privilege of prostituting young 'virgins' brought into the stations before they were handed over to troops. This is similar to the way geisha venues operated back in Japan: customers could pay more to prostitute girls in their first few months of internment. A Korean survivor, Hwang Kumju, testifies that '[t]he officers called for us three or four times a day for the first fortnight or so. The new girls were to serve the officers, as they were virgins. The officers didn't use condoms, so quite a few of us became pregnant quite early on'.[40] Joshua Pilzer describes the cultural rituals of comfort stations that were imported directly from Japan's civilian sex industry, and writes that '[t]he comfort women system was an extreme wartime extension of the Japanese and Korean colonial sex-and-entertainment industry, in which girls and women were often, as in the nonwartime sex industry, expected to sing, dance, and otherwise perform for clients in addition to sexual labor'.[41]

Comfort stations were designed by the military to replicate the format of brothels patronized by troops back home: a station in Manchuria displayed photographs of comfort women in the foyer area where soldiers waited, which replicated a standard practice of civilian brothels in displaying women's faces in wall-mounted photographs in reception rooms. The station's interior design and layout also mirrored, in the words of a former soldier, 'one of the Yoshiwara brothels back home'.[42] This fact is not surprising, considering comfort stations were set up and run for the military by the same pimps who had run sex industry venues back in Japan.[43] Not only were the same individual women prostituted through both civilian venues and comfort stations, but their broad population demographics were reproduced abroad; a Japanese survivor of civilian prostitution recalls of her later experience in a comfort station on Saipan that, 'just like the brothels back home in Japan', there were 'young women from the northern prefectures who had been sold by parents' in the station.[44] Venereal disease testing regimes for comfort stations, too, appear to have been modelled on practices of the civilian industry. Women were tested weekly and even twice-weekly and, similar to a stratagem used by civilian pimps,[45] comfort station proprietors inspected women themselves before sending them out for testing, and applied ointment and other measures to reduce inflammation and swelling in genitals to hide infection and hinder detection by authorities.[46] An account of a comfort station operating on Tokashiki in 1944 suggests that brothel-like organization of stations continued till the end of the war. In this station, soldiers would approach a 'reception desk' where they would pay for a numbered ticket, and then wait for their number to be called from a house next door to the station. They would then pass the ticket to the woman before prostituting her. At the end of the day, the station manager would tally up the number of tickets received by each woman, and allocate earnings on that basis. Similar to the practice in civilian brothels, these earnings would be offset against debts owed by the woman for supposed 'expenses' incurred in organizing their traffic from Korea to Tokashiki (often via Taiwan), as well as 'living expenses', 'clothing expenses' and interest accrued on money owing.[47] In other words, exactly like the civilian industry, women were bonded to comfort stations through manufactured debt which would barely subside because of stratagems like interest, fees and expenses.

The homeland sex industry was the blueprint and standard that guided the prostitution activity of Japanese men abroad, and this demand drove a traffic of women out of Japan by the same pimps and brokers who organized the domestic civilian industry. These same entrepreneurs assisted the military to create its wartime comfort station system. While the civilian characteristics of the military system might have faded in and out in certain times and areas of the war (in 1942, for example, Japanese troops in China were abducting local girls and locking them in single outdoor shacks for serial rape on empty rice sacks until they died or their families paid bribes to get them out),[48] the historical origins and logic of the system are evident in its early shape and organization, including in its initial establishment on the basis of women trafficked out of Japanese civilian prostitution. These overlapping organizational, operational, conventional and aesthetic aspects of civilian prostitution and the comfort stations reveal the historically important role of the civilian sex industry in the development of the military system. It also reflects, I argue, a process of 'military democratization' of Japan's civilian prostitution industry in the 1930s. Onozawa Akane uses the term *'heijunka'* ('levelling') to refer to democratized access to the prostitution of women sought by Japanese men in the war years, and this observation is the bedrock of the argument of this chapter.

The argument is that the democratization of prostitution that began in the Taisho years was perpetuated through military activity in the 1930s, centring on the development of comfort stations. These stations newly delivered an expanded population of Japanese men access to women for prostitution. Historians frequently emphasize the aggravation of socioeconomic-class and other hierarchies among men during wartime (e.g. conflict between conscript and officer-class men), but less considered are equality gains made in respect to prostitution rights via the development of military schemes like the comfort station system. In the China and Pacific wars, this system delivered significant sexual rewards to a wide cross-section of Japanese men in terms of socioeconomic background, rural/urban origin and age. The system was instigated by elite military men, and Yoshimi Yoshiaki writes that 'those responsible for setting up the comfort stations were all elite military personnel ... The decision to set them up was never made arbitrarily by army units in the field'.[49] This 'levelling' of Japanese male social relations forged through militarism was a devastating development for women and girls in Asia and the Pacific.

## The deployment of men out of Japan

The history of Japanese military and businessmen prostituting and pimping women in the Asia-Pacific, and the pre-war trafficking of Japanese women into areas of overseas male activity, makes difficult a clear-cut identification of the comfort station system as distinct from pre-war Japanese military and civilian systems of prostitution abroad. Nonetheless, as a starting point, we might refer to Yoshimi Yoshiaki's opinion that the first directly military managed comfort station established by the Japanese military with foreign ministry backing was initiated by the navy in 1932, with the army following suit in 1933. Notably, there were 102 Japanese women, compared to 29 Korean women, in the Shanghai brothel district where this first naval station operated, and it is likely that the majority of its internees at this early stage were women trafficked out of Japan.[50] Government agencies back home pitched in to help the military secure women for stations abroad. Hayashi Hirofumi writes that, at the army's request, the police bureau of Japan's home ministry ordered prefectural governors round up local women to send to China in 1938. The bureau even issued these women with travel documents to facilitate their overseas passage.[51]

This kind of official involvement in the transport of Japanese women abroad prompts historians like Kurahashi Masanao, Yuki Tanaka and Hayashi Hirofumi to draw a straight historical line between the international pre-war traffic of Japanese women for military prostitution and the later 1930s development of the comfort station system. There are certainly important observations to be made regarding the military's reliance on Japanese pimps already operating in Asia, as well as their pre-war trafficking networks, in developing and operating the wartime prostitution system. Furthermore, as mentioned in the book's introduction, Hayashi wrote a significant article in 1999 arguing that the origins of the comfort station system can be traced to the Siberian Intervention of 1918 when Japanese consulates in Manchuria, prior to the incursion, held meetings with foreign ministry staff to discuss an anticipated trafficking of women into the region with the influx of troops. Hayashi notes that, significantly, the army intervened in these talks to insist that no bans on the trafficking of Japanese women into the area be enacted, in spite of consular concerns that Japan's image abroad was likely to be tarnished by the traffic.[52] The army successfully argued that the traffic should not be impeded, and undertook to supply military doctors to inspect the women for venereal disease, so that they could be used by troops.[53] In citing this example, Hayashi highlights early historical evidence of Japanese military intent to become involved in facilitating prostitution in a way that is directly reflective of its later organization of the comfort station system.

While there are obvious parallels between the pre-war traffic of Japanese women for prostitution and their later 1930s traffic into comfort stations, this understanding of the origins of the military system tends to foreground the phenomenon of overseas sex trafficking as a historical cause of military sexual slavery. It thereby pushes into the background historical drivers of the development of the system that existed closer to home. In other words, the history of Japanese male demand for prostitution, and their prostitution of countrywomen at home, tends to be sidelined in discussions of military sexual slavery that locate its historical origins far away in the overseas trafficking networks of the pre-war years, and especially that organized under the banner of 'karayuki'. As described in previous chapters, the affordability and opportunity of prostitution expanded considerably among men in Japan in the 1910s and 1920s, and notably allowed a newly emerging class of working men flooding into Japan's cities sexual access to women through cheaper venues like *kafes*, with heightened levels of social tolerance and cultural acceptability. The fact that Japanese women were trafficked out of Japan when these men later travelled abroad in the twentieth century, and that elite military men committed themselves to supporting this traffic, is testament, I argue, to the strength of the demand for prostitution that had already been cultivated among Japanese men domestically by the 1930s. This demand was met for an extraordinarily broad base of men through the military's creation of the comfort station system of the China War.

## The military democratization of prostitution

Even in the 'tawdry' Taisho years, there were still young, rural men in Japan who did not have the money or opportunity to buy women for prostitution, even after enlisting as soldiers. By the time of the Russo-Japanese War, as Naoko Shimazu describes, democratized access to prostitution still had its limits among the Japanese male populace:

> Although there were small-scale officially condoned 'comfort houses' with Chinese and Japanese prostitutes near major encampments, they were often beyond the financial reach of lower ranking soldiers. When visiting Mukden, Private Tsuchida Shirohei wrote in his letter that 'I saw a brothel officially approved by the Japanese military authorities. For one visit, it cost three yen for the superior class, two yen for the medium class, and one yen for the lowest class. Although it was busy with highly paid people, for the likes of us it was too expensive.'[54]

With the advent of the China War, though, and the military's development of comfort stations, progress was made on behalf of these unfortunates; even poor, young men enlisting from rural areas could become prostitutors with certainty, frequency and at low cost. They even got the opportunity to become traffickers. Hayakawa Noriyo writes that, in the latter years of war, setting up comfort stations became a 'routine' duty of select army units, and oversight of the stations was transferred from consular police to the military.[55] The military made sure that enlistees could rest easy while exercising their prostitution rights; moreover, it operated a special security duty for the oversight of comfort stations, and required records be kept of men onsite to impede infiltration by guerrillas who would attack troops while they were off their guard.[56] While wartime access rights to comfort women were mediated through a rank- and class-based system of invented hierarchical 'privileges' among military men (e.g. higher ranking men were permitted sexual access in the evenings, but infantrymen had to use women in the mornings and afternoons), the China War nonetheless marked the first time in Japanese history that military enlistment came with near-guaranteed rights to the prostitution of women. For middle-class enlisting men, moreover, the military in wartime offered forms of sexual access usually available only to elite men – such as the 'geisha' format with its expensive wining and dining. A comfort station in Kadena on Okinawa, for example, operated like a geisha restaurant with alcohol and singing accompanied by the *shamisen* till late at night. It was available for patronage by troops as well as officers, and interned women from Okinawa's local civilian sex industry.[57]

In many cases, comfort stations were set up for common use by both officers and conscripts. While officers were prioritized over troops in the development of comfort stations, and also in the forms of sexual access granted to them (e.g. lengthier time frames permitted for accessing comfort stations, less restriction on amounts of time using women, women sequestered for their individual use), military command nonetheless went to extreme lengths to secure even rank-and-file troops access to stations. This access was planned for in detail, using substantial military resources. An army accounting officer, who went on to become head of Sankei Newspaper and Fuji Television after the war, recalls military comfort station development and operation was mapped out with scientific precision:

> At that time [when the comfort stations were being set up], we estimated the endurance of the women rounded up in local areas and the rates at which they would wear out. We analyzed which women were strong or weak in those areas, and then had to go so far as to determine 'how long they would be in use' from the time soldiers entered the rooms until they left – how many minutes for commissioned officers, how many minutes for noncommissioned officers, how many minutes for soldiers … (laughter) …[58]

Hayashi Hirofumi's 1994 compilation of collected excerpts from the memoirs and autobiographies of former military men describing personal involvement in the creation of comfort stations reveals an extraordinary level of commitment among officers to the task. While Hayashi's collection was compiled mainly to show direct military culpability for the trafficking of women, it also shows vividly the problems the military worked to overcome to secure women not just for officers but also underlings. Miyatani Shigeo, writing in 1985, for example, recalls praise he received from commanding officers after he ingeniously 'drew on memories of partaking in the illicit custom during former school days' to create a comfort station for officers through converting a commandeered local house (in an invaded town in central China) into a 'Japanese-style' brothel. Recognizing his initiative, officers then asked him to procure locally prostituted women to set up a comfort station for soldiers as well, which he was also able to do.[59] In another example, Hirahara Kazuo, writing in 1991, describes his experience late in the war in northern China in attending a meeting of military officers who were discussing concerns about the declining value of military scrip on issue, which was making it difficult to cover costs of retaining comfort women. To solve the problem, it was decided that the women would be allocated food and clothing directly by the military rather than be paid in scrip (which Hirahara recalls were actually items 'requisitioned' from the local population).[60]

These examples show great persistence and ingenuity on the part of the military in organizing military brothels in conditions of battle, privation and logistical difficulty. The strength of this commitment military-wide can be perceived in further research by Hayashi that calculates wartime transport volumes for condoms to army units around the Asia-Pacific, and the timing of these dispatches. Hayashi undertook this calculation to gauge the number of women who might have been victimized through comfort stations, and also to geographically assess where comfort stations might have been established. But his research additionally reveals an almost comical degree of military commitment to the prostitution rights of soldiers, even when these soldiers were in the midst of battle in the calamitous late years of war. Hayashi writes with some incredulity that condoms were dispatched to army divisions on their way to fight in the Battle of Midway in 1943, and also to troops on their way to Port Moresby and Guadalcanal.[61] Military command allocated significantly budgetary resources to the task, moreover. Hayashi notes that over nineteen million condoms were budgeted for by the army ministry in 1942 for 1.7 million soldiers, which he writes was calculated on the basis that soldiers would be afforded access to women through comfort stations once a month.[62] Accounts from survivors who had to wash condoms after use because of inadequate supply,[63] and also testimony that troops simply did not use them (with military doctors reporting that two out of ten comfort women on average were infected with venereal disease at any one time),[64] suggest that the military underestimated the rate at which its charges felt moved to act upon their entitlement to prostitute women. Indeed, an account by veteran Fusayama Takao published in 1983 describing an incident at a comfort station described to him by a subordinate in Singapore in 1942 shows the military losing control of troops as a result of the strength of this entitlement:

> After the first four or five men the women were going completely crazy and were crying out. They began pushing men away and said their bodies couldn't take any more. The soldier overseeing the station said we had to all leave and tried to herd us toward the door, but the line of waiting soldiers rose up and started to become violent. The supervising soldier began to fear for his life, so he tied the women's arms and legs to the beds and then re-opened the station door so all the soldiers could use them.[65]

## Military export of prostitution demand

Expansion in the demographic breadth of men afforded prostitution rights in the China War magnified the amplitude of sexual demand reverberating abroad during the war years, as Japanese military men were deployed to the mainland, the Korean peninsula and further afield in Asia and the Pacific. This situation in the 1930s and 1940s might be compared to a later phenomenon of the post-war period in which, as Catharine MacKinnon observes, imperialistic aims underpinned the failure of the US government to stop American pornographers expanding globally. She writes that 'the international pornography traffic means that American women are violated and tortured and exploited through its use' and, as a result, 'misogyny American style colonizes the world'.[66] This means that '[q]ualities characteristic of but not unique to the United States – including common and casual sexual violence and racism' are now, through pornography, 'promoted throughout the world as sex'.[67] Commenting on this phenomenon of imperialistically exported sexual values via militarism specifically, MacKinnon writes further that,

> when the army comes back, it visits on the women at home the escalated level of assault the men were taught and practiced on women in the war zone … sexual aggression against Asian women through prostitution and pornography exploded in the United States [after Vietnam]: American men got a particular taste for violating them over there.[68]

The conduct of the Japanese military might be seen as similar to that which MacKinnon ascribes to later military activity by American men by virtue of the fact the years of war were a time when 'misogyny Japanese style colonize[d] the Asia-Pacific'. Rather than digital technologies, though, it was male bodies on the ground that transmitted the Japanese-style misogyny of the twentieth century, which was anchored in prostitution according to people like Iwata Shigenori. While the following calculations of men deployed are only rough estimates, the numerical picture they paint illustrates the extent of Japanese male outreach abroad, and allows some conceptual grasp of the scale of prostitution demand that was physically transmitted to the Asia-Pacific region during the war years:

- More than 170,000 Japanese men were deployed to the Korean peninsula during the Sino-Japanese War in 1894.[69]
- 50,000 troops were dispatched to Taiwan in 1895.[70]
- 1,880 *kempeitai* military police were dispatched to Taiwan in 1895.[71]
- In 1915, there were 9,612 *kempeitai* on deployment within Japan, and to Korea, Taiwan, China, Manchuria and battlefield areas.[72]
- Over 400,000 troops were deployed to northern China during the Russo-Japanese War (1904–1905).[73]
- 70,000 troops were deployed for the 'Siberian' war of intervention in the Russian Revolution (1918–1922).[74]
- *Kempeitai* police forces in 1918 in Korea numbered nearly 8,000 men, plus another 5,400 special higher police.[75]
- Ten thousand soldiers of the Japanese occupying forces were organized in 1906 as the Kwantung Army.[76] Their numbers reached 700,000 by 1941.[77]
- A total of one million troops were deployed over the course of the China War beginning in 1937.[78]
- Total Japanese imperial army numbers deployed abroad by 1941 were 2,100,000, and by 1945 this number for the army was 6,400,000.[79]

Beatrice Trefalt's following summary of the dimensions of the geographical reach of Japanese military activity with the onset of the Pacific War is also worth citing in full for its illustration of the ballooning physical presence of Japanese men in the Asia-Pacific, as the late 1930s transitioned to the early 1940s:

To the north and west it [i.e. Japan] held, apart from Korea and Manchuria, an extensive part of China where the greater part of the Japanese Imperial Army was stationed and fought from 1937 onwards. To the south-west it held part of the whole of the countries then known as Burma, Siam, Indochina, Malaya and Singapore. To the south and south-east, apart from its colony of Taiwan, Japan held the Dutch East Indies, the Philippines, New Guinea and New Britain. In addition it also held many islands in the central Pacific: the Solomon Islands, the Marshall Islands, the Caroline Islands, the Marianas and the Bonin Islands (including Iwo Jima). In the north-east there were troops stationed on a part of the Aleutians. Even though Japanese-held territory was reduced considerably with the Allied advance from 1942 onwards, the nation's soldiers remained scattered over a wide area ... at the time when the Emperor announced to his subjects that the war was over, there were 5,470,000 soldiers on active duty in the Imperial army. Of those, 3,085,000 were overseas. The Navy had 2,241,000 troops in total, with close to 450,000 overseas.[80]

This overseas dispatch of large swathes of the Japanese male population in the 1930s and 1940s facilitated the physical export of the twentieth century Japanese male 'prostitution sexuality', I argue. As discussed in previous chapters, commentators like Iwata Shigenori think that Japanese men by the 1930s had cultivated a form of sexuality that drove the development of the comfort station system. A concrete example of how this mechanism worked might be seen in the way Japanese military command assessed movements in troop populations during the war. Yoshimi Yoshiaki describes a 1938 consulate document reporting that, 'with the great increase in military personnel stationed in the area due to the sudden outbreak of the Shanghai incident, the navy established naval comfort stations as a means to aid in supporting the comfort of those troops'.[81] From this account, military command appears to have viewed the stationing of personnel through a lens of prostitution demand, and took measures to procure women on that basis. Yoshimi suggests that this lens was adopted at the highest military levels: 'the names of the commissioned officers involved in setting up military comfort stations that have surfaced demonstrate that these officers were almost all members of the army elite'.[82] Even compared to policy action taken by the Japanese government nationally from 1900 to legalize large-scale brothel districts to cater to civilian male sexual access to women, and even to further legalize *kafe* and geisha venues in 1928, the Japanese military appears to have demonstrated a level of commitment to the male prostitution right that went above and beyond the call of duty in its level of aforethought, planning and resourcing. Explaining the military's inexplicable commitment in this regard perhaps requires historically specific attention be paid to the civilian conditions in which its leaders grew up. These conditions are evident in Suzuki's accusation that, for military officers in peacetime, 'using and paying for women as sexual objects was something they did as easily as taking a bath before breakfast'.[83]

## Democratized access to prostitution

The egalitarianism of the comfort station system is mostly overlooked by historians who are preoccupied with the multitude of invented rules and rituals that governed men's use of stations. Certainly, various features of male internecine social hierarchy (e.g. class, rank and nationality) were emphasized and upheld in the way comfort stations were set up and run. In some cases, sexual access was mediated according to the nationality background of prostituted women, and so Japanese women were sometimes sequestered for exclusive use by officers while Korean and Chinese women were interned in different venues for use by troops. These surface-level markers of male hierarchical social structuring perhaps should not be excessively emphasized, however, if we consider the extent of widespread and frequent access to women for prostitution for all levels of men the comfort station system established in the China and Pacific wars. Relative to this ambitious project of democratized prostitution access for millions of men, superficial rituals of male hierarchy and deference to superiors inbuilt in the comfort station system appear less significant than historians have cast them to date.

Nonetheless, the historical record does show intricate and pervasive adherence to rituals demarcating ranks and classes of men in the context of military prostitution, and a clear example of the extent of this fetishization is contained in two accounts by Japanese survivors of the stations. The first is from 'Kurosu Kana' who was trafficked by her pimp to north-eastern China from a geisha venue in Japan in 1931 at age 25. This pimp opened up a prostitution venue near the front line for use by military officers where Kurosu played musical instruments in a 'geisha' style. Kurosu testifies that her venue was differentiated from other comfort stations on the basis of its 'officers' club' status, which meant that it was also patronized by 'elite Korean and Manchurian business men'. Most crucially, it was distinguished from a venue down the road interning 'Korean women' where soldiers would go for 'mass sexual release' [*seiyoku shori kikan*].[84] A second Japanese survivor, 'Suzuki Fumi', describes being trafficked to Truk on a naval ship from Japan with nearly forty other women from the same brothel district where she was prostituted from a young age. She was indentured for a year and prostituted serially by conscripts on the island, but notes three women on her ship had been scheduled to be used exclusively by officers.[85]

The testimony of comfort station survivors is littered with similar accounts of the various demarcating rituals governing the operation of comfort stations according to military-created ranked-based rules, including, notably, a privilege afforded officers to rape women newly brought to comfort stations, and especially underage girls.[86] It is important to note, however, that these rules were not necessarily defining of the system's operation; Japanese women were more frequently prostituted by troops in exactly the same way as women of other nationalities. The above-mentioned Kurosu Kana, for example, was later prostituted by large numbers of men, including rank-and-file soldiers, and in abhorrent conditions. Even in cases where they were prostituted exclusively by officer-class men, they were not necessarily spared hardship and violence. A Japanese nurse who worked in an army hospital in Java said there were 'not a few' officers who were hospitalized with gonorrhoea, which, she noted, probably meant comfort women had also contracted the disease. But these women were not permitted to use the military hospital. Officers were frequent transmitters of STIs to comfort women because, more than troops, they were freely able to visit civilian brothels in nearby towns.[87] Korean survivor Mun P'ilgi testifies to the brutality of officers' conduct in prostituting comfort women: '[o]fficers who stayed overnight would ... keep harassing me, demanding sex several times, and allowing me no time to get off to sleep. There was one who came totally drunk and would throw up throughout the night, trying to climb on top of me at the same time. I was repulsed by this sort of behavior and really couldn't tolerate it'.[88] Unlike rank-and-file troops, moreover, officer-class personnel were allowed to consume alcohol in the stations, which made the risk of violence even higher, especially because officers would spend extended periods of time together in the stations, often till the early hours of the morning, eating and drinking with local businessmen, journalists, collaborators and politicians.[89]

It is important not to lose sight of the fact that even the lowliest of conscripts were furnished with sexual access to women at considerable expense and trouble to the Japanese military throughout both the China and Pacific wars. Civilian society had been only so successful in democratizing the male prostitution right, and I believe militarism operated to reduced economic-class based barriers to an extent that a more comprehensive democratization of the male prostitution right was achieved. Elite Japanese men gained access through militarism and war to a large and subordinated male population, which was then sequestered overseas away from their homes and families. This afforded elite men an opportunity to inculcate a hitherto unimaginably large portion of the Japanese male citizenry with the behaviours and habits of prostitution and other well-practiced behaviours of elite male sexuality around the time.

The democratization project was so complete that the military system that was developed abroad eventually came back to Japan in the form of comfort stations set up for troops sent home to defend the homeland. Japanese survivor Tanaka Tami who had been sold at age 11 in 1938 by her father to a Tokyo geisha house with an indentured contract until she was age 20 found herself in a comfort station attached to the Mobara naval air base that was built in Chiba prefecture in 1943. Comfort stations were launched near the base soon after in 1944, and Tanaka's pimp was one of the sex industry entrepreneurs asked by the military to set them up. He assigned Tanaka to a station that took the same name as the civilian brothel the pimp had been operating before. Tanaka recalls there were seven comfort stations in the area with around six women in each venue, all around her age, and all from the sex industry.[90] Democratized access to prostitution expanded during the war years was, therefore, secured not only for Japanese men abroad, but also those on home soil. Onozawa in 2010 described efforts by Japan's war ministry to encourage the development of homeland comfort stations that were affordable and accessible not just for factory-owning men who were making money out of the war, but also for workers. She describes the government's keenness that its planned comfort facilities (i.e. those discussed in Chapter Four) be developed on a *heijunka* (literally 'levelling') or egalitarian basis.[91] This concern stemmed from the fact that, by 1942 when rations were beginning to run short, a black market was operating in Japan on the basis of demand from men who had become rich through the manufacture of military supplies, and these men continued to patronize high-class geisha restaurants.[92] She cites a report by a police agency within the home ministry that was critical of former geisha restaurant owners who had been officially charged with setting up comfort facilities, but who were actually running businesses catering to these men in the same manner as before: charging high rates and allowing customers to pay large sums to exclusively access particular women. As a result, the new government-sponsored comfort facilities were unfortunately attracting a public reputation as exclusive, high-class venues. Onozawa concludes that these homeland facilities remained throughout the war accessible only to wealthy men, and so were not 'democratized' to any extent the ministry had hoped.[93] It is nonetheless significant that democratic intent officially underpinned their development.

## Democratized prostitution rights and the 'catharsis effect'

This enhanced democratized access to prostitution at home and abroad that came with Japanese militarism in the 1930s does not of course change the historical record of brutality, indignity and physical hardship meted out to imperial force conscripts, particularly lower class and young men, as well as Korean, Taiwanese and Okinawan enlistees. This brutality is much lamented by historians, and a major theme of the literature is that under-educated, poor and rural young

Japanese men were used as 'fodder' by military elites in perpetrating the China and Pacific wars, and were subject to the most horrendous of abuses from superiors and comrades. There is no doubt this was the case. Saburo Ienaga, for example, records that

> Military irrationality was … manifested in a despotic authoritarianism. Officers, although subject to restrictions, were still a privileged stratum at the top of the officer-NCO-enlisted man hierarchy. Differences of rank and junior subordination to seniors notwithstanding, the officer class in general had the status and authority of feudal lords. The privates, especially the new recruits, were at the miserable bottom of the pyramid. They had no human rights. They were nonpersons. Military education, training, and the daily routine of barracks life at the squad level was an unending stream of humiliation and rough treatment.[94]

Unsurprisingly, treatment as 'non-persons' was precisely correlated with socioeconomic background, because entry to officer ranks required prior educational achievement not possible for poor boys:

> Between the two world wars entry to secondary education was by selection. Only about a quarter of all boys could enter the elite five-year middle schools and about one half entered the upper elementary schools or supplementary vocational schools, both of which were usually attached to elementary schools. Graduates of middle schools, mostly of middle or upper-class origin, enjoyed the privilege of shortening their military service from two years to a year if they joined at their own expense. Moreover, they could be considered for commissions in the army; while the non-elite were almost all destined to be privates. Thus as elsewhere military status was linked to academic background.[95]

It is perhaps unfortunate, though, that the brutality of the Japanese military in the China and Pacific wars has been used by historians as an explanatory rationale for men's participation in military sexual slavery on the argued basis of their traumatized state. In other words, historians have taken the tragic and unjust history of military oppression of Japanese men and boys, and used it to rationalize the concurrent tragic and unjust history of sexual oppression of women and girls, both Japanese and foreign. They use this history to explain an apparent lack of compunction on the part of individual military men in prostituting women through comfort stations, and doing so in conditions that must have been more or less obviously atrocious to them as individuals. But it is worth pausing, I believe, to reflect on just how patently and obviously horrendous the situation of women was. Their conditions of enslavement must surely have been obvious to every single one of the men who prostituted them.

Yun Tu-Ri, for example, recalls of her time in a comfort station after a soldier had bashed her that, even after 'the wound on my bottom festered and I had such a high fever that I could not even lie on my back[,] ... I was forced to keep receiving soldiers'.[96]

This explanation of why 'brutalized' Japanese men participated in the sexual enslavement of women during war might be recognized as relying on a 'pressure valve' or 'catharsis' theory, which is articulated by Ienaga in the terms that '[m]en under constant pressure would explode in irrational, destructive behavior. Individuals whose own dignity and manhood had been so cruelly violated would hardly refrain from doing the same to defenseless persons under their control'.[97] In relation to the comfort station system specifically, acts of prostitution are described not only as expressions of 'outlet' for male emotional frustration, but also as a cheap form of institutional bribery to encourage continued pliancy among troops. In Suzuki Yuuko's words:

> In order to give outlet to the frustrations of troops, the military's prostitution strategy was extremely useful. Not only prostitution, but the sexual violence of troops like the rapes they perpetrated in Southeast Asia, were tolerated by the military, which looked the other way. As a result, the majority of soldiers acted out their resentment at the military on vulnerable women.[98]

But this argument tends to overlook the Taisho-era history of conscripts prostituting women back home in significant numbers even before they were deployed to the battlefield, and doing so with equal apparent disregard for victims. A former soldier interviewed by Tanikawa Mitsue in the early 1980s told her without apparent embarrassment that he prostituted women through Sapporo's brothel district as a military recruit between the years 1934 and 1938 without ever using condoms. He recalled that the women's names were written up on the brothel wall, with markings underneath to indicate how many men had bought them.[99] Even conceding the possibility that domestic military training imposed hardship on this enlistee to an extent requiring emotional 'outlet', the rampancy of the prostitution activity of civilian men in Japan's 'liberal' society of the 1920s where urban social conditions were relatively calm remains an explanatory challenge. As described in Chapter Two, in this pre-war environment a sex industry grew exponentially to cater to men prostituting women as part of their 'leisure' and 'recreational' activity in venues associated with drinking, dining and going away on holiday with friends. Surely, these conditions cannot be described as giving rise to any level of environmental stress among men that would require 'outlet'. Men prostituted women in venues around hot spring resort areas where they travelled in groups overnight, for example. Another one of Tanikawa's interviewees recalled with sadness a primary school friend who had died forty-eight years earlier from the effects of a sexually transmitted disease at age 17. The girl had been taken out of school to be trafficked to a *kafe* in a Sapporo hot springs resort. Taisho-era men on holiday without a care in the world prostituted her for three years before she was forced to return home ill to die.[100]

In a similarly high-spirited fashion, military officers, and even military doctors charged with inspecting comfort women for venereal disease,[101] had a widely documented penchant for prostituting women through comfort stations, even though these men were likely to have borne relatively light loads of hardship during the war, and so presumably not vulnerable to emotional overload like conscripts. The peculiar violence and abuse of officers towards comfort women is nonetheless recorded repeatedly in the accounts of Korean and Chinese survivors. Kim Tokchin recalls that, on the first night she was in a comfort station, she was 'dragged before a high-ranking soldier and raped'. Afterwards he patted Kim on the back and said she 'had to go through this experience whether I liked it or not, but that after a few times I would not feel so much pain'. 'We were taken here and there to the rooms of different high-ranking officers on a nightly basis. Every night we were raped'.[102] Similar accounts of officer-ranked male violence is also found in the testimony of Japanese survivors, who endured notably close-up experiences of these elite men through being interned for their exclusive use in some cases. Japanese survivor Takanashi Taka, for example, who was born in Shinagawa in 1904 and prostituted within Japan from ages 14 to 28, and then prostituted overseas from 1931 to 1939, ended up at age 36 in a brothel reserved for officers in the South Pacific. She was used exclusively by three army officers in this brothel. However, she notes that, after four to five months in this situation, she became so sick of their 'arrogance' that she chose to move to a comfort station operating for troops. While Takanashi's account does not document details of her treatment by the three officers, it is perhaps ominous that the alternative she chose – effectively, serial rape by multitudes of men – was preferable in her calculation to involvement with these three officer-class men.[103]

Rather than the popularly subscribed 'catharsis' theory, therefore, we might explain the rampancy of the prostitution behaviour of Japanese men during war by looking to the model set by elite men of the military command. Elite men went to great efforts to make sure their subordinates were furnished with ample opportunity to prostitute women and, in doing so, they reinvented whole swathes of the Japanese male population in their own image. I discuss later what benefits this delivered the Japanese male ruling elite once 'peacetime' resumed.

## Intra-military transmission of a 'prostitution sexuality'

Sheila Jeffreys describes in concrete terms how prostitution facilitates male 'bonding':

> [Men] are able to indulge in homosexual bonding through the sharing of women ... they may fuck a woman in another man's sperm either symbolically or literally. Prostitutes have in previous ages been called 'common women' meaning that they are held in common by men, like the common land. Such sharing helps form bonds of unity between those who share.[104]

Fucking women in other men's sperm is an unfortunately accurate description of a central feature of comfort station prostitution. Above all, the venues facilitated male prostitution of women en masse in 'gang'-rape (i.e. multiple-perpetrator rape) fashion. This characteristic of comfort stations is illustrated starkly in the testimony of survivors. Japanese survivor 'Shimada Yoshiko', for example, recalls that when she was trafficked to Manchuria in 1939 she was interned in a comfort station in a 'frozen village' near the Soviet border, which was managed by a private operator to serve 3,500 Japanese troops in the area. There were sixteen women in the brothel. Shimada was in that situation over one-and-a-half years.[105] Another Japanese survivor, 'Suzuki Fumi', in 1942 at age 18 was in a geisha venue when she was approached by a broker recruiting women to be trafficked to South Pacific comfort stations. After he paid off her debt to the venue in full, she travelled to Truk on a naval ship with nearly forty other women from the same prostitution district. Suzuki was prostituted by troops in a military brothel from the day after she arrived on Truk; troops came from ten in the morning 'one after the other'. Suzuki had time between men only to run to the basin to wash her genitals. When she returned, the next man would be waiting.[106] A third Japanese survivor, Takajima Junko, who was born in 1914 in a Yamagata village and indentured to a Tokyo brothel at age 17 in November 1937, was trafficked to China after her brothel association head was summoned by the army ministry to recruit women for transport, and to set up a brothel in Shanghai. She travelled with women who were mostly from Japan's north-eastern prefectures. The brothel where she ended up housed fifteen rooms where women lived and were prostituted. Takajima was examined by a military doctor on the day she arrived, and from the next day soldiers lined up outside the brothel to use her from nine o'clock in the morning. She got a break at noon for an hour, and also between five and seven o'clock in the evening. After this, officers used her between seven and nine o'clock. She was used by an average of fifteen men per day.[107]

If we understand prostitution as not a natural or inevitable male behaviour, we might question how Japanese troops, especially new and young conscripts, managed to learn and enact this particular activity with such brutal uniformity. As Jeffreys writes, 'how men gain the idea that they may buy and use a strange woman's body; and how they have learnt that such use is erotically exciting is a question that needs investigation'.[108] Feminist commentators have long been doubtful that individual perpetrators are able to replicate practices of violence against women without some kind of institutional training and backing. Judith Herman explains that

> [i]t is theoretically possible, of course, that each abuser might spontaneously re-invent the basic methods of coercive control for himself, but this seems quite unlikely, given the constancy and uniformity of these practices across class and culture. It is more likely that this knowledge is transmitted within all-male groups that promote an ideology of male dominance and contempt for women … In such groups, the exchange of women or a shared visit to a brothel is often the means by which male bonding and solidarity is affirmed. The ritual display of the power to command sex from women is also a common custom in many business and political enterprises and, of course, in armies worldwide … It is conceivable, then, that the prostitution industry, which operates in virtually every society, might be a primary vector for socialization in the practices of coercive control, and the pimp might be among the world's most common instructors in the arts of torture.[109]

In the case of the comfort station system, we might look to Iwata Shigeori's anthropological research described in Chapter Two to understand how military sexual slavery perpetrated through comfort stations was cultivated as a behaviour among Japanese troops. Iwata looked specifically at the wartime sexuality of married military men because, he writes, the sexual practices of older men are influential in terms of behavioural modelling. He notes that married men were found in numbers among *kobi* conscripts, and young men among the *yobi* conscripts of the imperial army. (Japan's pre-1945 recruits came from conscripts who served two years in all branches of the military, and after this period were called *yobi*, or who were reserves of the active army for a period of five years and four months. After this, and until the age of 40, they became *kobi*, or second-class reserves.) Looking specifically at the latter group, Iwata finds an account that describes older men arriving at battlefields in China far more concerned about sexual matters than younger troops, and eagerly frequenting comfort stations soon after engaging in battle, and even patronizing the stations singly by themselves rather than in groups. Iwata suggests that the account shows problems in the sexuality of married Japanese men already by the 1930s, and he supports this view with data showing men in older age brackets were the most frequent patrons of the 1920s sex industry (i.e. 22 per cent of all patrons were aged between 26 and 30, and this was the highest percentage of all age groups).[110] From this discussion, Iwata offers the view that leaders and decision-makers in the military were heavily influenced by a 'prostitution sexuality' developed in peacetime, and this guided their participation in the comfort station system. We might suggest that Iwata's research also points to older officer-class men being likely builders and developers of the system. These men went on to occupy positions of leadership in the military, and their behavioural model might be understood as the conduit that facilitated a 'prostitution sexuality' among military enlistees.

The operation of the military prostitution system relied crucially on information transfer between recruits, not just for correct personal conduct in comfort stations, but also for its patronage conventions. An ex-military policeman testified to researchers in the early 1990s that he had been stationed on Okinawa for little more than a month before a high-ranking elderly officer had shown him how to use a condom.[111] Significantly, it had not occurred to him before this to patronize a comfort station. Another veteran who had been stationed on Rabaul told researchers he had been forcibly ordered along to a comfort station by his unit leader, and when he later tried to run away from the cubicle he was dragged back into the room.[112] While none of this testimony lightens the weight of personal responsibility on these individual men for having prostituted women, the stories do point to evidence of senior-ranking men inculcating subordinates with practices of prostitution. A veteran who published a memoir in 1980 noted that units containing higher proportions of draftees who were older and had sexual experience were more likely to use comfort stations and commit sexual assault crime.[113] There are numerous accounts among veterans that the prostitution of women at comfort stations was their first sexual experience.[114] Kasahara Tokushi sees this process of information transfer between older and younger men as central to the culture of the Japanese military. He writes that,

> [i]n respect to the education of new recruits, older or higher ranking personnel would take young conscripts out into the field and teach them methods of 'commandeering' that involved looting food and supplies from Chinese farmers. If they came across local women, they would station the new recruits on 'lookout', get them to assist in restraining victims, and even involve them in raping them. Japanese military education comprised fundamentally the idea that new recruits

had to be trained in techniques of murder, looting, destruction and even to feel pleasure and a lack of criminal consciousness about humiliating and degrading women, before individuals could be deemed mature personnel and part of the group acting in coordination.[115]

Also important to information transfer was the fact that comfort stations afforded military men of a range of ranks an opportunity to exercise prostitution rights in concert, amongst an audience of mentors and peers. Suzuki Masahiro makes the point that the even the raping of local women that the Japanese military was infamous for, particularly in the China War, was carried out in groups and mostly took the form of 'gang rape' (i.e. multiple perpetrator rape), which Suzuki sees as equivalent to the format of the military prostitution system.[116] The operation of the stations in the context of all-male military deployment abroad facilitated a uniquely high degree of close-range observation and knowledge-sharing in relation to the specific practices of a 'prostitution sexuality', even compared to that exercised through Japan's civilian sex industry and its pornographic products. Koga Noriko cites an example of troops using a comfort station on Okinawa where men lining up outside the draped cubicles waiting to prostitute the women inside would 'jokingly' open the drapes to hurry-along the men in front who was already sexually using them.[117] A veteran who had been stationed on Rabaul in 1944 describes using a comfort station that had 'paper-thin' drapes rather than doors, and so all the men lining up waiting their turn could 'see everything' (*maru mie*) in terms of their comrades in front prostituting women in the cubicles.[118] This opportunity was one Japanese men had delighted in back in peacetime, even if in a more limited way. A Japanese survivor of civilian prostitution recalls that

> [t]here were three- and five-square metre rooms in the brothel that were for lone customers to be taken to, but the six-square metre rooms, and sometimes even the five metre ones, were partitioned with folding screens so that more than one woman could take customers into the room. People today will probably have difficulty believing this, but customers at the time had no qualms about this kind of arrangement when they visited a brothel; in fact some of the men found it stimulating, and visited brothels precisely in anticipation of using one of these partitioned rooms.[119]

We might think it extraordinary that hundreds and thousands of men beset by conflict, starvation, and physical pain experienced feelings of excitement at the prospect of sexually penetrating women they had no relational connection with, let alone in squalid conditions of extreme deprivation that were so obviously disregarding of their personhood. These conditions are well documented.[120] While, as Fujino Yutaka writes, prostitution must always be problematized for its own sake (*kaishun koso mondai ni*),[121] we might nonetheless reflect on the mind-boggling callousness of individual Japanese men in deciding to prostitute women in comfort stations who, for example, were pregnant:

> Kim Yonshil recounts that Japanese military men continued to line up to prostitute her friend in a late stage of pregnancy in a comfort station near the Russian border,[122] and Son Shin Do gave birth to two children after she was trafficked into a comfort station in northern China at age 16.[123]

Were seriously and obviously injured:

> Bark Young Sim remembers that one day when she was in severe pain and 'didn't respond to the demands of one officer' in a Nanjing comfort station, he cut her neck with a knife: 'blood poured out and soaked my whole body'. The officer still went ahead and sexually used her.[124]

Did not share a common language:

> Yi Poknyo was able to recall only two names of the men who prostituted her, even though she was in a comfort station in northern China for *eight* years.[125]

And were living in inhuman conditions:

> Gang Duk-Gyung lived in a tent and was prostituted outdoors on a mountainside in Toyama prefecture.[126] In one comfort station in North Korea, the women's rooms were 260 centimetres long and 180 centimetres wide – barely large enough for one person to move around in.[127] In June 1944, Japanese troops commandeered houses on Okinawa to use as comfort stations. They simply hung sheets from the ceilings of the houses to separate the rows of beds they had set out on which women were to be prostituted.[128]

We need not reach for abstract or complicated rationales to explain these examples of sexual callousness by Japanese men in war, I believe. Their conditions of battle may have been harsh, and Japanese 'military culture' bad, but Taisho-era history makes redundant any theoretically fancy correlations of these wartime factors with the sexual behaviour of troops. Put simply, Japanese men were already enacting the same sexuality in peacetime, and precisely the same examples of callousness are found in spades in accounts of pre-war civilian prostitution. For example, a former pimp interviewed by Tanikawa in the early 1980s recalled that women in his brothel were prostituted until the eighth month of pregnancy (and he knew of none who went on to raise these children).[129]

Yun found 'numerous' reports in Hakodate newspapers from the early 1920s mentioning suicide by Korean prostituted women and girls through jumping off a notorious sea cliff in the area. One of the reports, Yun notes, describes the naked body of a Korean girl who had been thrown off the cliff by her pimp after she attempted to resist the abuse of Japanese prostitution buyers.[130] A former pimp interviewed by Tanikawa in the 1980s noted that women who 'sold well' in his brothel usually had ten customers per day.[131] While the prevalence and frequency of similar acts of callousness and brutality might have escalated with the onset of war, we can perhaps explain this escalation in terms of expanded opportunity of sexual access to women, rather than on the basis of any peculiar mass psychology created by harsh battlefield conditions.

## Conclusion

The military democratization of the Japanese male 'prostitution sexuality' of the twentieth century was achieved in practical and logistical terms through the development of the comfort station system. The China War delivered prostitution rights to even the young, rural Japanese men who had not necessarily been part of the male colonization of cities achieved in the Taisho era. Nothing inherent to war or militarism led these men to become prostitutors, however. Rather, as I have argued, the military's leaders were loyal patriots of the sex industry and its practices and ideology even before the war started, and were evangelical in their efforts to create a system in the image of their sexual values when the opportunity of the China War arose. The origins of this evangelicalism might be explained in terms of feminist observations of the nature of the reproduction of patriarchal social organization. That is, older men teach younger men, and elite men teach subordinate men.[132] In creating comfort stations in the vision of Japan's homeland sex industry, and using Japanese women, elite military men were successful in organizing a system via which troops en masse were taught and trained in the practices of a prostitution sexuality. This sexual training was broad-based, intense and very well organized. No expense or trouble was spared in the development of the training facilities (i.e. comfort stations) in which the education was carried out. As a means of indoctrinating and disseminating a prostitution sexuality, the military system was highly efficient and effective, as evidenced by the millions of Japanese men who inexplicably made the decision to prostitute women while enlisted with the military. The system operated as a vehicle for the international promulgation of the gender-based harms of Japan's sex industry. These practices included prostitution, procurement, trafficking and indentured servitude. As the years of war progressed, women and girls throughout the Asia-Pacific came to experience what their Japanese sisters had endured for many years and decades not only on home soil, but also in colonial Korea and Taiwan. The next chapter examines this latter experience.

# Japan's Imperial Sex Industries and the Trafficking of Colonial Prostituted Women into Comfort Stations

> The Japanese government concealed its conscription of Asian women into military prostitution by 'embedding' them within a system of legal prostitution that distinguishes between women who are forced and women who choose to be in prostitution.[1]

Why Korean women were disproportionately targeted for trafficking into comfort stations during the China and Pacific wars is a question much discussed by academics and activists. It is widely thought that Korean women made up 80 per cent of victims of the military sexual slavery system. Whatever the exact ratio, and whether or not Chinese women were victimized in greater numbers,[2] there is no doubt Korean women were targeted at a rate disproportionate to their population ratio within the Japanese empire. They appear to have been targeted relatively more often than women in Japan's other colonies and controlled territories, moreover, and were also uniquely trafficked into comfort stations via a female wartime labour mobilization scheme (*joshi teishintai*) operating in Korea from 1944.

Explanations abound for the disproportionate representation of Korean women among military sexual slavery victims. The operation of the above-mentioned *teishintai* labour mobilization system is seen as having made Korean women vulnerable to trafficking in a systemized way. Another theory is that Korean women's assimilation within the Japanese empire made them sexually desirable to Japanese men. While Ueno Chizuko does not explicate any of the logic behind her claimed link between assimilation and desirability in this respect, she nonetheless writes that,

> [u]nder the assimilation policy of turning Koreans into Imperial subjects, former comfort women would have been given official Japanese names and made to wear yukata (cotton kimono) and take on the appearance of Japanese

women. Korean comfort women were welcomed by the soldiers exactly because they could act like Japanese women.[3]

A further suggestion advanced by Suzuki Hiroko is that the Japanese military preferred Korean women over Japanese women, because the internment of Japanese women in comfort stations would have reduced troop morale, and because the ideology of *ryousai kenbo*, in which Japanese women are exalted as 'good wives and wise mothers', circulated strongly in Japanese culture before the war, and so the military set aside its countrywomen for their reproductive utility. She explains that 'the military organized young Korean women and prostituted Japanese women into comfort stations rather than "pure" Japanese women because these Japanese women were seen as likely to remind troops of their families and relatives and therefore have a detrimental effect on the "fight for the emperor" spirit of soldiers'.[4] Even Yoshimi Yoshiaki in his early work was persuaded by this kind of wartime military rhetoric: that Japanese women were spared trafficking into comfort stations out of consideration for troop morale. He suggested that,

> if Japanese women who were not prostitutes were sent from Japan to China as comfort women, it would [have] exert[ed] a grave influence on citizens, and especially on families whose sons were stationed overseas. Also, if the sisters, wives or female acquaintances of soldiers stationed overseas came to the battlefields as comfort women, it would [have] probably destroy[ed] soldiers' sense of trust in the state and the army … Therefore, the rounding up of comfort women from Japan was extremely limited.[5]

Racism was behind the military viewing Korean women as suited to sexual exploitation, in Suzuki's opinion, and she suggests their large-scale trafficking into comfort stations amounted to an attack on their reproductive functioning that effectively comprised a slow-burn ethnic genocide policy against the Korean population. She writes that, 'while there were a few Japanese prostituted women trafficked into comfort stations, the military was concerned about population reproduction issues back in Japan, so didn't target other Japanese women for trafficking'. On the other hand, the military was indifferent, if not hostile, to the reproduction of the Korean population, in Suzuki's view, and so targeted Korean women for enslavement in a system that was likely to kill them, destroy their ability to have children, and stigmatize them to an extent they could no longer participate in Korean society as wives and mothers.[6]

One further explanation common in the historiography is that Korean women were trafficked into comfort stations in lieu of women in occupied areas to avoid raising the ire of local populations who might resent the military's targeting of their female family members for abduction and sexual enslavement. Suzuki suggests the fact that Korean women had been part of the Japanese empire since 1910, and were already subject to mobilization once war broke out, made their targeting less of a perceived risk for the military.[7] This risk was further lessened by the alleged fact that much of the military's prostitution of women took place in areas away from the peninsula from which Korean women were trafficked, and was therefore beyond the purview of any local community that might have retaliated.

Seungsook Moon proposes yet another rationale for the disproportionate targeting of Korean women: she claims non-prostituted Korean women were abducted, tricked and trafficked into stations because the Japanese military was aware that 'women in Korea's Confucian society were instilled with an education that valued rigid chastity', and so 'turned its attention to seventeen- to twenty-year-old Korean women as substitutes for Japanese sex workers ... who were chaste enough to be free of venereal disease and young enough to endure disease if it developed'.[8] In Moon's view, concerted efforts were made to traffic Korean young women and girls into comfort stations, and the military targeted this population precisely on the basis they were not 'sex workers'. This was, in the military's estimation, a prudent approach to organizing the wartime prostitution system in terms of minimizing venereal disease transmission among troops, which had been supposedly brought about by women entering comfort stations direct from the sex industry and bringing sexually transmissible infections with them. US historian Laura Hein in 1999 repeated this claim that the Japanese military 'targeted unmarried women and girls from the general population [for trafficking into comfort stations], rather than women who already worked as prostitutes, to keep down the incidence of venereal disease'.[9]

These numerous and varied explanations for the overrepresentation of Korean women in comfort stations might have some basis in the self-serving wartime rhetoric of the Japanese military, or in the war histories of Korean nationalists but, even setting aside the illogic and misogyny of some of the claims (e.g. that Japanese prostituted women were responsible for venereal disease transmission among troops), their historical factual bases might still be questioned. For example, Ueno's claim that Korean women were well assimilated within the Japanese empire, and so desirable to Japanese men as sexual substitutes for their countrywomen, might be challenged on the basis of documented primary school matriculation rates among the Korean female population during the war, which were so low as to render their Japanese language skills almost non-existent, and the extent of their 'assimilation' therefore dubious.[10] Indeed, the testimony of

Korean survivors indicates widespread Japanese language incomprehension.[11] More substantially, though, popular explanations for Korean overrepresentation among sexual slavery victims might be viewed sceptically in light of work by historians like Fujinaga Takeshi, Hayakawa Noriyo, Yamashita Yeong-ae, Zhu Delan (known in Japanese as Shu Tokuran) and Song Youn-ok showing Korean *prostituted* women trafficked into comfort stations in large numbers out of the sex industries of both Korea and Taiwan, particularly during the years of the China War. This chapter draws on their work to suggest military sexual enslavement is a historical crime that disproportionately affected *prostituted* members of the female Korean population, and the overrepresentation of Korean women among comfort station victims can be historically attributed to the long-standing operation of a civilian prostitution industry in the colony, which was mostly developed by Japanese men.

## Women who are forced and women who choose

The conventional historical wisdom of the comfort station system is that, different from Japanese women, Korean women and girls were trafficked into military brothels through non-sex industry channels, such as through trickery by mainstream labour market brokers commissioned by the military, abduction off the street, and familial manipulation by village leaders. This view persists to the current day with, for example, the South Korean Ministry of Gender Equality and Family's recently released online 'museum' on the sexual slavery issue claiming that the

> Japanese military mobilized Korean women as comfort women by luring them
> with promises of work, as well as via intimidation or violence, human trafficking
> and kidnapping. The women were defrauded with promises of 'work in factories'
> or offers of 'making a lot of money' into joining the military brothels.[12]

These methods of procuring Korean women and girls were certainly practised, and non-prostituted Korean women and girls were certainly targeted for trafficking, especially in the years of the Pacific War, and all these facts are well established in the testimony of survivors and in historical research. However, as the chapter later describes, there is also historical evidence of the large-scale trafficking of Korean women (as well as Japanese and Taiwanese women) out of prostitution venues on Korea and Taiwan, which hosted industrialized sex industry sectors from the time of Japanese colonization around the turn of the century.

Japan held various leased territories and colonies at different stages before and during the war, including Taiwan, Korea, Sakhalin, the Manchurian puppet state encompassing a number of provinces in north-eastern China, the Liaotung peninsula, and areas held by the South Manchurian Railway Company in China. Japanese men exported their homeland system of legalized prostitution to most of these areas. Prostitution was legalized in Taiwan in 1906, south Sakhalin in 1907,[13] Korea in 1916, and Kurahashi Masanao describes Dairen's sex industry as replicating the 'conventions and aesthetics' of the Japanese homeland industry.[14] Hata Ikuhiko agrees that Japan's legalized prostitution system was 'exported holus bolus' to Manchuria after its creation in 1932.[15]

By the time of the China War, some of these industries in Japan's colonies and territories had grown to a large and sophisticated scale on the efforts of Japanese prostitution entrepreneurs, and they interned Korean, Taiwanese, and Japanese women trafficked both domestically and within the Japanese empire. These women comprised a ready pool of victims for the military's prostitution scheme. As described below, the military capitalized on personal connections cultivated between prostitution entrepreneurs and officers who had been pre-war patrons of civilian geisha venues in the colonies; these connections allowed the military subsequently to enlist the help of pimps and traffickers (who were usually Japanese male long-term residents in the colonies) to move women directly from sex industry venues into comfort stations, often abroad. The military therefore relied on the civilian sex industries of Japan's colonies, and the Japanese sex industrialists who developed them, particularly those based in Korea and Taiwan, in developing its military sexual slavery system. As a result, I argue, Korean prostituted women came to be disproportionately represented among comfort station victims, because the civilian sex industries of Japan's colonies facilitated the bulk of the trafficking of women into comfort stations.

Apart from the work of the historians mentioned earlier, the experience of Korean survivors of sexual slavery is described in terms that mostly exclude reference to prostitution and Japan's pre-war colonial sex industries. This historical whitewashing of the experience of prostituted women is perpetrated by Korean as well as Japanese commentators alike. A paper published in October 2013 by Han Hye-in at the Center for East Asian History in Sungkyunkwan University explores the supposed difference between the systems deployed to procure Korean and Japanese women for comfort stations. According to Han, women in Japan were recruited by brokers who had been authorized to carry out the activity by the Japanese army in accordance with legislation governing labour recruitment, while women in Korea could be recruited by people who were also hiring nurses in keeping with regulations about Korean workers. In other words, in Han's view, 'Japanese comfort women were hired in the framework of state-sponsored prostitution, while in Korea recruitment of comfort women took place on a social level by job brokers'.[16] Even Yoshimi makes similar claims about an absence of sex industry involvement in the entry of Korean women into comfort stations:

> Licensed prostitution was an important source of income for operators [on Korea]. Thus while there were instances in which operators brought their prostitutes with them to the battlefields, they were generally loathe to part with their prostitutes. We can't say that unlicensed prostitutes never became comfort women, but this was probably rare because so many of them were afflicted with sexually transmitted diseases.[17]

This chapter challenges Han and Yoshimi's version of events through describing the pre-war history of sex industry development on Korea and Taiwan, and the Japanese military's subsequent engagement with (Japanese) local pimps and brokers in these colonial industries to procure women for trafficking into comfort stations. While Hata contends a sharp drop-off in sex industry profits in Korea in 1940 due to wartime 'decadence' restrictions provoked the mass trafficking of Korean prostituted women out of the country into comfort stations,[18] the chapter's discussion highlights the military's reliance on colonial civilian prostitution in the development of its sexual slavery system from the very start of the China War. Overall, it asserts that the history of Japanese imperialism is linked to the origins and creation of the comfort station system, but that this link is importantly mediated through the variable of colonial prostitution industry development.

Right-wing defenders of the Japanese military's historical record like Hata Ikuhiko (and also Park Yuha from a 'progressive' perspective) are keen to highlight the involvement of Korean pimps in procuring and trafficking women for comfort station internment. The work of the abovementioned historians, however, tends not to show significant involvement by Koreans in the organization of women, at least compared to Japanese pimps. In 2007, a group of right-wing MPs published an advertisement in the *Washington Post* defending the Japanese military on the basis of its purported efforts during the war to make sure women were not forcibly trafficked into comfort stations, and so claiming that any historical wrongdoing should be attributed to rogue sex industry entrepreneurs, especially Korean ones. The chapter does not necessarily challenge the suggestion that Korean (or Taiwanese or Chinese)[19] pimps might have been involved in the trade, but its focus remains on Japanese sex entrepreneurs based in the colonies and their relationships with the Japanese military. This focus emphasizes structural features supporting the organization of the military prostitution system from its early inception. The chapter sees links between Japanese military men and their fellow countrymen in the colonies who were running civilian sex industry businesses, as well as links between these pimps and colonial bureaucrats (also mostly Japanese men), as furnishing the system with an infrastructural base that was critical to its creation and operation on such a large and widespread scale in Asia and the Pacific.

## Japanese development of Korea's colonial sex industry

Historians like Fujinaga Takeshi over the past two decades have examined Japanese involvement in the development of Korea's colonial sex industry to connect this history to the subsequent creation and operation of the military prostitution system. Fujinaga suggests sex industry development on colonial Korea from the turn of the century meant pimping and trafficking networks were ripe for military cooptation by the time of the war.[20] This section summarizes the work of historians who have examined Japan's colonial sex industries, and notes that these industries in Korea and Taiwan developed early on through the trafficking of prostituted women out of Japan, and these women, too, along with Korean and Taiwanese prostituted women, thereafter became a major pool of victims of the wartime sexual slavery system.

The proportion of Korean victims who were trafficked out of prostitution into comfort stations is not numerically estimated in the historical literature, probably for reasons similar to those pertaining to Japanese survivors, as described in Chapter Two. Ueno Chizuko writes that concerted efforts have been made to highlight the non-prostituted status of Korean survivors of military sexual slavery, and these efforts are likely to be motivated by concerns about right-wing propaganda labelling survivors 'prostitutes' and suggesting they wilfully entered stations to earn money.[21] Suzuki notes the efforts of right-wing defenders of the Japanese military to 'locate the comfort women problem within the problem of prostitution', and suggests they do so for the purpose of 'degrading their individual existence and silencing them' through associating survivors with prostitution. She sees this strategy as successfully capitalizing on public approbation towards prostitution, and done in full knowledge of 'how hurtful being labelled a prostitute is for survivors'.[22]

Nonetheless, it is clear from the work of a number of historians that the Japanese military drew on Korean women prostituted in the legalized sex industries of Korea and Taiwan as a significant source of trafficking victims for comfort stations, especially during the years of the China War. Fujinaga writes unequivocally that legalized prostitution in colonial Korea formed the 'infrastructural base' of the comfort women system,[23] the export of Japan's legalized prostitution policy regime to Korea comprised the historical foundation of the system, and the trafficking of Korean women into comfort stations was organized primarily through sex industry recruitment.[24] He notes specifically that the creation of a comfort station network as part of Japan's southern China military campaigns from 1938 relied fundamentally on the existence of a large population of prostituted women on Taiwan, often trafficked there from Korea and Japan.[25] Song Youn-ok concurs that the mobilization of such large numbers of Korean women for trafficking into comfort stations was historically possible only because of the prior development of legalized prostitution on Korea from 1916 and the proliferation of its attendant trafficking networks.[26]

Contemporary advocates of justice for comfort station survivors might perceive efforts to emphasize this history as unnecessary or unproductive to the aims of the movement, or as inconvenient and distressing to survivors and their families, given that right-wing defenders of the Japanese military make mileage out of any historical hint of sex entrepreneur involvement in the sexual slavery system, as discussed earlier. They see this involvement as relieving the military of historical culpability. Hata, for example, writes that, '[t]he fact that no Japanese living on the Korean peninsula had sufficient command of the Korean language to deceive a Korean woman' must lead us to assume that 'the young women were deceived by Koreans – their compatriots'.[27] Tessa Morris-Suzuki challenges the suggestion Hata seeks to tacitly make: that the involvement of civilian brokers and traffickers in the organization of women for comfort stations lightens the weight of historical responsibility on the Japanese military. She responds that, 'even where women were recruited by third parties, this in no way diminishes the responsibility of the Japanese military on whose behalf the brokers were working'.[28] Further, I believe, involvement by civilian sex industry entrepreneurs might be seen as heightening the historical culpability of the Japanese military because of the likely implication that significant numbers of women were subject to sexual slavery in both civilian as well as military venues, and the Japanese military took advantage of this fact.

Their experience of sexual slavery was significantly determined by colonial sex industry development, both in respect of their civilian prostitution, as well as their subsequent entry into comfort stations. Indeed, the re-trafficking of Korean comfort station survivors into post-war civilian prostitution venues might also be identified as a significant legacy of colonial sex industry development, given the longevity of some of the Japanese-built red light districts within Korea in the post-war period, such as Nanchochon in Chucheon City, which was dismantled only recently in August 2013. The culpability of Japanese military and colonial authorities for the creation and development of the wartime system might be seen as aggravated by their support for and cooperation with civilian sex industrialists who enslaved not only women within the military system they helped to organize, but countless others in civilian venues, and profited from these activities. A more fulsome account of the wrongdoing of Japanese military men during the war might recognize this collusion with civilian pimps and traffickers, which was necessary to establishing and maintaining the operation of its sexual slavery system. The military, commercial, and administrative relationships Japanese men forged among themselves before and during the war to make possible the military sexual enslavement of tens of thousands of women is an aspect of historical wrongdoing that might be highlighted for the obscenity of its aforethought, planning, and coordination. The obscenity is compounded by Japan's history of colonial prostitution industry development, which goes back much further than the eight years of the China and Pacific wars.

Japanese pimps began developing the sex industry on Korea in earnest from the time of the Russo-Japanese War (1904–1905) through trafficking Japanese women to Seoul.[29] The war, and the military demand for prostitution it generated through the stationing of Japanese troops in the colonies, prompted the export of Japan's legalized prostitution policy model to both Korea and Taiwan.[30] Prostitution was legalized nationally in Japan in 1900, and this legislation became the blueprint for prostitution policy throughout the empire.[31] Japan acquired extraterritorial rights in Korean port areas in 1876, and shipping routes between the two countries opened up in the 1890s, which facilitated the trafficking of Japanese women into the country.[32] This traffic initially responded to military demand generated by the creation of bases in Korea after the Sino-Japanese War in 1894–1895.[33] As a result, ordinances regulating prostitution were introduced from 1904 for Japanese settlement areas in Pusan and Incheon and were administered by Japanese consulates. Yamashita Yeong-ae suggests these early regulatory measures were mainly for the purpose of raising funds for settler communities.[34] The ordinances were aggregated in one national piece of legislation legalizing the sex industry in Korea in 1916,[35] which was initially applied only to Japanese settlement areas, but was then extended to the whole country in 1919.[36] The trafficking of Japanese women into Korea peaked with the onset of the Russo-Japanese War and the signing of the 1905 protectorate treaty,[37] and by 1908 there were 2,839 prostituted Japanese women in the country.[38] By the 1920s, half of all prostituted women in Korea were Japanese.[39] Song suggests a reason for this was the lower minimum age permitted for women entering sex industry venues in Korea (17 years in Korea, compared to 18 years in Japan), which gave pimps a financial incentive to traffic girls out of Japan.[40] They were mostly trafficked direct from Japan's sex industry: Hata writes that 60 per cent of Japanese prostituted women in Korea in the 1920s had been previously prostituted, as compared to more than 50 per cent of prostituted Korean women who came from non-sex industry backgrounds.[41] This trend gradually changed over time, though: the number of Korean prostituted women overtook Japanese women in 1929 when circumstances in Korea's countryside declined, and starvation conditions made rural women and girls vulnerable to trafficking into cities.[42]

There were more Korean- than Japanese-owned prostitution venues in Seoul throughout this pre-war period, but the turnover of Japanese-owned venues was far higher, and the venues were far larger in size. Japanese sex industrialists were prominent members of settler communities in pre-war Korea and often had prior military experience of the Russo-Japanese War. Song suggests this experience meant that they were able to cultivate the connections among local military police that were needed to start large-scale prostitution ventures. They pimped Japanese as well as Korean women, but sold Korean women under Japanese names,[43] and persisted in this practice in their later operation of military comfort stations, as described in previous chapters. Their customers were mainly Japanese men, who comprised 80 per cent of sex industry patrons in pre-war Seoul, and who were responsible for twelve times the number of prostitution transactions as Korean men. When this number is adjusted for relative male population ratios in Korea in 1929, they were responsible for fifty-seven times the number of prostitution transactions, which amounted to over a million purchases in 1927.[44] Song notes they demanded sexual access mostly to Japanese women,[45] but their violence extended to all women in the sex industry, with reports of assault of Korean women common in newspapers in the 1920s. She offers the explanation that Japanese men felt a sense of entitlement to do things to women in the Korean sex industry they might not otherwise have dared back home.[46]

Korean women were organized in brothels in large numbers from the mid-1920s, primarily for the benefit of Japanese military, business, and government men.[47] As a result, Matsuoka Nobuo writes, between the years 1910 and 1937, the number of prostituted women in Korea grew nearly tenfold.[48] Fujinaga nominates more specifically the years between 1915 and 1925 as the period when the number of Korean as well as Japanese prostituted women in Korea rose.[49] He attributes the increase to 'expanded demand', which he sees as emanating from Japanese men colonizing the country.[50] Yamashita suggests that the number of Korean prostituted women grew five times between the years 1916 and 1920,[51] and Hata estimates 30,000 Korean girls were sold to brokers in the 1920s, often for trafficking out of the country.[52] Song observes *kafe* venues proliferating in Korea in the 1930s, following the 1920s trend in Japan (as described in Chapter Two), which reflected changing consumer preferences among Japanese men for prostitution mediated through unregulated venues. Notably, *kafes* were a major destination for girls trafficked into Korea's cities from the countryside around this time,[53] and Song suggests their lack of regulation facilitated the trade; policy measures to restrict the *kafe* prostitution sector in Korea were not introduced until 1934.[54] The number of Japanese pimps operating geisha venues in Korea also rose around this time, as did the number of Korean girls trafficked into geisha venues.[55] As a result, the total number of prostituted women and girls in Korea peaked at 18,000 in 1939 (with a population of roughly 24 million people).[56] While this number is small compared to the Japanese peak of 210,000 in 1937 (with a population of roughly 70 million people),[57] it is significant if we consider Korea did not have an industrialized prostitution sector before Japanese invasion, even if aristocrat Korean men had conducted a notorious but limited trade in women as '*kisaeng*' performing artists.

In fact, Japanese men integrated this prior-existing elite system of prostitution into the legalized industry when they colonized Korea. *Kisaeng* became part of the newly introduced regime, and live-in 'schools' were established for Korean girls to learn the traditional arts from a young age. Just like geisha houses (i.e. *okiya*) in Japan in the same period, though, these 'schools' were generally venues into which underage girls were trafficked for prostitution, often under the guise of adoption contracts.[58] In a 1999 book chapter looking at the representation of Korean *kisaeng* women in colonial era picture postcards,[59] Kawamura Minato of Hosei University argues that, whatever role scholars might ascribe to individual *kisaeng* in ancient Korean history as performers, 'courtesans', or the like, in its modern form *kisaeng*, was merely the product of Japanese male demand for a Korean equivalent of 'geisha' during the colonial occupation.[60] He notes that Japanese 'tourists, surveyors, scholars, and artists' who visited colonial Korea and saw the occupied territory as a 'fieldwork site' to 'exercise their spirit of adventure' and 'satisfy their intellectual curiosity' wrote about *kisaeng* in terms that promoted their use by Japanese men as geisha and prostitutes. He observes that *kisaeng*, along with Japanese geisha who were trafficked into the country after bans on their entry were lifted in the 1920s, were subjected to mandatory venereal disease examinations only after Japanese men came to occupy the country in 1910.[61]

## The pre-war trafficking of Korean women out of the colonial sex industry

Korean women were trafficked out of Korea to places within the Japanese empire from around the time of the First World War,[62] including to Manchuria from 1915,[63] and to Sakhalin and Taiwan from the 1920s.[64] Song estimates 5,000 women were trafficked in Korea each year from the mid-1920s, with 80 per cent destined for foreign sex industries.[65] These foreign industries included those in Japan-controlled areas in China, and Korean women were moved around repeatedly within the empire; in 1931, there were 1,173 detected trafficking cases involving Korean women, and among these were women who had been re-trafficked to Shanghai from the Chinese cities of Dalian and Qingdao.[66] Brokers operating in Korea had significant financial incentive to traffic women and girls out of the country: Song calculates they would have been able to live for two to three months on commissions earned from the trafficking of just two girls domestically, and for much longer if they trafficked the girls abroad.[67] Yamashita observes that the relatively low cost of indenturing Korean women and girls was also an incentive to their trafficking:

> The shift from recruiting Japanese comfort women towards recruiting Korean and Chinese women occurred under such market conditions. In other words, Japanese women were for higher-ranking officers, and Korean and Chinese women were assigned to the lower ranks and the prices charged were adjusted accordingly. This was not only because of ethnic discrimination but because they cost less in the first place due to these 'market' condition[s].[68]

While the pre-war trafficking of Japanese women throughout Asia and the Pacific has been well documented by historians of 'karayuki', and is even suggested to historically preface the development of the comfort station system (see Chapter Four), the similar trafficking of Korean women throughout the empire in a more recent historical time is less recognized as a precursor of the military sexual slavery system, even though their numbers relative to the (shorter) time period in which the *karayuki* traffic occurred might be comparable. The omission of this pre-war history from most accounts of Korean women's trafficking into comfort stations during the war now makes mysterious their disproportionate representation among victims to a degree that is perhaps not necessary or warranted. Inter-regional trafficking was precisely the logistical means used to establish the comfort station network, and this organizational method had been tried and tested prior to the outbreak of war using women and girls sourced from colonial Korea, and specifically its legalized sex industry, I argue.

From early on, Japan was a major destination country for trafficked Korean women. Song records the presence of Korean women in Osaka's sex industry in as early as 1910,[69] and cites newspaper reports from the 1920s of Korean girls being trafficked to Japan in groups of fifteen or more on the pretext of recruitment for factory work. Most of this work ended up delivering them into Japan's sex industry,[70] and there was also widespread trafficking (i.e. on-selling) of Korean girls out of factories into local prostitution venues.[71] Unsurprisingly, only a minority of employment advertisements targeting Korean women in the 1920s were for factory jobs; most openly advertised vacancies for Japanese bars, restaurants, and other prostitution-related venues.[72] These venues were often located around coal mining towns in Hokkaido or Kyushu.[73] Yun Chung-ok's survey of the Sapporo municipal government employment archives reveals Korean women in the sex industry of that city already by the 1920s, and she suggests these women were initially prostituted by Korean migrant male labourers in the area. By this time, there were reportedly five or six Korean restaurant brothels in the district, but Yun notes the venues became increasingly popular among local Japanese men by the early 1930s, and this escalation in demand promoted increased rates of trafficking of Korean women into the city thereafter. She cites a 1935 police report showing sixty-seven Korean sex industry venues in Sapporo by 1935, but estimates that there were likely to have been more than one hundred operating by this time.[74] We might speculate that this increased Japanese male demand for the prostitution of Korean women arose from their accumulated military experience abroad by this time, of which much was on the Korean Peninsula. As mentioned, Japanese men, including military men, became significant customers of the sex industry in Korea from the time of the Russo-Japanese War.

Whether sexual demand came from Korean or Japanese men, for the women prostituted the experience appears to have been unbearable. Yun describes a spate of suicides by Korean women reported in the mid-1930s at the Hakodate cliffs. They were by women from the local Korean red light district, and a 1935 newspaper report cited a reason for their deaths as 'protest' at abuse at the hands of 'Japanese people', which we might interpret to mean Japanese traffickers, pimps, and brothel customers. Local authorities banned the publication of reports of the suicides in 1943 but, before this, in 1940, Yun records classified advertisements regularly appearing in local newspapers seeking information on the whereabouts of Korean women who had escaped from brothels. The advertisements hauntingly describe the women's hairstyles and articles of clothing. This traffic in Korean women to Hokkaido persisted into the years of the Pacific War, and Yun notes a newspaper advertisement from January 1940 seeking a brothel proprietor to open a venue near a Hokkaido coal mine hosting 704 Korean male workers.[75] By this stage of the war, these workers are likely to have included significant numbers of men trafficked for the purpose of wartime labour: Brandon Palmer calculates there were 750,000 Koreans recruited for work in 'mines and wartime industries in Japan', and the formal conscription scheme was extended to the male Korean population in 1942.[76] Motivating the provision of prostituted women to these men might have been considerations similar to those described by Ogino Fujio in Chapter Three, whereby local authorities set up a comfort station at a mine in Toyama for the purpose of sexually placating Chinese slave labourers.[77] Gang Duk-Gyung's recollection that she lived in a tent and was prostituted outdoors on a mountainside in Toyama prefecture is jarring in the light of this history.[78] Concurrently at this time, Korean women were re-trafficked out of mining areas in Japan into mainland comfort stations, as Radhika Coomaraswamy notes in her 1996 United Nations Commission on Human Rights report: 'The first military sexual slaves were Koreans from the North Kyushu area of Japan'.[79]

Song describes the men organizing the pre-war traffic of Korean women and girls to Japan as mostly Japanese male long-term residents of Korea who had contacts among sex industrialists based in Japan, or Japanese factory owners with local connections that allowed them to on-sell Korean trafficked girls.[80] Alternatively, she writes, underage Korean girls were openly recruited for entry into geisha houses in Japan; there was no age restriction on Korean girls entering geisha houses on Korea or Manchuria, and the minimum age for Japan and Taiwan was set at a low 12 years.[81] While there was a ban in place on foreign women entering Japan's sex industry, this did not apply to Koreans after the 1910 annexation, and Japan in 1925 signed the International Convention for the Suppression of the Traffic in Women and Children on the condition it would not apply to women in its colonies.[82] This exclusion was significant because travel by Koreans to Japan for labour was deregulated in 1938, which put Korean women and girls at significant risk of trafficking into Japan's comparatively larger sex industry during the war years.[83] Rates of compliance with the ban on the trafficking of Japanese women were low, moreover, and Nishino Rumiko writes that, while the trafficking of women out of Japan's legalized sex industry into comfort stations was banned in law from 1925, the military's widespread participation in this criminal activity is shown in its supply of money in the form of advance credit loans to buy women out of civilian venues in Japan.[84] The exemption of Japan's colonies in the ratification of the Convention suited the business interests of pimps in these colonies, and their interests coincided with those of the military when the military contracted them to set up comfort stations, which is recognized by historians as a common method of organization of the venues.[85] A former military brothel proprietor on Truk who rang a national hotline set up by a Japanese women's organization in 1992 to collect information from the public on the military prostitution issue reported that he procured 200 Japanese women and 100 Korean women for trafficking by ship from the port of Yokosuka to set up two comfort stations on Truk during the war. He apparently procured 120 of these women from the Yoshiwara brothel district.[86]

While not likely to have been a significant vehicle of trafficking, historians suggest the 1944 extension of the *teishintai* system to the female Korean population, two years after the system had been formally operating to recruit Korean men for wartime labour since 1942, organized some Korean women and girls into military prostitution. Palmer writes that '[t]he Women's Volunteer Corps recruited single young women, making the organization an easy target of recruiters involved in military prostitution. Many women recruited by the corps ended up in brothels'.[87] He describes the Corps as follows:

> The Women's Volunteer Corps, created in April 1944, was a special work group for Japanese and Korean women. The corps' official purpose was to give women a chance to serve Japan prior to marriage. However, it was a means to compel women to perform labor duties. This organization functioned differently in Korea than in Japan. In Japan, the volunteer corps recruited unmarried women ages sixteen and older who had special skills; in Korea, too few women had

technical skills, so the organization focused on recruiting unskilled laborers; in some cases it recruited girls as young as fourteen … The corps mobilized women for agricultural and factory labor – often sending young girls to Japan on one-year contracts.[88]

The corps mobilized not only women in Korea, as is well documented, but also those residing in Japan during the war years. A male Korean resident of Japan (*zainichi*) who rang the above-mentioned hotline recalled his sister becoming a target of recruiters. His family had been living in Osaka in 1943 or 1944 when a Japanese military policeman came to their house and ordered his father hand over his 17-year-old sister to be recruited into the *joshi teishintai* system. When his father replied that she was scheduled to be married (and was therefore exempt from recruitment), the policeman demanded proof, which the father was fortunately able to hastily arrange.[89]

While the *teishintai* system is frequently nominated as a structural driver of the disproportionate trafficking of Korean women into comfort stations,[90] the sex industry emerges in the first-person historical testimony of traffickers as a more substantial hub of recruitment. A former navy transport division member reported to the above-mentioned hotline that, in late 1943 or early 1944, he had been involved in procuring women within Korea for entry into naval comfort stations. Some of the women he targeted were Japanese residents of Korea but, regardless of nationality, most came from the local sex industry (both brothels and *kafes*), in his testimony. According to his account, most of these prostituted women were Korean, and the sex industry was specifically the place he 'targeted' for comfort station recruitment. Even still, the women he recruited did not necessarily know they were going to be moved into comfort stations; he said they mostly believed they had been recruited for soldier entertainment or maid services.[91] He trafficked the women into comfort stations both in Japan and abroad. In another example, Yoshimi records 173 Japanese and 115 Korean women being given official permits to travel from Korea to Jinan in eastern China in 1938, after the Japanese military had conquered the area the year before. Of these, there were 76 Japanese and 101 Korean women who were sourced directly from the Korean sex industry. Yoshimi believes all the women were destined for sexual use in mainland comfort stations.[92] The sex industry was an important site of recruitment regardless of whether or not the Japanese military was directly involved in procurement. In some cases the military requested colonial authorities supply women for comfort stations, but in these cases bureaucrats would pass down the directive to local pimps and traffickers who would attempt to fill quotas. During the July–August 1941 China campaign, for example, the military requested the Korean colonial administration supply 20,000 women for entry into mainland comfort stations, in response to which between 3,000 and 8,000 women were trafficked out of Korea.[93] Fujinaga suggests it is likely many of these women were sourced from the local sex industry.

Another major trafficking destination for Korean women and girls was Taiwan, but historians are unsure as to why Japanese pimps relied on the trafficking of Korean women to build the Taiwanese sex industry, rather than sourcing victims locally.[94] They did of course traffic local Taiwanese women into brothels, as described further below, and Taiwanese prostituted women are likely to have been significant among trafficking victims on the mainland. By December 1943, 7,928 Taiwanese people lived in the southern China region, of which 33 per cent were women. Zhu Delan acknowledges some of these women would have been nurses, typists and housewives, but suggests the majority would have been in the sex industry, and especially in *kafes*.[95] Nonetheless, the presence of Korean and Japanese prostituted women on Taiwan in the pre-war period suggests cross-border trafficking was also a major procurement strategy of the industry in that colony. This traffic is perplexing in light of the fact Taiwan's colonial sex industry historically predates Korea's, so theoretically should have been more developed and organizationally integrated by the 1920s.[96]

Commentators offer a number of possible explanations for it. Zhu suggests the lower minimum entry age for prostitution venues in Taiwanese law provided Japanese pimps based in Korea with a financial incentive to traffic both Japanese and Korean girls under their control to Taiwan.[97] It is also possible that relatively stronger prostitution demand on Taiwan compared to Korea fuelled the traffic in later war years. Taiwan was not just a military staging post for the South Pacific at the start of the Pacific War, it was also an important gateway to southern China and Southeast Asia, so the number of deployed troops, business men, bureaucrats, and munitions factory workers increased year on year on the island.[98] As a result, sex industry businesses on Taiwan grew exponentially over the years 1937–1938,[99] with *kafes* notably booming from 1937.[100] Industry profits continued to rise throughout the war years, including between the years 1941 and 1942 when the revenue of the country's geisha sector doubled.[101] Zhu calculates the industry continued to grow year-on-year up until 1944 when the colonial administration enforced entertainment business bans in line with wartime anti-decadence policies.[102] Profit seeking might therefore have motivated Japanese pimps based in Korea to transfer their business activities to Taiwan, and this might have fuelled their trafficking of Korean and Japanese prostituted women to the island. Fujinaga suggests most men involved in the traffic of Korean women and girls to Taiwan were Japanese, and that it was Japanese pimps who originally initiated the trade.[103]

## Japanese development of Taiwan's colonial sex industry

A recognizable sex industry emerged on Taiwan after Japanese takeover of the country in 1895.[104] Travel from Japan to Taiwan was permitted mostly without restriction from 1896, and this is when the trafficking of Japanese women began, especially from Kyushu.[105] As mentioned, prostitution was legalized nationally in 1906, with the minimum entry age for women set at 16 years, but one of the first ordinances passed in the country after colonial administration began on 1 April 1896 related to prostitution, which indicates the depth of the commitment Japanese men brought to developing prostitution in the country.[106] As a result, there were more than 4,000 sex industry businesses on Taiwan by the late 1930s and early 1940s.[107] These businesses developed mainly around Japanese military bases on the island from 1910.[108] Fujinaga writes that Taiwan's pre-war sex industry was 'indistinguishable' from that of Korea in that demand for prostitution came primarily from Japanese military men due to large numbers of bases and troops deployed to the island.[109] There were 19,500 Japanese troops stationed on Taiwan during the war, which was more than the number deployed to Okinawa,[110] and the country's main sex industry district was converted to exclusive military use in 1941.[111]

On the eve of the China War in 1936, there were more than 7,000 prostituted women in Taiwan.[112] Of this, an average 758 Japanese women had entered the legal sector each year, plus another 1,000 Japanese women entering prostitution venues outside the legalized system.[113] Zhu suggests the industry on Taiwan 'democratised' in the 1930s to cater to different economic classes of men,[114] but started out catering to elite Japanese businessmen and colonial bureaucrats.[115] As in Korea, Fujinaga notes Taiwan's sex industry was patronized mainly by Japanese men.[116] This meant Japanese women were trafficked into Taiwan as 'geisha' from 1896, and the industry developed in the early decades in a 'Japanese-style' way.[117] Taiwanese prostituted women became victims of this trend; Zhu describes Taiwanese women being made to participate in Japanese events and wear kimonos, undertake Japanese language lessons, learn Japanese make-up application, perform traditional songs, and dance for Japanese troops.[118]

As the years progressed, Taiwan's sex industry fashioned itself to military demand; Shirota Suzuko was trafficked from Japan into a naval comfort station in the Taiwanese city of Magong. The station was part of a naval prostitution district hosting twenty comfort stations, each housing around fifteen women. Shirota describes her experience of military prostitution on Taiwan in haunting terms as 'completely absent of any human compassion or consideration', and after six months she managed to escape back to Japan, even if by this time her trafficking debt still had barely subsided.[119] Zhu suggests Japanese geisha venue (*ryouriten*) owners on Taiwan were 'semi-forced' by the military to convert their venues into stations for officers, and that others were 'forced' to commandeer schools and other public buildings to set up stations for troops.[120] She describes the case of a Japanese geisha venue owner on Taiwan being commissioned by the Japanese navy to set up a comfort station on Hainan Island in its capital of Haikou. The pimp had trouble sourcing a large number of women, even though the military gave him money to do so. This money was most likely for the purpose of buying women out of civilian sex industry debt bondage. The sex entrepreneur ended up trafficking sixty Japanese women he had debt bonded to his own prostitution business, plus another thirteen women controlled by other pimps.[121] Taiwanese women, too, were vulnerable to procurement into military prostitution by Japanese pimps, especially if they had any connection to the local sex industry. One of the first Taiwanese women to come forward as a comfort station survivor in the early 1990s, 'Mrs Kao', as she is identified in a 1998 English-subtitled documentary produced by the Taipei Women's Rescue Foundation, testifies she was employed as a 'geisha' at the time she was trafficked into a Burmese comfort station, but that this had involved only 'drinking and singing' and not prostitution. She was trafficked by a Japanese broker and attempted suicide upon realizing the situation she had been placed in. Nearly all of the fourteen Taiwanese survivors documented in the 1998 film explicitly report being either trafficked by Japanese brokers or interned in comfort stations that were managed by Japanese nationals, even when they had no prior connection to the sex industry.[122]

The trafficking of prostituted women out of Korea's sex industry to Taiwan peaked with the launch of Japanese military campaigns in southern China over the years 1938–1940.[123] Fujinaga suggests trafficking practices forged by the military during these campaigns established the logistical blueprint for the military's organization of women into comfort stations for the rest of the war.[124] The blueprint identified by Fujinaga, as well as Zhu, was one in which women were trafficked out of Korea's sex industry into the industry on Taiwan, and then re-trafficked to comfort stations on the Chinese mainland. Already by 1925, Korean women outnumbered their male countrymen on Taiwan; by 1932, the female ratio was one and a half times that of Korean men. Prostituted women made up a significant proportion of this population; around 40 per cent of Korean women on Taiwan were prostituted by the early years of the 1930s.[125] Taiwan's first Korean-style brothel ('restaurant') opened up in 1922,[126] and by 1937 there were fifty-eight such venues in the country.[127] Korean prostituted women on Taiwan were often under the control of Japanese pimps who had relocated their businesses to the island, which meant they were vulnerable trafficking into comfort stations, because it was these men the Japanese military most relied upon to organize its mainland stations after 1938.

Fujinaga questions why Korean women were mobilized via the Taiwanese sex industry instead of being directly trafficked from Korea into comfort stations, given the Korean colonial administration could have easily responded to requests from the military because Japanese pimps were well established in Korea by this time.[128] Historians have not reached consensus on an answer to this question, but Zhu's research shows significant financial support on offer from Taiwan's colonial authority to assist locally based Japanese pimps to set up comfort stations for the military. The colonial authority was staffed with Japanese bureaucrats and operated primarily to serve the interests of local Japanese businessmen and residents, as well as the military, and so exerted significant influence over commercial and administrative arrangements in the colony. The wartime loans scheme fostered a cooperative arrangement between local Japanese pimps and the military, given these pimps faced some level of commercial risk in establishing comfort stations in lieu of running their civilian enterprises (which were already meeting military demand for prostitution anyway). While this cooperative arrangement was auspiced by the Taiwanese colonial authority, the authority devolved management of the loans scheme to a state-owned enterprise, the Taiwan Colonization Company (TCC), which operated on the basis of Japanese financial investment and was staffed and managed by Japanese nationals. The TCC then sub-contracted the scheme to another smaller company.[129] The scheme offering loans to local pimps thereby operated at arm's-length from the colonial authority in order to protect its public reputation.[130] Zhu suggests the loans scheme was crucial to the ability of the Japanese military to mobilize so many pimps in such a short space of time to establish so many comfort stations.[131] Fujinaga similarly notes the effectiveness of the loans scheme in allowing the Japanese military to commission pimps to set up comfort stations on the mainland for its southern China campaigns.[132]

Similar to the situation in Korea, the authority also responded to military requests for the trafficking of women. Just after the commencement of the Guangdong campaign in 1938, for example, the Office of the Governor-General of Taiwan complied with a request from the Japanese military for the trafficking of 300 women from Taiwan into southern China comfort stations.[133]

The nationality background of women trafficked out of Taiwan into mainland comfort stations from 1938 reflects the pre-war historical picture of the trafficking of women within the Japanese empire. This trafficking, in turn, reflects the pre-war organization of civilian systems of prostitution within Japan and throughout the empire. To take one illustrative example, Fujinaga's research shows that, between November 1938 and January 1940, there were 828 Japanese, 528 Korean and 266 Taiwanese women trafficked on official papers out of Taiwan's sex industry into comfort stations in southern China.[134] That Japanese women were represented so significantly among victims is unsurprising, given the long pre-war history of their trafficking out of Japan into the colonial Taiwanese sex industry. According to Fujinaga's numbers, Korean women, too, featured prominently among trafficking victims out of Taiwan, and this suggestion is supported by other statistics. For example, between November and December 1938, Korean women accounted for fully 72 per cent of all departures from Taiwan, and this number includes at least 229 Korean women confirmed in historical records as destined for trafficking into mainland comfort stations.[135] While not all these women would have been prostituted in the Korean or Taiwanese sex industries before being trafficked via Taiwan into mainland stations, travel records from the time indicate many of them did in fact come from Korea's sex industry, because their employment status at the time of entering Taiwan was listed as 'barmaid', which was the conventional official euphemism used for women in prostitution around the time.[136] Korean women were re-trafficked out of Taiwan into mainland comfort stations in significant numbers notably after 1939.[137] In this year, 577 Korean women were trafficked to Taiwan, which Fujinaga suggests was mostly for the purpose of prostitution.[138] Roughly the same number were then trafficked out of the country to southern China (mainly Guangdong) within the same year.[139] Fujinaga suggests this coincidence of numbers shows a pattern whereby the Taiwanese sex industry was used as a clearinghouse for the trafficking of Korean and Japanese women into comfort stations.

Evidence of the trafficking of women out of Taiwan for the specific purpose of filling comfort stations can be further seen in the chronology of the campaigns that were launched by the Japanese military in the early years of the China War, which mirror trends in the trafficking of women. Fujinaga calculates that spikes occurred in the trafficking of Korean women out of Taiwan at two historical points: once between November 1938 and March 1939, and once between October and December 1939. These spikes, he suggests, mirrored developments in Japanese military campaigns: the frontline moved from northern to central China, culminating in the Guangdong campaign of October 1938, and the first trafficking peak coincides with the period immediately before this. The second peak coincides with the Nanning campaign.[140] Fujinaga writes that the timing of the two peaks might suggest the Japanese military pre-emptively organized the trafficking of women out of Taiwan, which hosted a large sex industry proximate to the southern China campaigns, to logistically prepare for the creation of comfort stations. By 1939, the 21st division of the Japanese military had around 1,000 comfort women under its control, which was roughly the same number (i.e. 1,166) recorded for official comfort station-related travel (i.e. with travel documents designated '*ianjo kankeisha*') for women out of Taiwan to the Chinese mainland between November 1938 and March 1939.[141] Fujinaga acknowledges that not all people travelling under the official designation of *ianjo kankeisha* (i.e. 'comfort station staff') would have been destined for sexual use in the stations (e.g. some would have been proprietors), but he compares the number of Korean women trafficked from Taiwan to southern China between November 1938 and January 1940 with the number of women who were trafficked into Taiwan's sex industry around the same time, and finds these numbers to roughly coincide. He therefore suggests there is some empirical basis to the possibility that trafficking took place from Korea into the Taiwanese sex industry primarily for the purpose of re-trafficking women into comfort stations on the Chinese mainland.[142]

## Conclusion

The discussion of this chapter has attempted to establish a framework for understanding the disproportionate targeting of Korean women for trafficking into comfort stations during the China and Pacific wars. The reason for the chapter's focus on Korean women, as opposed to the Japanese victims who are discussed in most of the rest of the book, was to introduce a cluster of literature that already contains the perspective of the book that the military system relied fundamentally on civilian prostitution in its development. This literature unequivocally establishes the fact that civilian colonial sex industries were crucial 'infrastructural bases' to the development of the wartime prostitution system.

Using existing research on the pre-war and wartime trafficking of Korean women, this chapter established a framework for understanding the place of colonial sex industry development in the creation of the military system. It suggested colonial civilian prostitution is historically linked to the military sexual slavery system in three ways: as a logistical blueprint for trafficking, as a source of victims, and as a wellspring of pimps and traffickers to organize the development of comfort stations on behalf of the military. As is emphasized throughout the book, the civilian sexual enslavement of women prior to their re-trafficking into comfort stations is understood to amplify the historical record of human rights violation by the Japanese military and bureaucracy, not lessen it. In other words, if the overrepresentation of Korean women among comfort station survivors is in part due to their mass organization in civilian prostitution before and during the war, as this chapter has suggested, this should strengthen the contemporary case for justice for survivors because it reveals an institutional basis to the history of military sexual slavery going back further than the eight years of war. It also makes clear the nature of the causal link between Japanese imperialism and the creation of the comfort station system, which this chapter suggests turns on colonial civilian sex industry development.

Even among those historians cited here who do acknowledge military reliance on civilian prostitution in the creation of the comfort station system, though, there are few who highlight any ongoing reliance on it throughout the years of war. Rather, as the next chapter observes, they suggest the military resorted to the trafficking of non-prostituted women as the pool of prostituted women came to be exhausted, as battleground areas moved to farther flung places, as transport logistics broke down and impeded trafficking efforts, and as the profit prospects of civilian pimps waned with worsening wartime conditions. The next chapter discusses the example of Okinawa in the final year of the Pacific War in counterpoint to this dominant view. Prostituted women on Okinawa were mobilized in large numbers for trafficking into comfort stations, both from the local sex industry as well as from Korea during this time, and their almost complete absence in the literature is observed in further and final evidence of the central contention of this book that scapegoating pervades and distorts historical accounts of the comfort station system.

# Okinawan Prostituted Women and Comfort Stations at War's End

The Battle of Okinawa ... is often referred to as one of the bloodiest battles fought in the Pacific War ... The battle was fought between 548,000 US troops ... and more than 110,000 Japanese troops ... but it also involved in various ways more than 400,000 local civilians pressed into service. Indiscriminate and relentless bombing and shelling from sea, air and land ... lasted three months, involved firing as many as fifty shells on average for each Okinawan resident, and killed civilians, babies, women, children and the elderly alike. The Battle of Okinawa killed over 210,000, including over 120,000 Okinawans out of the population of 460,000. Noncombatant Okinawan casualties ... far exceeded those of Okinawan members of Japanese defense forces ... The Battle of Okinawa also killed 65,908 soldiers from other prefectures of Japan and 12,520 Americans, along with smaller numbers of other nationalities. Some thousands of Koreans ... including men who had been mobilized to work for the Japanese military and women who were made into military sex slaves, were also killed.[1]

Military sex slaves of Okinawan and Japanese nationality were killed in the Battle of Okinawa but, as in the passage above, their deaths go usually unremarked upon in histories of the Pacific War. The reason for this, Koga Noriko explains, is that 'Okinawan and mainland Japanese "comfort women" are known to have histories of legalized prostitution, and so are overlooked in research on the Battle of Okinawa'. Bias distorts the literature, Koga suggests, because prostituted women on Okinawa are seen as having been 'legitimate' victims of comfort stations, though in reality they were victims of military sexual violence in equal measure to other women.[2] Indeed, even Ueno Chizuko, perhaps Japan's most well-known feminist, omits to mention the victimization of local prostituted women in the Battle of Okinawa in her remark that, 'because of the likelihood of rape by soldiers of the Imperial Army, the chastity of the women of Okinawa was "defended" at the sacrifice of Korean women.'[3] But Okinawan and mainland

Japanese women were 'sacrificed' in this way, too, and this chapter newly highlights their historical experience.

A second reason for their exclusion, the chapter suggests, is the perception of historians that the Japanese military sourced women from occupied and colonized female populations for trafficking into comfort stations at an escalating rate as the war years progressed. These local women and girls are seen as the true sex slaves: they were abducted, tricked, and threatened at gunpoint to enter the military prostitution system. Historians claim Japan's military became less and less able to source women from the sex industry as conditions of war worsened. Former police agency chief Yoshida Hidehiro writes bluntly, for example, that 'the military resorted to recruiting women among local populations overseas when they ran out of Japanese women'.[4] In other words, *non-prostituted* women and girls became victims of wartime sexual slavery as the military exhausted sex industry sources of prostituted women, or as various contingencies of war impeded access to them. This chapter reviews these claims and critiques them as a form of scapegoating. Their tacit suggestion, I argue, is that the tragedy of non-prostituted women and girls trafficked into comfort stations derives ultimately from historically inadequate numbers of prostituted women. Put differently, the victimization of non-prostituted women in comfort stations correlates positively with insufficient historical victimization of prostituted women. I condemn this logic as manifesting a form of scapegoating on the basis of its flawed premise that the two female populations existed in historical contrast, rather than in parallel.

The alternative perspective of the chapter is that the military sexual enslavement of non-prostituted women and girls was achieved precisely on the basis of the prior trafficking of prostituted women. These original victims were used to create the system and to develop it to the point where the military was able to subsequently enslave tens of thousands of non-prostituted women and girls. This did not mean, moreover, that prostituted women and girls were thereafter spared victimization. In its second half, the chapter briefly describes the history of prostituted women on Okinawa trafficked into comfort stations in the final year of the war. At least 136 stations operated on Okinawa and surrounding islands between 1944 and 1945, and among their victims were at least 500 Okinawan women trafficked from the local sex industry, plus an uncalculated number of Japanese prostituted women trafficked mostly from Kyushu. Both non-prostituted Korean women and girls, as well as those who had been in comfort stations on Taiwan, were also victimized in large numbers.[5] The Okinawan example offers an important illustration of the fact that prostituted women were *continuing* victims of Japanese military slavery throughout the China and Pacific wars. The example challenges a view popular in the literature that prostituted women were victimized in comfort stations only in the early years, such as that articulated by novelist and poet Itou Keiichi who writes that, in these early years,

> battlefield comfort women were so-called professionals who had voluntarily put their hands up after being approached by pimps with promises of high earnings. They were old hands at the trade, and it didn't matter to them how many men lined up. But, as the war went on and the deployment of soldiers continued, the military couldn't get enough volunteers or professional women with experience.[6]

This chapter describes the example of Okinawa in the final year of the war to highlight the Japanese military's continuing reliance on the civilian sex industry to organize its wartime prostitution scheme. As described below, without the resource of prostituted women already indentured in Okinawa's legalized civilian sex industry, the military would have had difficulty establishing so many stations on the island, and operating such a widespread system of sexual slavery in the desperate final year of the Pacific War.

## Condemning military sexual slavery for its lack of prostituted victims

Some progressive advocates of comfort station survivors appear to regret the fact the Japanese military was unable to source enough prostituted women to traffic into its wartime system. However tacitly made, their argument is clear: real sex slaves emerged only at the point the military was no longer able to source prostituted women. Jennifer Davies, for example, writes uncritically that, '[w]hen the supply of established prostitutes ran out, local civilians from a number of countries had to be recruited by force'.[7] Davies's suggestion, it seems, is that force did not underlie the trafficking of prostituted women into military stations. Yoshida Hidehiro suggests in equally uncritical terms that, because Japanese prostituted women were able to repay debts quickly and return home with money earned in the stations, there were not enough women left to be prostituted (*hitodebusoku*) in the wartime system, so the military had no choice but to recruit local women.[8] In other words, the military turned to the trafficking of non-prostituted women as the years of war progressed and the number of women pooled in the civilian sex industry dwindled, as logistically securing women from the industry proved difficult, or as Japanese prostituted women left stations and returned home thanks to the limited term of their contracts and all the money they earned.

Putting aside the dubious factual bases of these claims, the theme that underlies even critical comment in regards to the recruitment of non-prostituted women for comfort station internment is not that comfort stations enacted the sexual enslavement of women. Rather, criticism centres on the Japanese military's avarice: it was greedy in its demand for women, and so its means of procurement ended up inordinately and inappropriately targeting non-prostituted female populations. Historians imply that the true crime of the military system was not the system itself but the population it eventually targeted for internment. Even the trafficking of non-prostituted local women is described in relatively uncritical terms, as if it were an unfortunate but inevitable outcome of wartime resource shortages in the market of female sexual access. Even Yoshimi Yoshiaki, for example, presents uncritically archival evidence showing that the army made official plans to traffic local women into stations:

> In Southeast Asia and the Pacific region, transport was difficult, so the proportion of local women among comfort women was much higher. At a January 7, 1943 meeting of section chiefs, Chief of the Awards Section Kuramoto noted in regard to comfort stations built on orders from the Ministry of War that 'large numbers of comfort facilities have been built, but [women] imported from Japan are not well liked. Locals trained on site are more popular'.[9]

The historical record of military officers taking enthusiastic delight in raping local women into submission (i.e. 'training' them onsite) as a means of securing comfort station victims was perhaps behind the purported 'popularity' of local women over prostituted victims trafficked from Japan. This fact is abundantly established in the historiography: Chinese survivor Yin Yulin, for example, describes being stripped of her clothes and having an officer 'inspect' her body with a wax-dripping candle (which burnt her) as soon as she was brought to a comfort station. He then proceeded to rape her: 'He rose from the bed and returned repeatedly, torturing me almost the entire night. I was shaking in the dark the whole time and ever since then I have suffered from incurable trembling'.[10] This method of procurement was also cost-effective; as the years of war went on and the military faced budgetary constraints it was cheaper for unit commanders to source women from the local sex industry, or through brokers procuring local women via non-sex industry channels, than to negotiate with Japanese pimps to buy women out of their businesses on Japan, Korea or Taiwan. Some commentators lament the military having succumbed to such worldly considerations: novelist Sakakiyama Jun, who served in Burma in 1942, records in his 1963 memoir his concern that Japanese military police who were procuring women from a local village for comfort station internment were doing the station proprietors a disservice. These proprietors had arranged for the trafficking of Korean women into Burma to set up their station, but the actions of the military police were undermining their business plans, and meant they were not likely to realize anticipated profits. Sakakiyama expresses the view that the military had a responsibility to these pimps to make sure they made money out of their ventures (presumably because the military had contracted them in the first place).[11]

While Sakakiyama's concern for the financial position of pimps probably characterizes his viewpoint as a reactionary one, his objection to the inappropriate targeting of women for comfort station internment is shared in arguments put forward by some progressive historians, even if on the basis of different concerns. These historians condemn the military as at fault only to the extent it chose the wrong victims. Objections to the military trafficking local women into stations ultimately hinge on considerations of their prior prostituted status, rather than the fact of their military sexual exploitation. The near-total absence of Okinawan women in historical discussion of the wartime comfort station scheme reflects this perception of military prostitution as worthy of condemnation only to the extent it targeted non-prostituted victims. Hardships endured by Korean women in military prostitution on Okinawa are rightly discussed in the literature, but Korean women are widely believed, rightly or wrongly, to have been sourced from non-prostituted female populations. Tamashiro Fukuko even chastizes Okinawans for failing to assume enough historical responsibility for the sexual exploitation of Korean women on their soil without once mentioning the historical fact of the military sexual enslavement of local Okinawan women.[12]

## Prostituted victims till the very end

The suggestion that women from the sex industry were replaced by non-prostituted women sourced locally as the war years progressed overlooks the history of comfort stations on Okinawa in the final year of the Pacific War. Many of these victims were prostituted. There was already a significant civilian sex industry operating on Okinawa by 1944, and Shinozaki Yasuko describes the development of this industry at the turn of the century. Prostitution districts developed in Naha even before the 1879 Japanese annexation of Okinawa when the island began to attract sea-based traders as well as Japanese bureaucrats who were sent out to the territory on rotation for three-year stints. After the annexation, these districts grew as Japanese men poured into the island as politicians, bureaucrats, businessmen, fishermen, farmers and military personnel stationed at a base on the island. Shinozaki suggests these men generated demand for the prostitution of local Okinawan women, and this demand resulted in the development of Naha's major sex industry districts around the turn of the century.[13] By the time of the war, one of these districts, Tsuji, hosted 300 venues interning 3,000 women, most of whom had been sold into the industry as children.[14] Even on Miyakojima, which is located nearly 300 kilometres from Naha, there was a substantial sex industry operating by the time of the war, according to Mizutani Akiko. Already by the turn of the century, there was a legalized prostitution district on the island, mainly comprising geisha venues, but by 1913 this had grown to an additional nineteen restaurant-style venues housing nearly eighty women. This number doubled by the late 1920s, and by 1940 there were twenty restaurant-style venues, four *kafes*, and twenty geisha venues housing at least fifty-three women, and this excluded women who were being prostituted on the island without official registration.[15] Most of the women came from outside the prefecture, and their pimps were only temporary residents of the island. Even earlier than the colonial sex industries of Korea and Taiwan described in the previous chapter, therefore, Ryukyu women were trafficked into civilian prostitution in response to demand emanating in large part from Japanese men and were thereafter trafficked into comfort stations after these men returned in large numbers to Okinawa and surrounding islands in the final year of the war.

A description of the wartime operation of comfort stations on Okinawa is recalled in an extraordinary interview with the daughter of a former Miyakojima geisha restaurant owner, a woman called Kugai Yoshiko, conducted by a team of researchers in 2008. She relayed to the research team her teenage thoughts about a comfort station operating near to her home. Her home was attached to a geisha restaurant that was run by her father on the island. Kugai in her interview stressed the fact she had been made 'very sensitive' to poverty and discrimination because of having grown up around her father's geisha business (which she was not part of). She saw the poverty of the girls brought into the business, and the way they were treated.[16] As a result, she recalled in the interview,

> [w]hen I saw it (the comfort station) I got a shock. With so many soldiers
> lining up out front, I wondered what it was, they were there in droves ... [starts
> crying]. On Sundays and other days off soldiers with a leave-of-absence mark
> on their sleeves would descend on the station in large numbers and form long
> lines. I couldn't stand it. Seeing those men, it was beyond disgusting. I felt like

crying out for someone to help me. I got a shock when I realised the women had been brought there by someone who was controlling them through having taken advantage of the fact they had no education, no means of resisting and little ability to insist on their rights … I sympathised with them because I was a woman as well. My father owned a large geisha restaurant on Miyakojima called Azumatei. The difference between us and poor people on the island was huge, and I grew up with awareness of this fact. And also because my family was in the business, I was really aware of discrimination towards women like that [in the comfort station] … because of my father's business, I had some vague awareness of what it was they did. I hate it. Seeing all those men lining up in front of the station. Even now it makes me feel sick, and I've got a phobia about men. I was seventeen at the time. And the girls in the station were around the same age as me, I just couldn't comprehend why they had to be there, such vulnerable girls.[17]

They were there because Japanese military men arriving on Okinawa in 1944 harboured high expectations of sexual access to women in comfort stations. As already mentioned, one soldier stepping off a warship that had just sailed from Manchuria is recorded as exclaiming with apparent glee, 'so we get to make love to Okinawan women this time?'[18] Hon Yun Shin notes that the majority of these men had come from battlefields in China where, as described, comfort stations operated extensively.[19] It is likely they had been prostituting women as part of their military service for many years by the time of arrival on the island. Indeed, the decision of the military command in quickly organizing a network of comfort stations on Okinawa and its surrounding islands soon after April 1944 attests to the strength of the sexual entitlement that probably circulated among troops by this final year of the war. A lieutenant in Japan's 32nd regiment called a meeting with pimps from Naha's Tsuji prostitution district to appeal for their cooperation in organizing the trafficking of women out of the district into comfort stations. This prompted a rush of women to approach the Naha police station to formally submit applications for exit from the sex industry, as was legally possible for women who had fully paid off their 'debts' to pimps by this time in Japanese law. Unwillingness to enter the military prostitution system was behind this attempted mass exodus, but the military in response introduced new rules to restrict exit from the civilian sex industry. Only women who could prove marriage, illness or other conditions that made exit from the sex industry an absolute 'necessity' were granted permission to leave, and this rule prompted some women to forge marriage and medical certificates before their pimps had an opportunity to traffic them into military brothels.[20]

Crucial to the ability of women to leave the industry, however, was their capacity to repay existing debts to pimps (however dubious the basis of these debts), and only women who could do this qualified for legal exit. This was beyond the capacity of most prostituted women, and so some alternatively organized their own trafficking into geisha restaurants or *ryokan* traditional inns in regional areas away from the capital Naha. Even those women who were left in the Tsuji prostitution district after the military had undertaken a first-round of recruitment for trafficking into stations ended up entering military brothels after 10 October 1944, when the district was burnt to the ground in US area bombings. The Japanese military was thereafter able to set up new comfort stations as a result of the existence of this pool of women newly left destitute after the destruction of civilian prostitution venues.[21] As mentioned, it is estimated that more than 500 women were trafficked out of legalized prostitution on Okinawa into comfort stations on islands in the Ryukyu chain between 1944 and 1945.[22]

After the October bombings, private houses on Okinawa were newly commandeered by the military for the development of comfort stations. This usually involved hanging sheets from ceilings to separate cot beds on which women were lined up for prostitution. One of the largest houses in the village of Kuwae was quickly taken over by the military after the bombing, and its owner forced to move into a horse stable on the property. This resident recalls seven to eight women from Tsuji then being brought into the house by an Okinawan pimp, but the women were sequestered away and had no contact with anyone in the village, he recollects. A sign saying 'comfort station' was hung at the entrance of the commandeered house, with a 'no entry' warning to non-military personnel. He was also barred from entry.[23]

This practice of the military commandeering houses and local buildings (e.g. local government buildings or spinning factories) for the development of comfort stations means that there exists unusually detailed evidence of the military system's organization and operation via oral histories collected from Okinawans after the war. Particularly on islands like Miyakojima, the stations operated in close quarters to local communities and residents. In fact, the Japanese military attracted complaints from Okinawan residents about the operation of comfort stations in local areas for their negative public amenity effects. Locals complained about discarded condoms, and the possibility of children being exposed to the sight of men lining up outside military brothels.[24] Oral evidence from elderly residents of a Ginowan village records that 1,200 stationed infantrymen were given access to three homes and one storehouse in the village commandeered for conversion into comfort stations. On Saturdays and Sundays, thirty or more women were brought to these three venues for prostitution. The women were mostly but not all Korean. Even conservatively calculating an average of one prostitution transaction per month for each of these men stationed in Ginowan, this would mean the women (i.e. pegging their number at thirty) would be used by five men per day for eight days a month. It is likely, moreover, that they were being used by other men in other locations on the days they were not delivered to Ginowan.[25]

The pre-war Okinawan sex industry had been geographically contained to the capital and its nearby port area, but the onset of war meant it proliferated in militarized form to residential areas, and to further-flung islands in the archipelago. Existing prostitution venues on Okinawa were commandeered for conversion into comfort stations, and this included geisha restaurants. Koga writes that the military ordered geisha restaurant operators near Okinawa's main Untenkou port to convert their operations into comfort stations, and as a result the five to six women in each of these venues who had been trafficked into prostitution as children from the poor southern and central areas of Okinawa thereafter became comfort women.[26] This occurred also in Okinawa's northern areas. Koga writes that, from August 1943, northern area command officials would gather once a month at the geisha district for '*shucchou ian*' (out-of-town getaway trip) in the town of Nago. The former geisha restaurants had all been converted in military stations for officers. 'From five in the evening till eight the next morning the men would eat, drink and have their male needs catered to'.[27] Another venue in the area was designated for troops, and this venue was operated twice a week for their patronage.[28] Koga describes a lieutenant stationed in northern Okinawa in February 1945 procuring women for the establishment of a comfort station in the area. He apparently paid inducements to local geisha restaurant and *ryokan* (traditional inn) proprietors for the transfer of their women.[29] The women were then prostituted six days a week from noon onwards by men stationed in the area. Some were made into 'field wives' (*genchi tsuma*) for military officers, especially those who had originally come from geisha venues on the Japanese mainland with skills in music and dance.[30]

In another example, in a village called Tsukayama, the local government office was taken over for use as a comfort station, and more than ten women from the Tsuji brothel district were interned there. On weekends, soldiers lined up in front of the station for two blocks, and the women inside could be heard crying out in distress '*kurushii*' '*kurushii*'. An Okinawan girl who had been sold into the island's prostitution district at age 14 after one of her family members fell ill, called 'Miyahira Tsuru', was trafficked into this comfort station in November 1944. The station was managed by a former comfort woman who had been prostituted in the Southwest Pacific. Miyahira came to be infected with sexually transmitted disease in the station and was thereafter transferred to a hospital in Shuri. After the US landing on Okinawa, she was assigned to nursing, cooking, cleaning, and other duties with a Japanese military unit hiding out in one of the island's many caves.[31]

Just like Korean women holed up in stations on the island, once conditions of battle became too intense to operate military prostitution venues in the open, prostituted Okinawan women were transported to caves where Japanese troops hid out in the final months of the war, including those who had been prostituted by officers in 'geisha restaurant'-type stations. These women were forced to administer to the sick and wounded, carry water, cook for troops, as well as be sexually used. Conditions in the caves were dire, and women were often killed by US bombing or gassing when carrying out errands to and from the caves. Comfort women were assigned the most dangerous and taxing tasks. They were allocated little food, and very few are thought to have survived the experience. They died of starvation, injury in US raids, or as a result of forced 'suicide' by Japanese military men. Local Okinawans recall feeling 'very sorry' for the women in that situation. Historians have found evidence of official directives from the Japanese military instructing units to 'abandon' the women once they were no longer useful to the unit.[32]

While oral histories contain evidence of local Okinawans feeling sorry for military prostituted women on the islands and even offering them assistance, Koga notes that the 'mindset' of the Japanese military in regards to the utility of prostituted women for the 'protection' of other women from sexual assault spread among locals. As a result, in May 1945, as reports of US military men raping local Okinawan women rose, Koechi village responded to the suggestion of a local pimp to open a brothel that would be marketed specifically to US troops and would house Okinawan prostituted women. This was before the end of the Pacific War, and before the well-known Recreation and Amusement Association network of brothels for US troops were established on the Japanese mainland in 1946. The biggest house in Koechi was commandeered for the purpose, and US troops thereafter lined up in long rows outside the venue. The women used in the venue were prostituted by ten or more men each day, and reportedly described the experience as 'harrowing'. The comfort station continued to operate for one month before local residents were taken into US detention after the cessation of hostilities.[33] Even in the US detention camps, furthermore, there is record of one Japanese woman, 'Sachiko', being prostituted by US troops in exchange for food and other necessities, which she would share with the other former comfort women interned in the camp.[34]

## Japanese prostituted women on Okinawa

Japanese prostituted women from prefectures outside of Okinawa were also trafficked into comfort stations on the island, according to Koga, from 'Kyushu, and especially Nagasaki, Fukuoka and other areas in northern Kyushu'.[35] A station for officers set up in Tomigusuku interned more than ten women trafficked from a geisha venue in Kyushu who were flown to Okinawa by plane. Military officers took full advantage of comfort stations on Okinawa even in the final year of the war; one local Shuri district police officer recalls cautioning Japanese officers leaving a comfort station in the early hours of each morning around 1 or 2 am, because they were drunk and noisy. He got into an argument with an officer over the warning, even though the operating hours of the station officially ended at 11 pm.[36] While pimps from the Tsuji prostitution district appear to have been mostly Okinawan collaborators with the Japanese military in the development of comfort stations,[37] there is evidence of involvement also by Japanese mainland pimps. A Tokyo pimp in his thirties named 'Suzuki' set up a station on Aka Island in November 1944, for example, using seven Korean women and taking over two houses in the area for the purpose.[38]

## Conclusion

This chapter has offered a brief snapshot of comfort stations operating on Okinawa in the final year of the war and shown evidence of their operation relying on the trafficking of women out of the local civilian sex industry. The Japanese military negotiated directly with pimps on Okinawa for this traffic to take place soon after troops arrived on the island in 1944. While Korean women and girls were also significant victims of military prostitution on Okinawa, and have received some historical attention for this enslavement,[39] prostituted Okinawan and Japanese women trafficked into comfort stations on Okinawa in the final year of the war are almost totally overlooked in the historiography. This is because of their prostituted and therefore 'deserving' status, according to Koga Noriko, but this chapter has additionally observed that historians believe prostituted women were trafficked into comfort stations only in the early years of the system's operation. The historical example of Okinawa, however, shows that the Japanese military continued to rely on civilian prostitution systems for the development of stations and the trafficking of women into them. In the case of Okinawa, Japanese men contributed to the development of the civilian industry before the war through their political and bureaucratic activity on the island in a similar way they exported demand for prostitution to the colonies of Korea and Taiwan. Comfort station development on Okinawa might be understood in parallel to the history of military sexual enslavement of Korean and Taiwanese women described in the previous chapter in that its origins similarly reside in colonial sex industry development. Just like Korea and Taiwan, women and girls on Okinawa were made vulnerable to the prostitution demands of Japanese men first through civilian sex industry development in the pre-war period, and then in the subsequent war years during which time the military was able to capitalize on the existence of a sex industry operating on the island to enslave local women in comfort stations.

# Conclusion: Sexual Slavery and the Crucible of Contemporary Japan

Japan today is a frightening place. We've got these ex-military men who have the gall to stand for parliament handing out their business cards at polling booths, just full of themselves and riding high in their civilian lives (Japanese 'Ms Yamamoto' speaking in 1974 after recounting a wartime experience of Japanese military men attempting to blackmail her to enter a comfort station).[1]

We know of Lieutenant Nakasone's role in setting up a comfort station thanks to his 1978 memoir, 'Commander of 3,000 Men at Age 23'. At that time, such accounts were relatively commonplace and uncontroversial – and no obstacle to a political career. From 1982 to 1987, Mr. Nakasone was the prime minister of Japan.[2]

... the world must re-examine the social conditions of this case [of the comfort station system], examine how ignoring such tragedies has allowed Japan to achieve its position today, and take positive steps to protect the world from similar things ever happening again.[3]

The failure to settle these claims [in relation to the comfort women] more than half a century after the cessation of hostilities is a testament [*sic*] to the degree to which the lives of women continue to be undervalued. Sadly, this failure to address crimes of a sexual nature committed on a massive scale during the Second World War has added to the level of impunity with which similar crimes are committed today (former United Nations Special Rapporteur, Gay J. McDougall, writing in 1998).[4]

... the prostitution and rape-tolerant culture of Japan today is stronger than even before the war. In the more than half-century since the end of the war, Japan has fortunately not directly participated in another battle but, looking at the state of today's culture, if the country were to again mobilise for war, it surely wouldn't be just us who would fear a resulting eruption of violence among young Japanese men.[5]

Statistics describing rates of prostitution buying among men in different parts of the contemporary world are an easy reference point for understanding the state of Japanese male society before the war that, this book argues, drove the creation and development of the military prostitution system of the China and Pacific wars. In first making this comparison with present-day Japanese society, this concluding chapter seeks to imagine the causes of military sexual slavery as they might inhere in peacetime society, which is likely to be the context most familiar, relevant, and accessible to readers. It is the context likely to be the most immediately and productively available, I believe, for addressing latently circulating drivers of military sexual slavery, including possibly in Japan today. The analysis of the chapter is offered in counterpoint to the reigning orthodoxy of even the feminist literature that military prostitution develops heuristically as a product of war and as a function of harsh conditions endured by men in battle. Different from this understanding, the chapter draws on the history of the comfort station system to describe its civilian heart as a step towards tackling its peacetime antecedents. At this heart, the chapter reiterates, is military prostitution facilitated by, firstly, the scapegoating of civilian prostituted women, and, secondly, an urge prevailing among elite men in peacetime patriarchal society to democratize and consolidate the male prostitution right through activities like war and militarism.

## The Taisho era rebooted?

While easily comparable statistics on prostitution buying are not available for the Taisho era, we might start with the reported figure that 61,000 prostitution transactions were carried out in Japan per day in 1928, as mentioned in Chapter Two. If we conservatively estimate that one-tenth of these transactions were undertaken by unique individuals daily, then around 6 per cent of the Taisho-era Japanese male population of roughly 31.5 million men might have been prostitution buyers. Perhaps ominously, this figure is small compared to contemporary statistics. A survey published in the year 2000 on prostitution buying rates among Japanese men found 12 per cent of respondents had purchased a woman in the past year.[6] This percentage is at the very high end of similar surveys taken of male populations in other industrialized countries, only matched by Spain. In comparison, men in Australia and the Netherlands, which are countries known for their large sex industries and prostitution-tolerant cultures, prostitute women at rates of roughly 2 and 3 per cent, respectively, over a twelve-month period.[7] Japanese men currently stand out in the rich world as rampant prostitution buyers, and in Asia are trumped only by men in the sex industry-saturated country of Thailand. A survey by the pro-feminist Study Group on Men and Prostitution in Japan in 1998 found 46 per cent of respondents had purchased a woman for prostitution at some point in their lives.[8] Eight years later, a survey by the National Women's Education Center of Japan found more than 40 per cent of respondents had bought a woman at some point.[9]

High rates of prostitution buying are recorded among limited populations of Japanese men travelling abroad as tourists to countries like South Korea and Thailand in the post-war period,[10] even higher than the above-mentioned rate for contemporary Japanese society. But to find prostitution buying rates for a broad-based population of Japanese men that are anywhere close to those of contemporary figures, we have to go back to comfort station visitation rates during the China War. To take one example, during the first ten days of February 1938, there were 25,000 Japanese troops stationed in Nanjing. There were two comfort stations in the area designated for troops, one hosting 141 women and the other 109 women. In the first ten days of February, 5,734 men patronized the latter station. This figure rose to 8,929 troops for the 11–20 February period.[11] While exact figures are not available for the former comfort station hosting 141 women, even if we conservatively estimate this station generated only an additional 50 per cent of unique visitors over the period to add to those of the latter station, the proportion of Japanese troops buying women for prostitution in Nanjing in 1938 equalled around 35 per cent. This figure is hauntingly similar to prostitution buying rates for contemporary Japanese society. Of course, the intensity of prostitution buying among men during the war was much higher, given the military's supply of condoms for one prostitution transaction per month per man,[12] and the proportion of men having experience of prostituting women is likely to have risen exponentially over the years of war. Also, the time periods forming the basis of the comparison are vastly different – twenty days in the Nanjing example and 'lifetime experience' in the case of the National Women's Education Center of Japan survey. Nonetheless, that even a hint of similarity exists between the prostitution behaviour of Japanese men in wartime and that of contemporary peacetime might pull us up short and lead us to question any particularizing of the sexual behaviour of Japanese men during the China and Pacific wars as uniquely arising out of militarism and the harsh conditions of battle.

The age demographics behind contemporary prostitution buying rates among Japanese men are not likely to allay fears like those expressed at the top of the chapter about a likely outbreak of sexual violence if fascistic social conditions were to again arise in Japan. The major finding of a quantitative study published in 2008 was that Japanese '[m]en in their 50s, who spent their adolescence before the enforcement of anti-prostitution laws, had high prostitution acceptability. Those in their 20s and 30s ... also showed high rates'.[13] The authors attribute this observed similarity between the two generations of men to the phenomenon of child prostitution (*enjo kousai*) that proliferated in Japanese society during the adolescent years of the latter group, and the legally unconstrained sex industry of the early years of the men aged in their fifties. In other words, the researchers suggest that similarity between the two generations of men in terms of practices and attitudes towards prostitution can be explained by similar states of sex industry growth prevailing during their respective teenage years. In the case of the former group, a police transcript from the late 1990s provides a jarring illustration of the nature of the behaviour that was normalized during these years, and which continues to cast a long shadow on Japanese society even today.[14] The transcript records the experience of a 16-year-old girl who was bought by a man after school and taken to a hotel at around 4.30 pm in the afternoon. The man penetrated her vaginally and then ejaculated into her mouth. The girl told police that, while she gave the man her pager number afterwards, she never responded to any of his numerous subsequent calls because, 'no matter how much I wanted his 20,000 yen, I found him so unspeakably revolting that I never wanted to have sex with him ever again (*hyougen no shiyou ga nai gurai kimochi no warui hito...*)'.[15]

We might wonder about boys going through adolescence in twenty-first-century Japanese society now that barely any basis of comparison remains between the sex industry of today and that of even the 1990s. Different from twenty years ago, today in Japan the internet makes buying an underage girl for prostitution as simple as responding to a call for a 'spare room for the night' on social media,[16] and accessing locally produced pornography made of Japanese women and girls that is unimaginable in its violence and degradation is now possible at all times and in all places via hand-held devices. Advances in technology and an almost complete absence of government regulation of the sex industry in either its real-world or cyber forms combine to produce escalating rates of demand for prostitution among Japanese men, which now drives the growth of an industry large even by US standards.[17] The industry currently responds to demand for not only the widespread prostitution and pornification of adult Japanese women, but also girls. Japan's national police agency detected more than one thousand underage girls posted for prostitution on social networking sites in one sting against offenders in 2006.[18] The agency in 2007 then conducted a survey of 206 girls aged between 12 and 17 years who they had detected during online child prostitution investigations, and found 40 per cent of them had been prostituted by ten or more men via the sites.[19]

In this environment, unsurprisingly, there is no declining demand among Japanese men for sexual access to children, especially girls; between the years 1994 and 2004, the number of rapes, attempted rapes and sexual assaults of children aged *under twelve years* increased by 70 per cent.[20] Schools in Japan have become prominent sites of sex-offending activity. Kaneko Yumiko, a middle school welfare officer with 36 years' experience in schools, in 2011 announced at a conference that school administrators and staff were having difficulty combating incursions by sexual predators onto school grounds, and responding to reports of male harassment of female students as they walked to and from school. In 2001, she took a straw poll of female students at her own school and found more than one-third had been harassed while wearing their school uniforms, and this harassment centred specifically on their status as female students – Kaneko recorded regular incidents of 'groping' (i.e. sexual assault) on commuter trains, ejaculate thrown on to the girls' uniforms from behind, and solicitations from men in cars, including attempted abduction. Kaneko further noted that her school attracted ongoing incidents of girls' underwear being stolen from swimming pool change rooms by outsiders, and had problems with unidentified men bringing cameras onto campus for the purpose of 'upskirting' on school fete and festival days.[21]

Perpetrators of these kinds of crimes in Japan are likely to have come of age in an environment that was permissive of pornography consumption among even children. The purchase of pornographic materials by minors has been widely permitted in Japan with only minimal regulation and public action since at least the early 1990s. The selling of manga comic books with incest and other child sexual abuse themes to underage consumers through convenience stores was not prohibited till 2010, and only through prefectural ordinance, and with little enforcement of its provisions to date.[22] This is in spite of twenty years of recognition of the social problems this causes. In 1992, Mugishima Fumio of Teikyo University (and the then-head of Japan's Child Welfare Association) surveyed 2,217 junior and senior high-school students in five prefectures. His study shows the pervasiveness of pornography consumption that had already spread among Japanese male youth by these early years. Of the 14-year-old boys he surveyed, roughly two-thirds had seen a 'pornographic magazine' (e.g. manga), and one-third a pornographic film. Among the 16-year-old boys surveyed, these figures rose to 89 per cent having seen a pornographic magazine, and 74 per cent a film. (These figures are particularly notable for the fact the internet was not yet pervasive in Japan at this time. Similar figures were not recorded in Australia until a decade later, and not until internet usage rates were high in that country.)[23] On the basis of these findings, Mugishima issued the strongly worded warning that

> the large social issue we now face with the explosion in pornographic comic book consumption among youth in Japan in the last three or four years is a problem unprecedented in our history. These books are produced in order to provoke sexual curiosity among youth, and this is occurring in an environment in which youth are concurrently being influenced by sex industry-related phone services and karaoke venues that have sprung up since 1991.[24]

Mugishima was prescient in issuing this warning, but it went unheeded. Early and sustained exposure to the sex industry (both in the form of pornography and prostitution) by large sections of the Japanese male population since the 1990s now produces a society in which reports of serious, coordinated and diverse sex offending by Japanese men and boys has become everyday fare, as Imanishi Hajime wrote in 2007.[25] One example among many is the Fukushima city rapes of 2001, where a 16-year-old boy broke into women's homes and raped, assaulted and tied them up. The boy victimized thirty different women over a one-year period in this way. A total of 130 pornographic films were found in the boy's room at the time of his arrest, and he testified in court that these films of women being raped had inspired him to commit the crimes.[26]

The increasing normalization of sexual violence among men and boys towards ever-expanding populations of women and girls in contemporary Japan is a problem recognized, though, only in the dullest terms by government. Japan's post-war governments have benignly tolerated and even actively supported sex industry development in the country. Chubu University's Seiko Hanochi notes the government's post-war funding of the sex industry as a part of efforts to bolster the tourism sector, for example:

> The sex industry was considered part of the service industry, classified as a service provided to individual customers. It was partially financed under a 1963 law, which awarded 'financing and other support measures to small and middle industries'. This government support, intended for industrial development, funded the modernization of the Japanese sex industry.[27]

Fujino Yutaka at Toyama University is similarly critical of Japan's post-war governments for materially supporting the sex industry. He observes that local governments in Toyama and Okinawa incorporated plans for sex industry development into their regional economic promotion policies of the 1970s, and this paved the way for the proliferation of sex industry businesses in Japan's regional areas.[28] Feminist legal theorist Tsunoda Yukiko also condemns the government for undermining the spirit of the 1958 *Prostitution Prevention Law* by pre-emptively permitting prostitution to take place in hostess venues through enacting an 'entertainment industry' law in 1954.[29] The Osaka no fujin hogo jigyou o mamoru kai (Osaka women's shelter protection association) in its 1985 publication further criticizes Japanese police for not enforcing the 1958 law, as well as Japan's public servants for failing to do anything about a society in which 'women's degraded social status causes them to suffer bad pay and conditions in work and low living standards'.[30] The Association raises these conditions specifically as having given rise to a society favourable to sex industry activity.[31] Feminist lawyer Ida Emiko similarly decries the government's implementation of the law, which, she suggests, while not being perfect in its construction, would have reduced the size of the industry if it had been applied to those 'aiding and abetting' prostitution, as she suggests was intended in the law's drafting.[32]

There are, of course, innumerable differences between the society of the Taisho era and that of Japan in both the post-war period and today in terms of social initiatives against sexual violence that reflect modern human rights ideas, as well as concern for victim welfare. For example, the Gender Equality Bureau within Japan's Cabinet Office over the last few years has issued statements that appear to define prostitution as a form of violence against women.[33] As mentioned, some local governments share this view, and the Gender Equality Centre of the Fukushima Prefectural Government in 2003 assisted a team of researchers from Nagoya University to examine male attitudes towards prostitution in the prefecture with a view to questioning, in their words, the assumption that men have a 'natural' right to 'consume' women in the sex industry.[34] There are also civil society groups, like the Anti-Pornography and Prostitution Research Group (APP), People Against Pornography and Sexual Violence (PAPS), the Violence Against Women in War Research Action Center (VAWW-RAC), the *Seibouryoku o yurusanai onna no kai*, the Anti-Prostitution Association of Japan, and Okinawa Women Act Against Military Violence, that persist in campaigning against the sex industry, even if in an environment of ridicule and abuse from both the right and left sides of Japanese civil society.

The combined work of these local groups might be better recognized within Japan and abroad as comprising a critical peacetime bulwark against the re-emergence of, in a possible future time of war, the sexual violence of Japanese men that characterized the China and Pacific wars. The groups work within the crucible of contemporary Japan, which fosters tolerance and even celebration of male sexual victimization of women and girls. As this book argues, peacetime tolerance of prostitution is a notable precursor to the development of military sexual slavery. This does not mean, though, that I draw any straight historical line between the prostitution of the wartime military system and the sex industry of contemporary Japan. Indeed, the discussion of the book is silent on any such causal connection between the past and the present, and, in fact, I see no need for any such historical pattern to be evidenced over the course of modern Japanese history.

Instead, this book has encouraged recognition of the prostitution of contemporary peacetime society as 'civilian sexual slavery' to advance the view that conditions of female sexual servitude prevailing in non-wartime societies have some connection to the systems of military sexual slavery that develop in war. Confronting the casual prostitution habits of men in civilian society, I believe, is crucial to understanding and combating the sexual violence that seems to 'inevitably' arise in extraordinary times of social emergency or war. The argument I make in this regard is not original: Morita already made it more than fifteen years ago:

> When the comfort women system is divorced from peacetime as a peculiar problem of war, or is understood exclusively as a product of the wayward activities of the Japanese military before the war, a true understanding of the system cannot be reached, and solutions found. The system is fundamentally linked to violence and abuse of women both before and after the war.[35]

## Scapegoated victims of military sexual slavery

Distinctions emphatically drawn between the phenomenon of civilian prostitution in the Taisho era history and the sexual slavery of the Showa military years have given rise to an injustice against, particularly, Japanese victims of the comfort station system, given their mostly prostituted status before entering military stations. These victims, through their association with Taisho-era prostitution, are imagined to have entered comfort stations easily and willingly, and therefore not suffered the real harms of sexual slavery. This observation is not restricted to Japanese victims; the same injustice is replicated for women of other nationalities who were prostituted in civilian systems before being trafficked into comfort stations, as discussed in Chapter

Five for women in Korea and Taiwan's colonial sex industries. Chapter One described the deprecating and demeaning discourse that continues to surround prostituted victims, and the role of this discourse in legitimizing the struggle for 'justice for comfort women' as a respectable campaign against militarism, racism, and colonialism, rather than a campaign against male sexual entitlement. The legitimizing potency of the former framing, as Sheila Jeffreys notes, is that 'militaries can be held accountable [for military prostitution]', but 'pinning down the culprits [for civilian prostitution] may require attacking the rights of men in general to prostitute women'.[36]

Reticence on the part of campaigners to 'attack the rights of men in general to prostitute women', both in the past and present, has led to the scapegoating of prostituted victims of the comfort station system, I suggested in Chapter One, and this scapegoating is perpetrated by both right-wing defenders of the Japanese military as well as left-wing defenders of civilian prostitution as 'sex work'. Again, this point is expertly made by Morita:

> Conservatives legitimise sexual abuse during wartime in the name of the state (as needed for the morale of troops), and liberals legitimise it in peacetime in the name of the state in terms of individual free choice (and so prostitution should be legalised). The relationship between political conservatism and political liberalism is less one of opposition and more one of jurisdiction ... Conservatives suggest that calling women 'sex slaves' in the comfort women system denies their subjectivity and is demeaning of them. Sexual liberals in Japan today defend civilian systems of prostitution in much the same terms that conservatives defend the wartime prostitution system: That it protects women from rape, that women gain esteem through serving men, that women in prostitution are in a position of control over men through their sexuality ... The arguments of sexual liberals leave no basis for fundamentally challenging the basis of the comfort women system. They only leave room for challenging the way the system operated ...[37]

The 'scapegoat' theory described in the book and used centrally to understand the place of Japanese and other prostituted women in the contemporary 'justice for comfort women' movement is discussed in terms originally articulated by Andrea Dworkin and Margaret Baldwin. Even though Japanese prostituted women were the original victims of military sexual slavery, and their experiences clearly illustrate foundational aspects of the nature and origins of the comfort station system, their history is sidelined, and their existence denied as not truly representing the sexual slavery of the system. Paradoxically, as described in Chapter Four and elaborated upon in Chapter Six, it is imagined that prostituted women were trafficked into stations only in the early years of the system's operation, and only as a stop-gap measure before more suitable, less diseased, younger and more racially marginalized women and girls could be sourced. Their early internment in comfort stations is seen as incidental to the development of the system, and not fundamentally indicative of its core reliance on the operation of civilian prostitution and the peacetime sex industry. The Trojan horse of the Taisho-era sex industry, which paved the way for the military system to develop and encompass an ever-expanding population of women, whether these women were trafficked, blackmailed, coerced or abducted, is lost sight of when the system's original prostituted victims are scapegoated. The existence of this pool of women, who were already at the mercy of pimps and traffickers with whom the military could collaborate in order to organize its wartime system, was essential to its development, which was initially organized via the trafficking of women out of Japan, or the trafficking of prostituted Japanese women already on the mainland as 'karayuki'. The pre-existing sex industry-organization of these women and the infrastructure and logistical resources of civilian sexual slavery allowed for the military system's creation and development. It is surely not going too far to say that, without this existing sex industry base, the sexual slavery harms subsequently visited upon tens of thousands of non-prostituted women during the war might not have been historically possible.

The internment of Japanese women in comfort stations is seen as incidental to their individual life histories: their military prostitution is often not recognized as inflicting any additional violation on them, given their prior prostitution, and is not seen as representing any notable human rights harm, given their purported prostitution in 'officers clubs' and their different pathways into stations compared to underage victims who might have been abducted or physically forced. That prostituted victims of the military sexual slavery system invariably faced sexual violence and trauma over longer periods of their lifetimes compared to other victims, were disproportionate victims of sexual abuse from a young age (e.g. often trafficked as children), and were victimized by their fellow countrymen (often in the same brothels as women of other nationalities), are considerations not canvassed in the literature as potentially qualifying Japanese women for special historical consideration. While these facts do not trump any of the backgrounds or circumstances of other victims of the system, the discussion of this book aims to combat misogynistic myths circulating about prostituted victims of military sexual slavery, particularly Japanese victims, which over decades have served to minimize their enslavement and experience of harm, and which to date has obstructed most of them coming forward to claim rightful recognition and restitution as survivors.

## Military reductionism

This book has challenged the 'military reductionism' that is found in even feminist scholarship that suggests sexual violence in wartime derives fundamentally from militarism and is an essential outgrowth of the harsh conditions of battle. It is a view of military sexual slavery that overlooks Morita's aforementioned observation that the comfort station system was 'fundamentally linked to violence and abuse of women both before and after the war'. This oversight, I argue, serves to whitewash the experience of prostituted women and girls during the period of Taisho-era 'demokurashii' who were victims of precisely the same practices of sexual violence that are now widely and rightly decried as 'slavery' in relation to the subsequent context of war. Only if we underestimate or deny the sexual enslavement of women and girls in Taisho-era civilian systems of prostitution, which are described in Chapter Two, can we suggest that it was the later conditions of war that *uniquely* generated military sexual slavery. These same systems operated in peacetime Japanese society but, different from prostitution in wartime, their reality as sexual slavery is obscured by retrospectively applied ideologies of 'choice' and self-serving defences of 'sex work'. In terms of the social and political functioning of prostitution for the benefit of male sex class interests, little substantive difference exists between systems that operate in either peacetime or wartime, as Morita further notes:

> The sexual violence against women that proliferates in war is continuation by military means the sexual violence and abuse that is visited upon women in peacetime. In war, this violence is more extreme, wide ranging, debased, and targets a broader base of women. However, the lower the social status or more extreme the objectification of women in peacetime, the more likely men in wartime are going to use sexual violence to regain their 'personal subjectivity'. This is due to the fact that in everyday life in peacetime these men structure themselves around the control of women, particularly sexual control.[38]

Chapter Two highlighted the similarity of experience that women and girls in the Taisho-era sex industry, both in brothels and *kafes*, endured, as compared to the later experience of their sisters in comfort stations. The sexual control that pimps, traffickers, and prostitution buyers exercised over these women and girls is easily recognizable as organizing a civilian system of sexual slavery, and one that operated throughout Japan on an expanding scale in the pre-war years. The unfortunate failure of historians like Sheldon Garon to comprehend the sexual slavery of the Taisho era, and to instead imagine women in this period to have achieved a degree of sexual liberation, has clouded comprehension of causes of the subsequent development of military sexual slavery, I argue. Misapprehension of the extent of sexual enslavement of Japanese women during the Taisho years has caused the military system to have become historically walled-off from pre-existing conditions in Japanese society, where men had become rampant prostitution buyers and the sex industry had grown to an unprecedented size over the 'tawdry' years of Taisho. This historical quarantining of the comfort station system has led historians to dedicate unwarranted amounts of attention and research to causes of the system lying outside of Japan and far away from the pre-war social conditions of the sex industry and Japanese women. The 'karayuki' system, colonial invasion, racism, and venereal disease are problems certainly all factoring in the historical context of the system's development, but these factors are ultimately peripheral to the simple matter of male sexual demand for the prostitution of women cultivated in pre-war Japanese society, and their habituated practice of buying women that became ultimately central to male fraternal relationships in war.

The 'personal subjectivity' that practices of sexual violence like prostitution allow men to exercise in times of war and peace is the observation that underpinned the argument of Chapter Four which was that military activity affords men an opportunity to 'democratize' existing civilian prostitution rights, and that elite men have an interest in capitalizing on the opportunity. It is not the contention of this book that civilian conditions of male sexual violence are 'unleashed' in an explosive, uncontrolled way once the fetters of peacetime society come off with the onset of war and fascism. Rather, militarism is more calmly recognized as affording ruling-class men an opportunity to 'democratise' their civilian prostitution rights through acculturating a broader base of the male population to the culture and practices of buying women. In other words, while prostitution buying rates might be high in civilian society, especially among elite men, war nonetheless affords them an opportunity to expand these rates, because of factors like male segregated and intensely concentrated living environments in the military, and a battlefield absence of social scrutiny, especially from women. While militarism might provide an opportunity for elite men to consolidate class and economic domination over poor and young men in various ways, these men concurrently have an interest in solidifying the bonds of male-class membership across as broad a base of the male citizenry as possible, and prostitution is a practice well suited to achieving this aim as a practice bolstering of individual male 'personal subjectivity'. The chance to strengthen and broaden bonds of male-class membership through developing a military sexual slavery system that 'democratically' allows different classes men acting in concert to exercise their personal subjectivity against the interests and welfare of women is a useful opportunity presented by war, and its outcomes serve the interests of elite men once 'peacetime' society resumes. Greater cohesiveness in the male civilian population forged through a prolonged experience of communal sexual use and abuse of women is an outcome useful for the subsequent peacetime aims of elite men, including economic exploitation and repeat military venture. In the case of the comfort station system, the discussion of Chapter Four highlighted the central role of elite, officer-class men in both establishing the system and acculturating subordinates to its use. The chapter's discussion recognized that while the system operated according to various rules of male hierarchy (e.g. different venues for different ranks of men), it nonetheless served a remarkably broad base of Japanese troops, and elite men went to a great deal of trouble and effort to ensure that it did.

It is this observation of Chapter Four, I believe, that critically links the discussion of the book to contemporary Japanese society and comprises its major theoretical contribution. This observation, which challenges alternative explanations characterized by their military reductionism, understands peacetime society as harbouring a masculinist incentive or demand for war on the basis of the opportunity war and militarism affords elite men to 'democratise' or further expand the reach of their prostitution rights. This temptation in peacetime society is not universal or inevitable – it is wholly contingent on the existence of a civilian sex industry that already inculcates a proportion of the male population, and especially the ruling male class, to the habits and culture of prostituting women. For the military democratization thesis to hold, there must exist in peacetime society a pre-existing commercial sexual organization of women that can be democratized. In other words, incentives to expand and disseminate the civilian male prostitution right through enacting systems of military sexual slavery in times of war exist only when conditions prevail in peacetime that make this particular means of male fraternal bonding possible. Defeating this possibility, therefore, through dismantling civilian prostitution systems and resisting peacetime cultures of female sexual exploitation, is the approach recommended as an outcome of the insights generated by this book's examination of the history of the comfort station system.

## A historical view of civilian sexual slavery

Reflecting on past historical events to generate insights about contemporary society is a well-worn practice of historians, and there exist a number of examples of historians of modern Japan drawing on insights from the war years to explain aspects of post-war Japanese society. Hazama Hiroshi in 1996, for example, argued that 'corporate warriors' (*kigyou senshi*) – who he defined as the men born before or during the war who numerically dominated Japan's white collared workforce until the mid-1960s[39] – were responsible for disseminating a new 'work ethos' (*roudou eetosu*) in Japanese society in the post-war period.[40] Hazama refers to these men as 'corporate warriors' to emphasize the fact of their wartime military experience. He writes that the values corporate warriors took on during the war years – including values of personal sacrifice and love of nation – came not only to shape Japanese companies and work culture in the era of high speed economic growth but also influence wider Japanese society. He calculates that nearly half of all men in white-collar work in Japan in 1965 were born either before or during the war,[41] and he distinguishes these corporate warriors from the 'company men' (*kaisha ningen*) who did not experience the war, and who were not greatly represented in Japanese companies until after 1965.[42] Hazama interviewed 105 Japanese men of a range of ages, including the men he labels corporate warriors, and asked them how their experience of war and occupation (if they had any such experience) might have shaped their attitudes towards work. His survey aimed to pinpoint generational differences in attitudes towards work, and thereby understand how the values and attitudes of men born before and during the war might have influenced Japanese society in the period before 1965.[43]

Hazama writes that the most prevalent value expressed by survey respondents who were born either before or during the war was that 'sacrificing oneself to work for the company on behalf of the [prosperity of the] nation is a natural thing to do'.[44] Moreover, he notes that while survey respondents born after the war generally indicated they were able to put behind them their experiences of poverty during Japan's post-war occupation, Hazama reports that the men who experienced the war were likely to have made these experiences the centre of their lives, and have had them fundamentally guide their attitudes and actions thereafter.[45] It was this latter category of men, who were heavily influenced by the war, who led Japanese companies until at least 1965. Hazama notes that these men commonly declared in interviews that men should 'work like crazed animals', 'give up one's life for one's work', 'expect death at work', and 'die on the job in fulfilment of true Japanese manhood'.[46] He contends that the leading role that corporate warriors played in companies after the war meant that these ideals of personal self-sacrifice for the 'greater good' came to set the tone for working life in Japan, both for younger and older men in companies, and also for men outside of white collared work.

Hazama carried out his research in 1996 to attempt to explain Japan's 'extraordinary' corporate culture and labour market conditions of the high-speed economic growth era, which notably featured the phenomenon of *karoushi* (death from overwork). He therefore limited his exploration of the 'wartime values' of corporate warriors to the attitudes that guided their work 'ethos' in the 1960s and did not consider any implications of his study for the state of sexual politics inhering in post-war Japan. Drawing on events from Japan's past to warn of or explain developments in the present in this way is a methodology expertly used by historians like Hazama, and one endorsed by John Dower who observes that '... many of the characteristics and accomplishments of postwar Japan are deeply rooted not merely in the prewar period, but more precisely in the dark valley of early Showa ... developments that took place in conjunction with Japan's fifteen-year war proved to be extremely useful to the postwar Japanese state'.[47] Unfortunately, though, it is an approach rarely seen in analyses of sexual politics in contemporary Japanese society: the extreme and sustained social inequality of Japanese women in the post-war period continues to perplex commentators who generally fail to consider the possibility of state capitalisation on arrangements of sexual politics forged during war.

Even when feminist historians of the wartime sexual slavery system consider its implications for post-war sexual politics in Japan, they usually constrain their focus to the *kisaeng* sex tourism of Japanese men to South Korea and Southeast Asian countries from the 1970s. This tourism is suggested to be a directly identifiable manifestation of sexual practices and habits cultivated among Japanese men during the war. For example, in a 1993 article titled 'Bijinesu senshi no juugun ianfu tachi' (Comfort women for corporate warriors), Ieda Shoukou expresses the opinion that the comfort station system and *kisaeng* prostitution tourism are parallel phenomena in Japanese history.[48] Suzuki Yuuko and Matsui Yayori frequently make the same observation. The only historian who appears to have further stretched insights going back to the *pre-war* period to consider conditions of sexual politics prevailing in contemporary Japan is Imanishi Hajime of Otaru University of Commerce, who prefaces his masterful 2007 monograph on Japanese sex industry development in colonial Korea with an introductory chapter discussing at length the state of male sex offending against women and girls in contemporary Japan. Imanishi's decision to introduce his comprehensive historical work of the 1910s and 1920s in this way is probably unprecedented in both the English and Japanese historical literatures, and he is clear he made a deliberate decision to undertake the work to shed light on the nature of Japanese male society today:

> The sexual standards and culture that envelop us developed over the course of history. This book considers both pre-war society and its history of prostitution to examine the problems of contemporary Japanese sexual culture ... In what other country in the contemporary world do you see commercial ventures dedicated to the filming of young girls, or pornographic magazines aimed at teenagers sold in mainstream bookstores? Even though we worry constantly about the problem of an 'ageing society' we don't do anything to protect children.[49]

Fujino Yutaka is perhaps the only other historian to have directly linked problems of prostitution in contemporary Japan to systems of sexual exploitation operating in the country before the war:

> Under the guise of 'free choice', prostitution to this day has continued to diversify and develop in Japan. It is used for the purpose of 'entertaining' in the bureaucratic and business worlds, and underpinned the 'high speed growth' that characterised Japan's economy in the 1960s and 1970s. The fact that men in Japan's parliament are known to pay money to retain individual women for sexual access is scandalously reported in the media from time to time. But the Japanese state continues to benignly oversee the 'sexual comfort' of its male citizens. Under the 'righteous cause' (*daigi*) of 'free choice', prostitution has continued to be accepted. Certainly, prostitution in Japan today looks externally different from the prostitution that existed before the war and in the early postwar years. In these years the daughters of poor farming families were sold into prostitution to reduce the number of mouths to feed, and war widows went into prostitution to find a way to look after their children. Today, on the other hand, poverty is rarely cited as behind women's entry into prostitution. It's now widely believed that prostitution takes the form of '*enjo kousai*' where underage girls, including those in junior and senior high school, exercise free will in carrying out prostitution for the sake of earning large amounts of money. But is this the form it really takes? ... in order to attract customers the sex industry promotes an idea of itself as 'fun and safe' so that buyers of prostitution can avoid feelings of culpability. The buyers convince themselves of the fact that women 'sell themselves' in prostitution as a means of liberating their sexuality.[50]

Apart from Imanishi and Fujino's work, the historical experience of local Japanese women in being organized into large-scale systems of prostitution both before and during the war is mostly forgotten in academic discussion of prostitution in post-war Japan. Even feminist historical writing tends to be solely concerned with the plight of *foreign* women trafficked into the country's sex industry. Matsui Yayori – who otherwise takes a critical feminist view of prostitution – wrote in a 1995 monograph that hostess bars traffic women in from abroad, because young Japanese women have more opportunity in the mainstream job market compared to 'fifteen to twenty years ago', and so trafficking takes place in order 'to make up for the shortage of young women'.[51] Matsui provides no evidence for her belief that Japanese women enter the sex industry at declining rates, though, and offers no discussion of the plight of local women in Japan's sex industry. While she does call Japanese men a 'giant parade of lechers' in her 1984 chapter 'Why I oppose *kisaeng* tours', Matsui still contends there is 'something fundamentally different' about Japanese men's *kisaeng* prostitution tours compared to their buying of 'the bodies of bath girls or bar hostesses in their own country'.[52] She does not elaborate on why she considers Japanese men's prostitution of women abroad to be different from their prostitution of women at home, but this sentiment is echoed in a lot of the feminist literature on *kisaeng* tourism.

Vera Mackie in her 2003 monograph is generous in the space she dedicates to the plight of foreign women in Japan's post-war prostitution industry, but the only local Japanese women she considers are those prostituted by US troops on Okinawa.[53] This format for discussing prostitution in post-war Japan, where a discussion of foreign women trafficked into Japan's sex industry is followed by an examination of local Japanese women prostituted by US troops on Okinawa, is replicated in a number of feminist texts.[54] When the prostitution of local Japanese women is discussed, their victimization is often not recognized. Particularly in discussions of 'enjo kousai' or 'compensated dating' from the 1990s and 2000s, as Fujino explains above, underage Japanese teenage girls are commonly framed as active and willing participants in their own prostitution.[55] The only other context in which Japanese women are discussed in relation to the local sex industry is hostess bars (e.g. *kyabakura* and *pinku saron*), but the prostitution of these women is usually minimized or overlooked. Sugita's observation that commentators are likely to see Japanese women as having 'chosen' to enter the local sex industry, and therefore fail to see them as victims of prostitution,[56] applies to most academic comment on the prostitution of local women in post-war Japan to the present.

This failure to take seriously the prostitution of local women generates a skewed perspective on the history of the comfort station system when the situation of foreign women trafficked into Japan's sex industry is imagined to be the closest contemporary parallel of events in the Showa era. Fukushima Mizuho suggests confusingly that

> [t]here is a parallel between comfort women and Asian women today who are deceived into coming to Japan and are then forced to work as prostitutes against their wills. Both of these groups are deluded by the same seductive voice: if you come to Japan, you will easily find well-paid jobs.[57]

The historical veracity of this argued parallel is highly questionable, given the large-scale trafficking of women out of Japan and its colonies into comfort stations all over the world during the war years. The military system was very much a product of the sexual exploitation of women within the Japanese empire throughout the war. This kind of understanding of the history of the comfort station system: that it was a product of overseas military activity, interned only foreign women, and operated through stations in remote locations far removed from Japan and Japanese women, blocks recognition of the possibility that, in terms of sexual politics, social conditions exist domestically in Japan today that are similarly conducive to the emergence of a system of large-scale military sexual slavery system in the event of war as existed in the Taisho era.

Scholars like Imanishi consider the prostitution practices and attitudes of Japanese men in pre-war modern history with a view to making comment on the state of male sexuality in contemporary Japanese society. His approach is not shared in this book. Rather, its viewpoint aligns with Morita Seiya's suggestion that similar social conditions of female sexual servitude and male prostitution sexuality prevail across the two time periods: that contemporary conditions in Japan are conducive to similar outcomes as those of the Showa era. This book builds on Morita's unique methodology to consider sex industry conditions inhering in Japan in the Taisho era and traces their influence on the creation, subsequent development, and sustained operation of the military comfort women system throughout the years of the China and Pacific wars. It examines the system as an endpoint of the state of sexual politics during the period, and not as an isolated emergence of sexual slavery, nor as a turning point in the history of sexual politics in Japanese society. It does not consider, in the way Imanishi and Hazama do, the effects of the history of the comfort station system on the state of Japanese society today. While we might agree with Imanishi and Hazama that these outcomes are visible in the prostitution culture of present-day Japan, the observations of this book alternatively follow Morita's example pointing precisely in the opposite direction. That is, the comfort station system is understood to have been historically 'inevitable' only to the extent a similar state of male sexuality prevailing in peacetime would likely to generate similar forms of sexual slavery in the event of war or military mobilization. It is the view of the author and groups she is involved with in Japan, such as the Anti-Prostitution and Pornography Research Group, that conditions of civilian sexual slavery prevail in Japan today to an extent dwarfing even those of the Taisho era. This state of affairs currently inflicts untold harm on women and girls residing in Japan, as well as populations of women in Asia. It is a state of affairs pregnant with the potential for magnified and escalating human rights harms against these same women if the Japanese government continues on its current trajectory towards militarism and war, and Japanese men continue in their current habits of rampant prostitution and pornography activity. This potential repetition of history, if for no other reason, imposes a burden of responsibility on us all to recognize the civilian sexual slavery of 'peacetime' Japanese society and do something about it. This book was written in contribution to that effort.

# Notes

## Introduction

1 Kinoshita Naoko, 'For the sake of encounters with Japanese "Comfort Women" victims', in Iwasaki Minoru, Chen Kuan-Hsing and Yoshimi Shunya (eds), *Cultural Studies de Yomitoku Asia*, Tokyo: Serica Shobo, 2011, p. 119.

2 'Excerpt from Dr. Suki Falconberg's book ....', http://www.leapnonprofit.org/Phil%20article%20Suki%20Falconberg.htm

3 Shirota Suzuko, *Mariya no sanka*, Tokyo: Nihon Kirisuto Kyoudan Shuppan Kyoku, 1971, p. 2.

4 Ibid., p. 34.

5 Ibid., p. 35.

6 Ibid., p. 87.

7 Ibid., p. 46.

8 Katharine Moon, *Sex among allies: Military prostitution in U.S.-Korea relations*, New York: Columbia University Press, 1997, p. 156.

9 See volume compiled by the Korean Council for Women Drafted for Military Sexual Slavery by Japan and the Research Association on the Women Drafted for Military Sexual Slavery by Japan (translated by Young Joo Lee; edited by Keith Howard), *True stories of the Korean comfort women: Testimonies*, London; New York: Cassell, 1995.

10 Peipei Qiu, Zhiliang Su and Lifei Chen, *Chinese comfort women: Testimonies from imperial Japan's sexual slaves*, New York: Oxford University Press, 2014, p. 38.

11 Hirao Hiroko, 'Senjika "Shina tokou fujo" no ki', *Sensou Sekinin Kenkyuu*, Vol. 61, 2008, p. 11.

12 Ibid.

13 Nishino Rumiko, 'Naze ima, Nihonjin "ianfu" na no ka?', *Baurakku Tsuushin*, No. 2, December 2012, p. 5.

14 Ibid., p. 4.

15 Kinoshita Naoko, 'Victimization of Japanese "comfort women": Opinions and redress movements in the early 1990s', in The Tokai Foundation for Gender Studies (ed), *Gender studies*, Nagoya: The Tokai Foundation for Gender Studies, No. 14, 2011, pp. 89–113.

16 Yoshimi Yoshiaki, '"Kouno danwa" to "ianfu" seiko no shinsou kyuumei', in Risaachi Akushon Sentaa (ed), *'Ianfu' basshingu wo koete*, Tokyo: Ootsuki Shoten, 2013, p. 7.

17 Hirai Kazuko, 'Nihon gun "ianjo" kara senryou gun "ian shisetsu"/"akasen" e',
   presentation handout at VAWRACC Soukai Shimpojiumu, 'Nihon jin "ianfu" no
   choushuu/taiguu/sengo', p. 3, 21 September 2013 (on file with author).

18 Yoshimi Yoshiaki and translated by Suzanne O'Brien, *Comfort women: Sexual
   slavery in the Japanese military during World War II*, New York: Colombia
   University Press, 2000, pp. 127–128.

19 Jan Ruff-O'Herne, *50 years of silence*, Sydney: Editions Tom Thompson, 1994.

20 Katharine Moon, 'South Korean movements against militarized sexual labor', *Asian
   Survey*, Vol. 39, No. 2, 1999, pp. 310–327.

21 Yoshimi, '"Kouno danwa" to "ianfu" seiko no shinsou kyuumei', p. 5.

22 Tessa Morris-Suzuki, 'Letters to the dead: Grassroots historical dialogue in
   East Asia's borderlands', in Tessa Morris-Suzuki, Morris Low, Leonid Petrov
   and Timothy Y. Tsu, *East Asia beyond the history wars: Confronting the ghosts of
   violence*, London: Routledge, 2013, p. 91.

23 Mark Driscoll, *Absolute erotic, absolute grotesque: The living, dead, and undead in
   Japan's imperialism, 1895–1945*, Durham, NC: Duke University Press, 2010.

24 Andrea Dworkin, *Scapegoat: The Jews, Israel, and women's liberation*, New York:
   Free Press, 2000, p. 312.

25 Hayashi Hirofumi, 'Japanese comfort women in southeast Asia', *Japan Forum*,
   Vol. 10, No. 2, 1998, pp. 212–213.

26 See Shouhei Imamura, Imamura Productions and Kino International Corporation,
   *Karayuki-san: The making of a prostitute*, New York: Kino International, 1980.

27 Vera Mackie, 'Militarized memories and sexual silences: Writing about military
   prostitution in the Second World War', *Japanese Studies*, Vol. 16, No. 2–3,
   1996, p. 63.

28 Antje Kampf, 'Controlling male sexuality: Combating venereal disease in the New
   Zealand military during two world wars', *Journal of the History of Sexuality*, Vol. 17,
   No. 2, May 2008, pp. 235–258.

29 Kelly Askin, 'Comfort Women: Shifting shame and stigma from victims to
   victimizers', *International Criminal Law Review*, Vol. 1, No. 1/2, 2001, pp. 13–14.

30 Suzuki Masahiro, 'Sensou ni okeru dansei no sekushuariti', in Ningen to Sei
   Kyouiku Kenkyuu kyougikai Dansei Keisei Kenkyuu Purojekuto, *Nihon no otoko
   wa doko kara kite doko e iku no ka: Dansei sekushuariti keisei kyoudou kenkyuu*,
   Tokyo: Juugatsusha, 2001, p. 108.

31 Catharine MacKinnon, 'Rape, genocide, and women's human rights', in Alexandra
   Stiglmayer (ed), *Mass rape: The war against women in Bosnia-Herzegovina*,
   Nebraska: University of Nebraska Press, 1994, p. 12.

32 Catharine MacKinnon, *Are women human? And other international dialogues*,
   Cambridge, MA: Harvard University Press, 2007, p. 37.

33 Morita Seiya, 'Senji no sei bouryoku heiji no sei bouryoku', *Yuibutsuron Kenkyuu
   Nenshi*, Vol. 4, November 1999, p. 115.

34 'Clinton says "comfort women" is incorrect term', *Chosun Ilbo*, 9 July 2012, http://english.chosun.com/site/data/html_dir/2012/07/09/2012070900793.html

35 Susan Kay Hunter, 'Prostitution is cruelty and abuse to women and children', *Michigan Journal of Gender and Law*, Vol. 95, 1993, p. 95.

36 Caroline Norma and Melinda Tankard Reist (eds), *Prostitution narratives: Stories from the sex trade*, Melbourne: Spinifex Press, 2016.

37 Morita Seiya, 'Poruno to ha nani ka, poruno higai to ha nani ka', in Poruno higai to sei bouryoku wo kangaeru kai (eds), *Shougen: Gendai no sei bouryoku to poruno higai*, Tokyo: Tokyo-to Shakai Fukushi Kyougikai, 2010, pp. 50–51.

38 Qiu, Su and Chen, *Chinese comfort women*, p. 65.

39 Rachel Moran, *Paid for: My journey through prostitution*, Melbourne: Spinifex Press, 2013, pp. 111–112.

40 Catharine MacKinnon, 'Trafficking, prostitution, and inequality', *Harvard Civil Rights-Civil Liberties Law Review*, Vol. 46, 2011, p. 273.

41 Ibid., p. 274.

42 Sugita Satoshi, *Danken shugiteki sekushuariti: Poruno baibaishun yougoron hihan*, Tokyo: Aoki Shoten, 1999, p. 172.

43 Fujino Yutaka, *Sei no kokka kanri: Bai-baishun no kin-gendaishi*, Tokyo: Fuji Shuppan, 2001, p. 288.

44 'Yegeurina', 'There is no such thing as voluntary or involuntary: Can it really ever be a choice?' p. 15 in Salim Center (translated by Yunmi Lee), booklet (self-published) on file with author.

45 Dworkin, *Scapegoat*, p. 314.

46 Kurahashi Masanao, *Juugun ianfu mondai no rekishiteki kenkyuu: Baishunfugata to seiteki doreigata*, Tokyo: Kyouei Shobou, 1994.

47 Sandra Wilson, 'Rethinking the 1930s and the "15-Year War" in Japan', *Japanese Studies*, Vol. 21, 2001, pp. 155–164.

48 Hayashi Hirofumi, 'Shiberia shuppei ji ni okeru Nihon gun to "karayukisan"', *Sensou Sekinin Kenkyuu*, Vol. 24, 1999, p. 18.

49 Sorano Yoshihiro, 'Kitachousen moto juugun ianfu shougen', *Ekonomitsuto*, Vol. 70, No. 49, 1992, p. 34.

50 Koga Noriko, 'Okinawa-sen in okeru Nihon gun "ianfu" seido no tenkai (2)', *Sensou Sekinin Kenkyuu*, Vol. 61, 2008, p. 64.

51 Sorano, 'Kitachousen moto juugun ianfu shougen', p. 34.

52 Shirota, *Mariya no sanka*, p. 67.

53 Hayashi, 'Japanese comfort women in southeast Asia', pp. 212-214.

54 Maria Rosa Henson, *Comfort women: Slave of destiny*, Metro Manila: Philippine Center for Investigative Journalism, 1996, p. xvi.

55 Sorano, 'Kitachousen moto juugun ianfu shougen', p. 34.

56 Nishino Rumiko, *Juugun ianfu no hanashi: Juudai no anata e no messeeji*, Tokyo: Akashi Shoten, 1993, p. 83.

57   Hayashi Hirofumi, 'Japanese military comfort houses and Overseas Chinese "comfort women" in South-east Asia (summary)', http://www.geocities.jp/hhhirofumi/eng05.htm

58   Hayashi Hirofumi, 'Rikugun ianjo kanri no ichi sokumen: Eisei sakku no koufu shiryou wo tegakari ni', *Sensou Sekinin Kenkyuu*, Vol. 1, No. 1, 1993, pp. 12–19.

59   Yoshimi, *Comfort women*, p. 29.

60   Shimojuu Kiyoshi, *Miuri no nihonshi: Jinshin baibai kara nenki boko e*, Tokyo: Yoshikawa Kobunkan, 2012.

61   Park Hyun, 'Bill related to comfort women passed in US congress', *The Hankyoreh*, 17 January 2014, www.hani.co.kr/arti/english_edition/e_international/620209.html

62   UNESCO, 'Nomination form International Memory of the World Register Archives about "Comfort Women": The Sex Slaves for Imperial Japanese Troops', http://www.unesco.org/new/fileadmin/MULTIMEDIA/HQ/CI/CI/pdf/mow/nomination_forms/china_comfort_women_eng.pdf

63   'Kaigai de baishun suru Kankokujin josei, Nihon 5man nin Beikoku 3man nin, Beiou de shakai mondai ka', 28 May 2012, http://news.searchina.ne.jp/disp.cgi?y=2012&d=0528&f=national_0528_040.shtml

64   Jeong nam-ku, 9 June 2013, 'Inside Japan's growing xenophobic right-wing', *The Hankyoreh*, http://english.hani.co.kr/arti/english_edition/e_international/591008.html

65   Shared Hope International, 'Japan: Culture and crime promote commercial markets of sexual exploitation', http://www.sharedhope.org/files/demand_japan.pdf, p. 1.

66   Office To Monitor and Combat Trafficking in Persons, *Trafficking in persons report 2009*, http://www.state.gov/g/tip/rls/tiprpt/2009/123136.htm.

# Chapter 1

1   BBC TV, *Against pornography: The feminism of Andrea Dworkin*, Sydney, NSW: SBS, 1992.

2   Matthew Carney, 'Return of the samurai: Japan steps away from pacifist constitution as military eyes threat from China', *Foreign Correspondent*, 19 August 2014, Australian Broadcasting Corporation, http://www.abc.net.au/news/2014-08-19/japan-expands-their-military-amid-growing-tensions-with-china/5672932

3   Hata Ikuhiko, *No organized for forced recruitment: Misconceptions about comfort women and the Japanese military*, 2007, p. 16, http://www.sdh-fact.com/CL02_1/31_S4.pdf

4   'New NHK head's "comfort women" remark stirs controversy', *Japan Today*, 26 January 2014, http://www.japantoday.com/category/national/view/new-nhk-heads-comfort-women-remark-stirs-controversy

5   Matsumura Toshio, 'Biruma no tokoro "juugun ianfu"', *Doko*, No. 1589, 1999, p. 18.

6   Japan Women for Justice and Peace, 'What is "comfort women"?', http://nadesiko-action.org/wp-content/uploads/2013/01/nadeshiko_zWeb.pdf

7   Yasuhara Keiko, 'Bunseki ripouto: Ianfu ni tsuite', in Juugun Ianfu 110ban Henshuu Iinkai (eds), *Juugun ianfu 110ban: Denwa no mukou kara rekishi no koe ga*, Tokyo: Akaishi Shoten, 1992, p. 87.

8   Nishino Rumiko, 'Naze ima, Nihonjin "ianfu" na no ka?', *Baurakku Tsuushin*, No. 2, December 2012, p. 4.

9   Andrea Dworkin, *Scapegoat: The Jews, Israel, and women's liberation*, New York: Free Press, 2000, pp. 311, 316–317.

10  Margaret Baldwin, 'Split at the root: Prostitution and feminist discourses of law reform', *Yale Journal of Law and Feminism*, Vol. 5, No. 47, 1992, p. 83.

11  Ibid., p. 117.

12  Ibid., p. 119.

13  Ibid., pp. 119–120.

14  Morita Seiya, 'Senji no sei bouryoku heiji no sei bouryoku', *Yuibutsuron Kenkyuu Nenshi*, Vol. 4, November 1999, p. 115.

15  Yuki Tanaka, *Japan's comfort women: Sexual slavery and prostitution during World War II and the US occupation*, London; New York: Routledge, 2002, p. 52.

16  Katharine Moon, 'Resurrecting prostitutes and overturning treaties: Gender politics in the "anti-American" movement in South Korea', *The Journal of Asian Studies*, Vol. 66, No. 1, February 2007, p. 131.

17  For a comprehensive description of this history, see Katharine Moon, 'South Korean movements against militarized sexual labor', *Asian Survey*, Vol. 39, No. 2, 1999, pp. 310–327.

18  Matsui Yayori, 'Why I oppose the kisaeng tours', in Kathleen Barry, Charlotte Bunch and Shirley Castley (eds), *International feminism: Networking against female sexual slavery, Report of the Global Feminist Workshop to Organize Against Traffic in Women, Rotterdam, the Netherlands, April 6–15 1983*, New York: International Women's Tribune, 1983, p. 70.

19  Ibid., p. 71.

20  See Takasato Suzuyo, *Okinawa no onnatachi: Josei no jinken to kichi guntai*, Tokyo: Akashi Shoten, 1996.

21  Bang-Soon L. Yoon, 'Imperial Japan's comfort women from Korea: History & politics of silence-breaking', *Journal of Northeast Asian History*, Vol. 7, No. 1, 2010, p. 27, http://www.historyfoundation.or.kr/shtml/include/filedownload. asp?sidx=239&fname=J7_1_A1.pdf.

22  Quoted in Ibid., p. 22.

23  Yoon, 'Imperial Japan's comfort women from Korea', pp. 26–27.

24  Alice Yun Chai, 'KOREA. Modern period', in Helen Tierney, *Women's studies encyclopedia*, Westport, CT: Greenwood Electronic Media, Vol. 2, p. 824.

25  Suzuki Hiroko and Kondou Kazuko, *Onna tennou-sei sensou*, Tokyo: Orijin Sentaa, 1989, p. 207.

26  Takahashi Kikue, *Sei shinryaku o kokuhatsu suru kiisen kankou*, Tokyo: Kiisen Kankou Ni Hantai Suru Onnatachi No Kai, 1974.

27  Kinoshita Naoko, 'For the sake of encounters with Japanese "comfort women" victims', in Iwasaki Minoru, Chen Kuan-Hsing and Yoshimi Shunya (eds), *Cultural Studies de Yomitoku Asia*, Tokyo: Serica Shobo, 2011, p. 117.

28  Ibid., p. 111.

29  Ibid., p. 113.

30  Ibid., p. 115.

31  Ibid., p. 120.

32  Fujino Yutaka, *Sei no kokka kanri: Bai-baishun no kin-gendaishi*, Tokyo: Fuji Shuppan, 2001, p. 292.

33  Nishino, 'Naze ima, Nihonjin "ianfu" na no ka?', pp. 4–5.

34  Ibid., p. 6.

35  Hirai Kazuko, 'Zasshi ni hyoushou sareta Nihonjin "ianfu" kara miete kuru mono', p. 11, presentation handout on file with author, 29 September 2012, VAWWRAC Soukai Shimpojiumu, 'Nihon jin 'ianfu' no higai jitai ni semaru!'.

36  Hiroko Tabuchi, 'Women forced into WWII brothels served necessary role, Osaka mayor says', *The New York Times*, 13 May 2013, http://www.nytimes.com/2013/05/14/world/asia/mayor-in-japan-says-comfort-women-played-a-necessary role.html?_r=0

37  'Hashimoto shi "fuuzoku josei he no sabetsu da" Ishihara shi "machigattenai"', *Asahi Shinbun*, 14 May 2013, http://www.asahi.com/politics/update/0514/OSK201305140009.html

38  Tabuchi, 'Women forced into WWII brothels served necessary role, Osaka mayor says'.

39  'Ianfu mondai, fuuzokugyou wo meguru Hashimoto shi no hatsugen youshi', *Asahi Shinbun*, 13 May 2013, http://www.asahi.com/politics/update/0514/OSK201305130144.html?ref=reca

40  'Hashimoto shi "fuuzoku josei he no sabetsu da" Ishihara shi "machigattenai"'.

41  See, for example, Hata Ikuhiko, 'No organized or forced recruitment: Misconceptions about comfort women and the Japanese military', Society for the Dissemination of Historical Fact, 2007, http://www.sdh-fact.com

42  Sugisaka Keisuke, *Tobita no ko: Yuukaku no machi ni hataraku onnatachi no jinsei*, Tokyo: Tokuma Shoten, 2013, p. 4.

43  Nishino, 'Naze ima, Nihonjin "ianfu" na no ka?', p. 4.

44  Tessa Morris-Suzuki, 'Freedom of hate speech; Abe Shinzo and Japan's public sphere', *The Asia-Pacific Journal*, Vol. 11, No. 8.1, 25 February 2013, http://www.japanfocus.org/-Tessa-Morris_Suzuki/3902

45  'Stop undermining Kono statement', *Japan Times*, 25 June 2014, http://www.
    japantimes.co.jp/opinion/2014/06/25/editorials/stop-undermining-kono-
    statement/#.VFNosfnLe4E

46  Study Team on the Details Leading to the Drafting of the Kono Statement etc.,
    *Details of exchanges between Japan and the Republic of Korea (ROK) regarding
    the comfort women issue – From the drafting of the Kono Statement to the Asian
    Women's Fund*, 20 June 2014, http://www.mofa.go.jp/files/000042171.pdf

47  Nishino, 'Naze ima, Nihon jin "ianfu" nano ka?', p. 3.

48  Morita, 'Senji no sei bouryoku heiji no sei bouryoku', p. 121.

49  Chunghee Sarah Soh, 'The Korean "comfort women" tragedy as structural violence', in
    Gi-Wook Shin, Soon-Won Park and Daqing Yang (eds), *Rethinking historical injustice
    and reconciliation in northeast Asia*, New York: Routledge, 2007, p. 17.

50  Chunghee Sarah Soh, 'The Korean "comfort women": Movement for redress', *Asian
    Survey*, Vol. 36, No. 12, 1996, pp. 1238–1239.

51  Ibid., p. 1239.

52  Chunghee Sarah Soh, 'From imperial gifts to sex slaves: Theorizing symbolic
    representations of the "comfort women"', *Social Science Japan Journal*, Vol. 3, No. 1,
    April 2000, p. 60.

53  Shu Tokuran (Delan Zhu), *Taiwan soutokufu to ianfu*, Tokyo: Akashi Shoten, 2005,
    p. 20.

54  Melissa Farley, 'Prostitution and the invisibility of harm', *Women & Therapy*,
    Vol. 26, Nos. 3–4, 2003, pp. 247–280.

55  Chunghee Sarah Soh, *The comfort women: Sexual violence and postcolonial memory
    in Korea and Japan*, Chicago: University of Chicago Press, 2008, p. 181.

56  Ibid., p. 194.

57  Morita, 'Senji no sei bouryoku heiji no sei bouryoku', p. 116 quoting Oogoshi
    Aiko.

58  Chunghee Sarah Soh, *The comfort women*, p. 194.

59  Yuha Pak, *Teikoku no ianfu: Shokuminchi shihai to kioku no tatakai*, Tokyo: Asahi
    Shinbun Shuppan, 2014.

60  Kamala Kempadoo, 'Globalization and sex workers' rights', *Canadian Women's
    Studies*, Vol. 22, No. 3/4, 2002/3, p. 143, http://pi.library.yorku.ca/ojs/index.php/
    cws/article/viewFile/6426/5614

61  See Seiya Morita, 'Pornography, prostitution, and women's human rights in Japan',
    in Christine Stark and Rebecca Whisnant (eds), *Not for sale: Feminists resisting
    prostitution and pornography*, North Melbourne: Spinifex, 2004, pp. 64–84.

62  Sugita Satoshi, *Danken shugiteki sekushuariti: Poruno baibaishun yougoron hihan*,
    Tokyo: Aoki Shoten, 1999.

63  Kajsa Ekis Ekman, *Being and being bought: Prostitution, surrogacy and the split self*,
    Melbourne: Spinifex Press, 2013.

64  Chimoto Hideki, 'Roudou toshite no baishun to kindai kazoku no yukue', in Tazaki Hideaki (ed), *Uru shintai kau shintai: Sekkusu waaku ron no shatei*, Tokyo: Seikyuusha, 1997, p. 178.

65  See Dara Culhane, 'Their spirits live within us: Aboriginal women in downtown eastside Vancouver emerging into visibility', *American Indian Quarterly*, Vol. 27, No. 3/4, Special Issue: Urban American Indian Women's Activism (Summer–Autumn, 2003), pp. 593–606.

66  Kim Il-myon Kim, *Guntai ianfu: Sensou to ningen no kiroku*, Tokyo: Tokuma Shoten, 1992.

67  Laura Hein, 'Savage irony: The imaginative power of the "military comfort women" in the 1990s', *Gender & History*, Vol. 11, 1999, p. 340.

68  Andrea Dworkin, *Life and death: Unapologetic writings on the continuing war against women*, New York: The Free Press, 1997, p. 141.

69  Takasaki Ryuuji (ed), *Hyakusatsu ga kataru 'ianjo' otoko no honne: Ajia-zen'iki ni 'inanjo' ga atta*, Tokyo: Nashinokisha, 1994, p. 124.

70  Commission on Human Rights, 4 January 1996, *Report of the Special Rapporteur on violence against women, its causes and consequences, Ms. Radhika Coomaraswamy, in accordance with Commission on Human Rights resolution 1994/45; Report on the mission to the Democratic People's Republic of Korea, the Republic of Korea and Japan on the issue of military sexual slavery in wartime*, p. 15, http://www.awf.or.jp/pdf/h0004.pdf

71  Suzuki Yuuko, *Sensou sekinin to jendaa*, Tokyo: Miraisha, 1997, p. 51.

72  Alice Yun Chai, 'Asian-Pacific feminist coalition politics: The chongshindae/jugunianfu ("comfort women") movement', *Korean Studies*, Vol. 17, 1993, p. 69.

73  Maria Höhn and Seungsook Moon, *Over there: Living with the U.S. military empire from World War Two to the present*, Durham: Duke University Press, 2010, p. 42.

74  Yun Chung-ok and Suzuki Yuuko, *Heiwa o kikyuushite: 'Ianfu' higaisha no songen kaifuku e no ayumi*, Musashino-shi: Hakutakusha, 2003, p. 23.

75  Yumiko Mikanagi, 'Women, the state, and war: Understanding issue [*sic*] of the "comfort women"', Kokusai kirisutokyo daigaku, *Shakai Kagaku Jaanaru*, Vol. 48, 2002, p. 45.

76  Ueno Chizuko (translated by Beverley Yamamoto), *Nationalism and gender*, Melbourne: Trans Pacific Press, 2004, p. 92.

77  Hirai Kazuko, 'Zasshi ni hyoushou sareta Nihonjin "ianfu" kara miete kuru mono', p. 11 presentation handout on file with author, 29 September 2012, VAWWRAC Soukai Shimpojiumu, 'Nihon jin "ianfu" no higai jitai ni semaru!'.

78  Nishino Rumiko, 'Higai sha shougen ni miru "ianfu" renkou no kyousei sei', in Sensou to Josei he no Bouryoku Risaachi Akushon Sentaa (ed), *'Ianfu' basshingu wo koete: 'Kouno danwa' to Nihon no sekinin*, Tokyo: Otsuki Shoten, 2013, p. 36.

79  Yoshimi Yoshiaki, '"Kouno danwa" wo dou kangaeru ka', in *Sensou to Josei he no Bouryoku Risaachi akushon sentaa* (ed), *'Ianfu' basshingu wo koete: 'Kouno danwa' to Nihon no sekinin*, Tokyo: Otsuki Shoten, 2013, p. 3.

# Chapter 2

1   Catharine MacKinnon, 'Sexual abuse as sex inequality', in Catharine MacKinnon (ed), *Women's lives, men's laws*, Cambridge, MA: Harvard University Press, 2007, p. 152.

2   Amihud Gilead, 'Philosophical prostitution', *Journal of Social Sciences*, Vol. 6, No. 1, 2010, p. 90.

3   Charles Schencking, *The Great Kanto Earthquake and the chimera of national reconstruction in Japan*, New York: Columbia University Press, 2013.

4   William Beasley, *The rise of modern Japan: Political, economic and social change since 1850* (revised edn), New York: St. Martin's Press, 2000, p. 122.

5   Ibid., p. 126.

6   Andrew Gordon, *A modern history of Japan: From Tokugawa times to the present*, New York; Oxford: Oxford University Press, 2003, p. 140.

7   Mark Ramseyer and Frances Rosenbluth, *The politics of oligarchy: Institutional choice in imperial Japan*, Cambridge: Cambridge University Press, 1998, pp. 160–161.

8   Tetsuo Najita, *Japan: The intellectual foundations of modern Japanese politics*, Chicago; London: University of Chicago Press, 1974, p. 103.

9   Janet Hunter, *Concise dictionary of modern Japanese history*, Berkeley; Los Angeles; London: University of California Press, 1984, p. 217.

10  Elise Tipton, *Modern Japan: A social and political history*, London: Routledge, 2002, p. 109.

11  Carol Gluck, 'Introduction', in Carol Gluck and Stephen Graubard (eds), *Showa: The Japan of Hirohito*, New York; London: W.W. Norton & Company, 1992, p. xiii.

12  Barbara Sato, *The new Japanese woman: Modernity, media, and women in interwar Japan*, Durham; London: Duke University Press, 2003; Miriam Silverberg, 'The modern girl as militant', in Gail Bernstein (ed), *Recreating Japanese women, 1600–1945*, Berkeley, Los Angeles and Oxford: University of California Press, 1991, pp. 239–266.

13  Sato, *The new Japanese woman*, p. 27.

14  Janet Hunter, 'Women's labour force participation in interwar Japan', *Japan Forum*, Vol. 2, No. 1, 1990, p. 107.

15  Muta Kazue, 'The new woman in Japan', in Margaret Beetham and Ann Heilmann (eds), *New woman hybridities: Femininity, feminism, and international consumer culture, 1880–1930*, London: Routledge, 2004, p. 2017.

16  See Frances Olsen, 'Statutory rape: A feminist critique of rights analysis', *Texas Law Review*, Vol. 63, No. 3, 1984, pp. 393–394: 'For many years women were forced into unequal and oppressive "community" under the control first of their fathers and then of their husbands. Nor is forced community just a problem of the past for women. Men force community upon women when they make sexual advances to coworkers and subordinates or pester women strangers with unwelcomed conversations. A rapist may believe he is seeking community with his victim, especially if she is his wife or social friend'.

17  Joan Kelly, *Women, history and theory: The essays of Joan Kelly*, Chicago: University of Chicago Press, 1984, p. 17.

18  Sheila Jeffreys, *The spinster and her enemies: Feminism and sexuality, 1880–1930*, North Melbourne: Spinifex Press, 1997, p. 192.

19  Iwata Shigenori, 'Nihonjin dansei no sei koudou to sei ishiki', *Rekishi Hyouron*, Vol. 4, 1998, p. 36.

20  Vanessa B. Ward, 'A Christian challenge: Chou Takeda Kiyoko and feminist thought in modern Japan', *Women's History Review*, Vol. 21, No. 2, 2012, pp. 281–299.

21  Mark Ramseyer, 'Indentured prostitution in imperial Japan: Credible commitments in the commercial sex industry', *The Journal of Law, Economics, & Organization*, Vol. 7, No. 1, 1991, p. 113.

22  Ibid., p. 91.

23  Ibid., p. 106.

24  Ibid., p. 92.

25  Sheldon Garon, *Molding Japanese minds: The state in everyday life*, Princeton, NJ: Princeton University Press, 1997, p. 95.

26  Ibid., p. 96.

27  Ibid., p. 92.

28  Ibid., p. 107.

29  Elise Tipton, 'Cleansing the nation: Urban entertainments and moral reform in interwar Japan', *Modern Asian Studies*, Vol. 42, No. 4, 2008, p. 722.

30  Miriam Silverberg, *Erotic grotesque nonsense: The mass culture of Japanese modern times*, Berkeley: University of California Press, 2007, p. 75.

31  Onozawa Akane, *Kindai Nihon shakai to koushou seido: Minshuushi to kokusai kankeishi no shiten kara*, Tokyo: Yoshikawa Koubunkan, 2010, p. 717. See also Yoshida Hidehiro, 'Nihon baishun shi: Henkan to sono haikei (2) Taisho/Showa shoki no baishun joukyou: Sono haikei to torishimari', *Jiyuu*, Vol. 41(12), No. 478, 1999, p. 141 for indication that customers could pay a fee to *kafe* proprietors to take women outside the venues.

32  Miriam Silverberg, 'The cafe waitress serving modern Japan', in Stephen Vlastos, *Mirror of modernity: Invented traditions of modern Japan*, Berkeley: University of California Press, 1998, p. 225.

33  Tanikawa Mitsue, *Mono iwanu shougitachi: Sapporo yuukaku hiwa*, Sapporo-shi: Miyama Shobou, 1984, pp. 116–120.

34  Hayakawa Noriyo, 'Koushou sei to sono shuuhen: Tokyo-fu wo chuushin ni', *Sensou Sekinin Kenkyuu*, Vol. 17, 1997, pp. 56–58.

35  Fujino Yutaka, *Sei no kokka kanri: Bai-baishun no kin-gendaishi*, Tokyo: Fuji Shuppan, 2001, p. 63.

36  Onozawa, *Kindai Nihon shakai to koushou seido*, p. 82.

37  Ibid., p. 97.

38  Takao Fukumi, *Teito ni okeru baiin no kenkyuu* (reprinted 1999), Tokyo: Hakubunkan, 1928, p. 226.

39  Onozawa, *Kindai Nihon shakai to koushou seido*.

40  Hata Ikuhiko, *Ianfu to senjou no sei*, Tokyo: Shinchousha, 1999, p. 28 notes advance payments were less than brothels, and age restrictions more loosely enforced than for brothels.

41  See Masanao Kurahashi, *Juugun ianfu to koushou seido: Juugun ianfu mondai sairon*, Tokyo: Kyouei Shobou, 2010; Ryuuji Takasaki, *100-satsu ga kataru 'ianjo', otoko no honne: Ajia zen ' iki ni 'ianjo' ga atta*, Tokyo: Nashinokisha, 1994, p. 124.

42  Kate Millet, *Sexual politics*, New York: Ballantine, 1970, p. 122.

43  Ibid., p. 279.

44  Andrea Dworkin, *Pornography: Men possessing women*, New York: Perigee Books, 1981, p. 207.

45  Ibid., p. 207.

46  Ibid., p. 208.

47  Ann Snitow, Christine Stansell and Sharon Thompson, *Powers of desire: The politics of sexuality*, New York: Monthly Review Press, 1983.

48  Cecilia Segawa Seigle et al., *A courtesan's day: Hour by hour*, Amsterdam: Hotei, 2004; J.E. De Becker, *The Nightless city, or the history of the Yoshiwara yuukaku*, Tokyo: Charles E. Tuttle, 1971; Liza Dalby, *Geisha*, London: Vintage, 2000.

49  Shimojuu Kiyoshi, *'Miuri' no Nihon shi: Jinshin baibai kara nenki-boukou e*, Tokyo: Yoshikawa Koubunkan, 2012.

50  Sone Hiromi, 'Prostitution and public authority in early modern Japan', in Hitomi Tonomura, Anne Walthall and Haruko Wakita (eds), *Women and class in Japanese history*, Ann Arbor: Center for Japanese Studies the University of Michigan, 1999, pp. 169–185.

51  Onozawa, *Kindai Nihon shakai to koushou seido*, p. 87.

52  Ibid., pp. 86–87.

53  Fujino, *Sei no kokka kanri*.

54  Kim Il Myon, *Nihon josei aishi: Yuujo, jorou, karayuki, ianfu no keifu*, Tokyo: Gendaishi Shuppankai, 1980, p. 259.

55 Hyunjung Choi, Carolin Klein, Min-Sup Shin; Hoon-Jin Lee, 'Posttraumatic Stress Disorder (PTSD) and Disorders of Extreme Stress (DESNOS) symptoms following prostitution and childhood abuse', *Violence Against Women*, Vol. 15, No. 8, 2009, pp. 933–951.

56 Quoted in Kim, *Nihon josei aishi*, p. 259.

57 Ibid., p. 259.

58 Fukumi, *Teito ni okeru baiin no kenkyuu*, p. 227.

59 Yoshida, 'Nihon baishun shi', p. 145.

60 Fukumi, *Teito ni okeru baiin no kenkyuu*, p. 27.

61 Kusama Yasoo, *Jokyuu to baishoufu*, Tokyo: Nihon Tosho Sentaa, 1982, p. 51.

62 Ibid., pp. 87–88.

63 Ibid., p. 287.

64 Sheila Jeffreys, *The industrial vagina: The political economy of the global sex trade*, London: Routledge, 2009, p. 155.

65 Kusama, *Jokyuu to baishoufu*, p. 28.

66 Ibid., p. 29

67 Ibid., p. 36.

68 Fujino, *Sei no kokka kanri*, p. 100.

69 Yoshida, 'Nihon baishun shi', pp. 142–143.

70 Ibid., p. 142.

71 Cited in Hata, *Ianfu to senjou no sei*, p. 35.

72 Yoshimi Kaneko, *Baishou no shakaishi*, Tokyo: Yuuzankaku, 1984, p. 12.

73 Hata, *Ianfu to senjou no sei*, p. 36.

74 Sayo Masuda (translated by G.G. Rowley), *Autobiography of a geisha*, New York: Columbia University Press, 2003, p. 51.

75 Tanikawa, *Mono iwanu shougitachi*, p. 182.

76 Hayakawa, 'Koushou sei to sono shuuhen', p. 56.

77 Ibid., p. 56.

78 Kusama, *Jokyuu to baishoufu*, pp. 262–263.

79 Tanikawa, *Mono iwanu shougitachi*, p. 102.

80 Fukumi, *Teito ni okeru baiin no kenkyuu*, p. 70.

81 Ibid., pp. 71–72.

82 Kusama, *Jokyuu to baishoufu*, p. 267.

83 Fukumi, *Teito ni okeru baiin no kenkyuu*, p. 258.

84 Kusama, *Jokyuu to baishoufu*, p. 139.

85 Ibid., p. 142.

86 Ibid., p. 122.

87 Tanikawa, *Mono iwanu shougitachi*, pp. 64–65.

88 Kanzaki Kiyoshi, 'Shoujo geisha no jinshin baibai', *Heiwa*, Vol. 1, 1955, p. 81.

89 Ibid., p. 78.

90    Tammy Heilemann and Janaki Santhiveeran, 'How do female adolescents
      cope and survive the hardships of prostitution? A content analysis of existing
      literature', *Journal of Ethnic and Cultural Diversity in Social Work*, Vol. 20, No. 1,
      2011, pp. 57–76.

91    Yoshimi, *Baishou no shakaishi*, p. 179.

92    Nishino Rumiko, 'Naze ima, Nihonjin "ianfu" na no ka?', *Baurakku Tsuushin*,
      No. 2, December 2012, p. 4.

93    Takayasu Yae, 'Onna no Rabauru kouta', in Senchuu-ha Group (eds), *Zoku
      senchuu-ha no yuigon*, Tokyo: Kai Shobou, 1979.

94    Kinoshita Naoko, 'For the sake of encounters with Japanese "comfort women"
      victims', in Iwasaki Minoru, Chen Kuan-Hsing and Yoshimi Shunya (eds),
      *Cultural Studies de Yomitoku Asia*, Tokyo: Serica Shobo, 2011, p. 120.

95    Hirai Kazuko, 'Zasshi ni hyoushou sareta Nihonjin "ianfu" kara miete kuru
      mono', p. 10 presentation handout on file with author 29 September 2012,
      VAWWRAC Soukai Shimpojiumu, 'Nihon jin 'ianfu' no higai jitai ni semaru!'.

96    Nishino, 'Naze ima, Nihonjin "ianfu" na no ka?', p. 5.

97    Masutomi Masaisuke, 'Gotaiten to geigi mondai', *Kakusei*, October 1915, p. 24.

98    Ibid., p. 24.

99    Ibid., p. 25.

100   Ibid., p. 24.

101   Shirota, *Mariya no sanka*, Tokyo: Nihon Kirisutokyoudan Shuppankyoku, 1971,
      pp. 25–27.

102   Masuda, *Autobiography of a geisha*.

103   Ibid., p. 76.

104   Ibid., p. 70.

105   Tanikawa, *Mono iwanu shougitachi*, pp. 8–9.

106   Korean Council for Women Drafted for Military Sexual Slavery by Japan and the
      Research Association on the Women Drafted for Military Sexual Slavery by Japan
      (translated by Young Joo Lee; edited by Keith Howard), *True stories of the Korean
      comfort women: Testimonies*, London; New York: Cassell, 1995; Peipei Qiu,
      *Chinese comfort women: Testimonies from imperial Japan's sex slaves*, New York:
      Oxford University Press, 2014.

107   Tanikawa, *Mono iwanu shougitachi*, pp. 34–35.

108   Ibid., p. 50.

109   Ibid., pp. 113–114.

110   Ibid., pp. 64–65.

111   Ibid., p. 66.

112   Ibid., p. 68.

113   Ibid., p. 68.

114   Ibid., p. 69.

115   Ibid., p. 70.

116  Ibid., p. 71.

117  Ibid., p. 71.

118  Ibid., p. 84.

119  Ibid., p. 85.

120  Ibid., p. 198.

121  Ibid., p. 199.

122  Ibid., p. 200.

123  Ibid., p. 201.

124  Ibid., pp. 34–35.

125  Ibid., p. 177.

126  Ibid., p. 37.

127  Frederick R. Dickinson, *World War I and the triumph of a new Japan, 1919–1930*, Cambridge; New York: Cambridge University Press, 2013.

128  Miho Matsugu argues that, '[g]eisha were governed by contracts similar to those for prostitutes, by which male family heads transferred the women to their new owners'. 'In the service of the nation: Geisha and Kawabata Yasunari's Snow Country', in *The courtesan's arts: Cross-cultural perspectives*, New York: Oxford University Press, 2006, p. 246.

# Chapter 3

1  Yoshimi Kaneko, *Baishou no shakaishi*, Tokyo: Yuuzankaku, 1992, p. 37.

2  Shimokawa Koushi and Hayashi Hiroko, *Yuukaku o miru*, Tokyo: Chikuma Shobou, 2010, p. 95.

3  Quoted in Kano Mikiyo, 'The problem with the "comfort women problem"', *Ampo: Japan-Asia Quarterly Review*, Vol. 24, No. 2, 1993, p. 42.

4  Suzuki Yuuko, 'Ima, mimi kakete kioku kizumu toku', *Human Rights*, Vol. 111, 1997, p. 26.

5  Onozawa Akane, 'Shiryou ni miru Nihonjin "ianfu" no choushuu no jitai', VAWW-RAC Soukai Shinpojiumu, 'Nihon jin 'ianfu' no higai jitai ni semeru!', 29 September 2012, presentation handout on file with author, p. 5.

6  Yoshiaki Yoshimi and Suzanne O'Brien, *Comfort women: Sexual slavery in the Japanese military during World War II*, New York; Chichester: Columbia University Press, 2000, p. 142.

7  Michael A. Barnhart, 'Japan's economic security and the origins of the pacific war', *Journal of Strategic Studies*, Vol. 4, No. 2, 1981, p. 108.

8  Kerry Douglas Smith, *A time of crisis: Japan, the great depression, and rural revitalization*, Cambridge: Harvard University Asia Center; distributed by Harvard University Press, 2001, p. 326.

9    Minami Orihara and Gregory Clancey, 'The Nature of Emergency: The Great Kanto earthquake and the crisis of reason in late imperial Japan', *Science in Context*, Vol. 25, 2012, pp. 103–126.

10   Richard J. Smethurst, *A social basis for prewar Japanese militarism: The army and the rural community*, Berkeley: University of California Press, 1974, p. 8.

11   Iwata Shigenori, 'Nihonjin dansei no sei koudou to sei ishiki', *Rekishi Hyouron*, Vol. 4, 1998, p. 163.

12   J.A. Mangan and Takeshi Komagome, 'Militarism, sacrifice and emperor worship: The expendable male body in fascist Japanese martial culture', *The International Journal of the History of Sport*, Vol. 16, No. 4, 1999, p. 192.

13   Yoshimitsu Khan, 'Schooling Japan's imperial subjects in the early Showa period', *History of Education: Journal of the History of Education Society*, Vol. 29, No. 3, 2000, p. 220.

14   Jeremy Phillipps, 'City and empire – Local identity and regional imperialism in 1930s Japan', *Urban History*, Vol. 35, No. 1, 2008, p. 120.

15   Ibid., p. 124.

16   Emily Horner, 'Kamishibai as propaganda in wartime Japan', *Storytelling, Self, Society*, Vol. 2, No. 1, 2005, p. 21.

17   Ibid., pp. 21–31.

18   See Suzuki Yuuko, '*Jugun ianfu*' *mondai to seibouryoku*, Tokyo: Miraisha, 1993.

19   Melissa Farley, *Prostitution and trafficking in Nevada: Making the connections*, San Francisco: Prostitution Research & Education, 2007.

20   Kano, 'The problem with the "comfort women problem"', p. 41.

21   Iwata, 'Nihonjin dansei no sei koudou to sei ishiki', p. 29.

22   Ibid., p. 36.

23   Ibid., p. 38.

24   Iwata Shigenori, 'Yobai to kaishun', *Nihon Minzoku Gaku*, Vol. 158, No. 186, 1991, p. 160.

25   Ibid., p. 160.

26   Ibid., pp. 147–149.

27   Ibid., p. 150.

28   Ibid., p. 150.

29   Ibid., p. 158.

30   Yoshida Hidehiro, 'Nihon baishun shi: Henkan to sono haikei (2) Taisho/Showa shoki no baishun joukyou: Sono haikei to torishimari', *Jiyuu*, Vol. 41(12), No. 478, 1999, p. 147.

31   Mark Forbes, 'Sex city', *The Age*, 1 March 1999, p. 11.

32   Kusama Yasoo, *Jokyuu to baishoufu*, Tokyo: Nihon Tosho Sentaa, 1982, p. 9.

33   Ibid., p. 11.

34   Ibid., p. 13.

35  Iwata, 'Nihonjin dansei no sei koudou to sei ishiki', p. 36.

36  Ibid., p. 28.

37  Iwata Shigenori, 'Nihon dansei to sei koudou to sei ishiki: 1910-1930 nendai wo chuushin ni', *Rekishi Hyouron*, Vol. 4, 1998, p. 28.

38  Itou Takashi, 'Nihon kaigun ianjo no rekishi teki hakken', *Toitsu Hyouron*, Vol. 411, 1999, p. 65.

39  Koga Noriko, 'Okinawa-sen in okeru Nihon gun "ianfu" seido no tenkai (2)', *Sensou Sekinin Kenkyuu*, Vol. 61, 2008, p. 68.

40  Toshiyuki Tanaka, *Japan's comfort women: Sexual slavery and prostitution during World War II and the U.S. occupation*, London: Routledge, 2000, p. 59.

41  Fujino Yutaka, *Sei no kokka kanri: Bai-baishun no kin-gendaishi*, Tokyo: Fuji Shuppan, 2001, p. 148.

42  Kanzaki Kiyoshi, *Baishun: Ketteiban Kanzaki repouto*, Tokyo: Gendaishi Shuppankai, 1974, p. 20.

43  Ibid., p. 22.

44  Ibid., p. 23.

45  Ibid.

46  Melissa Farley, Emily Schuckman, Jacqueline M. Golding, Kristen Houser, Laura Jarrett, Peter Qualliotine and Michele Decker, 'Comparing sex buyers with men who don't buy sex: "You can have a good time with the servitude" vs. "You're supporting a system of degradation"', paper presented at Psychologists for Social Responsibility Annual Meeting, 15 July 2011, Boston; San Francisco: Prostitution Research & Education, 2011, http://www.prostitutionresearch.com/pdfs/Farleyetal2011ComparingSexBuyers.pdf

47  Andrea Dworkin, *Pornography: Men possessing women*, London: The Women's Press, 1981.

48  Melissa Farley and Vanessa Kelly, 'Prostitution: A critical review of the medical and social sciences literature', *Women & Criminal Justice*, Vol. 11, No. 4, 2000, p. 54.

49  Rae Langton, *Sexual solipsism: Philosophical essays on pornography and objectification*, Oxford: Oxford University Press, 2009.

50  Catharine MacKinnon, 'Rape, genocide, and women's human rights', *Harvard Women's Law Journal*, Vol. 17, 1994, p. 13.

51  Mark Driscoll, *Absolute erotic, absolute grotesque: The living, dead, and undead in Japan's imperialism, 1895–1945*, Durham: Duke University Press, 2010, p. 185.

52  Mark McLelland, *Love, sex, and democracy in Japan during the American occupation*, New York: Palgrave Macmillan, 2012.

53  Stewart Lone, 'The Japanese Military during the Russo-Japanese War, 1904–05: A reconsideration of command politics and public images', STICERD/International Studies, Discussion Paper No. IS/98/351, 1998, p. 15, http://www.russojapanesewar.com/aspects.pdf

54  Stewart Lone, *Provincial life and the military in imperial Japan: The phantom samurai*, Abington: Routledge, 2010, p. 49.

55  Naoko Shimazu, *Japanese society at war: Death, memory and the Russo-Japanese war*, Cambridge; New York: Cambridge University Press, 2009, p. 90.

56  Maki Fukuoka, 'Selling portrait photographs: Early photographic business in Asakusa, Japan', *History of Photography*, Vol. 35, No. 4, 2011, p. 368.

57  Korean Council for Women Drafted for Military Sexual Slavery by Japan and the Research Association on the Women Drafted for Military Sexual Slavery by Japan, (translated by Young Joo Lee; edited by Keith Howard), *True stories of the Korean comfort women: Testimonies*, London; New York: Cassell, 1995, p. 189.

58  Senda Kakou, *Juugun ianfu*, Tokyo: Koudansha, 1993, p. 142.

59  Bang-Soon L. Yoon, 'Imperial Japan's comfort women from Korea: History & politics of silence-breaking', *Journal of Northeast Asian History*, Vol. 7, No. 1, 2010, p. 15.

60  Cynthia H. Enloe, *Bananas, beaches & bases: Making feminist sense of international politics*, Berkeley: University of California Press, 1990.

61  Junichi Saga, *Memories of silk and straw: A self-portrait of small-town Japan*, Tokyo; New York: Kodansha International; Distributed in the U.S. through Harper & Row, 1987, p. 165.

62  Fujime Yuuki, *Sei no rekishigaku: Koushou seido, dataizai taisei kara baishun boushihou, yuusei hogohou taisei e*, Tokyo: Fuji Shuppan, 1997, p. 147.

63  Ibid., p. 147.

64  Imanaka Yasuko, 'Guntai to koushou seido', in Hayakawa Noriyo (ed), *Shokuminchi to sensou sekinin*, Tokyo: Yoshikawa Koubunkan, 2005, p. 42.

65  Shimazu, *Japanese society at war*, p. 38.

66  Imanaka, 'Guntai to koushou seido', p. 47.

67  Ibid., p. 42.

68  Lone, *Provincial life and the military in imperial Japan*.

69  Shimokawa and Hayashi, *Yuukaku o miru*, p. 95.

70  Kanzaki, *Baishun: Ketteiban Kanzaki repouto*, p. 19.

71  Fukuda Toshiko, *Yoshiwara wa konna tokoro de gozaimashita: Kuruwa no onnatachi no shouwashi*, Tokyo: Bungensha, 2004, p. 137.

72  Kanzaki, *Baishun: Ketteiban Kanzaki repouto*, pp. 75–77.

73  Ibid., p. 114.

74  Fukuda Toshiko, *Yoshiwara wa konna tokoro de gozaimashita*, p. 133.

75  Ibid., p. 134.

76  Tanikawa Mitsue, *Mono iwanu shougitachi: Sapporo yuukaku hiwa*, Sapporo-shi: Miyama Shobou, 1984, p. 126.

77  Ibid., p. 53.

78  Kanzaki, *Baishun: Ketteiban Kanzaki repouto*, p. 19.

79  Yoshida, 'Nihon baishun shi', p. 148.

80  Hirai Kazuko, 'Zasshi ni hyoushou sareta Nihonjin "ianfu" kara miete kuru mono', p. 10 in presentation notes on file with author, 29 September 2012, VAWW-RAC Soukai Shinpojiumu, 'Nihon jin 'ianfu' no higai jitai ni semeru!'.

81  Onozawa Akane, 'Shiryou ni miru Nihonjin "ianfu" no choushuu no jitai', p. 6 in presentation notes on file with author, 29 September 2012, VAWW-RAC Soukai Shinpojiumu, 'Nihon jin 'ianfu' no higai jitai ni semeru!'.

82  Ogino Fujio, 'Toyama ken in okeru "roumu ianfu" ni tsuite', *Sensou Sekinin Kenkyuu*, Vol. 6, 1994, p. 66.

83  Ibid.

84  Onozawa Akane, *Kindai Nihon shakai to koushou seido: Minshuushi to kokusai kankeishi no shiten kara*, Tokyo: Yoshikawa Koubunkan, 2010, p. 238.

85  Ibid., p. 256.

86  Ibid., pp. 241–242.

87  Ibid., p. 244.

88  Ibid., p. 250.

89  Ibid.

90  Ibid., p. 251.

91  Ibid., p. 254.

92  Ibid., p. 255.

93  Ibid., p. 252.

94  Ibid., p. 265.

95  Ibid., p. 279.

96  Ibid.

97  Ibid., p. 256.

98  Ibid., p. 255.

99  Yun Chung-ok and Suzuki Yuuko, *Heiwa o kikyuushite: 'Ianfu' higaisha no songen kaifuku e no ayumi*, Musashino-shi: Hakutakusha, 2003, pp. 54–55.

# Chapter 4

1  Suzuki Yuuko, *Chousenjin juugun ianfu: Shougen Showa shi no danmen*, Tokyo: Iwanami Shoten, 1991, pp. 2–3.

2  Okamura Toshihiko quoted in Kano Mikiyo, 'The problem with the "comfort women problem"', *Ampo: Japan-Asia Quarterly Review*, Vol. 24, No. 2, 1993, p. 42.

3  Quoted in Ryuuji Takasaki, *100-satsu ga kataru 'ianjo', otoko no honne: Ajia zen' iki ni 'ianjo' ga atta*, Tokyo: Nashinokisha, 1994, p. 74.

4  On the Chinese mainland at least. See Masanao Kurahashi, *Kita no karayukisan*, Tokyo: Kyouei Shobou, 1989, p. 76.

5  Mark Driscoll, *Absolute erotic, absolute grotesque: The living, dead, and undead in Japan's imperialism, 1895–1945*, Durham: Duke University Press, 2010, p. 61

suggests Chinese traffickers were initially involved but this claim is unusual in the literature.

6  Kurahashi, *Kita no karayukisan*, p. 120.

7  MacMillan Reference Books, *Japan: An illustrated encyclopedia*, Kodansha, 1993, p. 748.

8  Kurahashi, *Kita no karayukisan*, p. 40.

9  Ibid., p. 66.

10  Ibid., p. 54.

11  Ibid., p. 126.

12  Ibid., p. 73.

13  Stephanie Limoncelli, *The politics of trafficking: The first international movement to combat the sexual exploitation of women*, Stanford: Stanford University Press, 2010, p. 85.

14  Kurahashi, *Kita no karayukisan*, p. 77.

15  Ibid., p. 101; Yoshimi Kaneko, *Baishou no shakaishi*, Tokyo: Yuuzankaku, 1984, p. 179 notes that women were first trafficked out of sex industry districts in northern areas of Kyuushu like Nagasaki into comfort stations abroad.

16  Tanikawa Mitsue, *Mono iwanu shougitachi: Sapporo yuukaku hiwa*, Sapporo-shi: Miyama Shobou, 1984, p. 165.

17  Yun Chung-ok and Suzuki Yuuko, *Heiwa o kikyuushite: 'Ianfu' higaisha no songen kaifuku e no ayumi*, Musashino-shi: Hakutakusha, 2003.

18  Hirao Hiroko, 'Senji ka "Shina tokou fujo" no ki', *Sensou Sekinin Kenkyuu*, Vol. 61, 2008, p. 13.

19  Ibid.

20  Suki Falconberg, 'Where in the name of all that is holy are the comfort women? An open letter to Ken Burns on "the War – An intimate history"', 28 September 2007, http://womensspace.wordpress.com/2007/10/02/where-in-gods-name-are-the-comfort-women-an-open-letter-to-ken-burns-on-the-war-an-intimate-history/

21  Julie Cwikel and Elizabeth Hoban, 'Contentious issues in research on trafficked women working in the sex industry: Study design, ethics, and methodology', *Journal of Sex Research*, Vol. 42, No. 4, p. 307.

22  Song Youn-ok, 'Nihon no shokuminchi shihai to kokka teki kanri baishun: Chousen no koushou wo chuushin ni shite', *Chousen Shi Kenkyuu Kai Ronbun Shuu*, Vol. 32, 1994, p. 85.

23  Kurahashi, *Kita no karayukisan*, p. 52.

24  Driscoll, *Absolute erotic, absolute grotesque*, p. 61.

25  Kurahashi Masanao, *Juugun ianfu mondai no rekishiteki kenkyuu: Baishunfugata to seiteki doreigata*, Tokyo: Kyouei Shobou, 1994.

26  Kim Il Myon, *Guntai ianfu: Sensou to ningen no kiroku*, Tokyo: Gendaishi Shuppankai, 1977, pp. 70–73.

27 Onozawa Akane, *Kindai Nihon shakai to koushou seido: Minshuuishi to kokusai kankeishi no shiten kara*, Tokyo: Yoshikawa Koubunkan, 2010, pp. 49, 53.

28 Kim Pu-ja and Song Youn-ok, *'Ianfu', senji seibouryoku no jittai*, Tokyo: Ryokufuu Shuppan, 2000, pp. 66–91; Nishino Rumiko, 'Nihonjin ianfu: Dare ga dono youni choushuu sareta ka', in VAWW-NET Japan (eds), *Nihon gun sei dorei sei wo sabaku 2000nen josei kokusai senpan houtei no kiroku: Jisshou sareta senji seibouryoku ni okeru higai to kankeisei*, Vol. 3/4, Tokyo: Rokufu Shuppan, 2000, p. 67.

29 Suzuki Yuuko, *'Jugun ianfu' mondai to seiboryoku*, Tokyo: Miraisha, 1993, p. 27.

30 Hata Ikuhiko, *Ianfu to senjou no sei*, Tokyo: Shinchousha, 1999, p. 31.

31 Fukuda Toshiko, *Yoshiwara wa konna tokoro de gozaimashita: Kuruwa no onnatachi no Showashi* (reprinted 2010), Tokyo: Shufu To Seikatsusha, 1986, p. 139.

32 See filmed comment about Chinese village chiefs supplying the Japanese army with women most likely taken from the local sex industry at 'If we don't face our past, we're bound to repeat the same mistakes'. Japanese wartime medical orderly reports on army's role in maintaining 'comfort women' system, David McNeill introduction, Matsumoto Masayoshi testimony (Japanese and English transcript and video of testimony), translation by Miguel Quintana, http://www.japanfocus. org/-David-McNeill/4202

33 Hirao, 'Senji ka "Shina tokou fujo" no ki', p. 11.

34 Ibid., p. 13.

35 Ibid., p. 15.

36 Korean Council for Women Drafted for Military Sexual Slavery by Japan and the Research Association on the Women Drafted for Military Sexual Slavery by Japan (translated by Young Joo Lee; edited by Keith Howard), *True stories of the Korean comfort women: Testimonies*, London; New York: Cassell, 1995, p. 190.

37 Joshua Pilzer, 'Music and dance in the Japanese military "comfort women" system: A case study in the performing arts, war, and sexual violence', *Women and Music: A Journal of Gender and Culture*, Vol. 18, No. 1, pp. 1–23.

38 Yoshiaki Yoshimi and translated by Suzanne O'Brien, *Comfort women: Sexual slavery in the Japanese military during World War II*, New York; Chichester: Columbia University Press, 2000, p. 75.

39 Takasaki, *100-satsu ga kataru 'ianjo', otoko no honne*, p. 147.

40 Korean Council for Women Drafted for Military Sexual Slavery by Japan and the Research Association on the Women Drafted for Military Sexual Slavery by Japan, *True stories of the Korean comfort women*, p. 74.

41 Joshua Pilzer, 'Music and dance in the Japanese military "comfort women" system: A case study in the performing arts, war, and sexual violence', *Women and Music: A Journal of Gender and Culture*, Vol. 18, 2014, p. 4.

42 Hayashi Hirofumi, 'Sensou taiken ki/butai shi ni miru "juugun ianfu"', *Sensou Sekinin Kenkyuu*, Vol. 5, 1994, p. 31.

43 Hon Yun Shin, 'Okinawa sen to Chousenjin "ianfu"', in Nikkan Kyoudou 'Nihon gun ianjo' Miyakojima Chousadan (eds), *Senjyou no Miyakojima to 'ianjo'*, Okinawa: Nanyou Bunko, 2009, p. 27.

44 Tamai Noriko, *Hinomaru o koshi ni maite: Tekka shoufu, Takanashi Taka ichidaiki*, Tokyo: Gendaishi Shuppankai, 1984, p. 41.

45 Tanikawa, *Mono iwanu shougitachi*, p. 211.

46 Tamai, *Hinomaru o koshi ni maite*, p. 74.

47 Tamai, 'Okinawa sen in okeru Nihon gun "ianfu" seido no tenkai (4)', p. 63.

48 Peipei Qiu, Zhiliang Su and Lifei Chen, *Chinese comfort women: Testimonies from imperial Japan's sex slaves*, New York: Oxford University Press, 2014.

49 Yoshimi and O'Brien, *Comfort women*, p. 58.

50 Ibid., p. 44.

51 Hayashi Hirofumi, 'The structure of Japanese imperial government involvement in the military comfort women system', *Kanto Gakuin University*, p. 6, http://opac.kanto-gakuin.ac.jp/cgi-bin/retrieve/sr_bookview.cgi/U_CHARSET.utf-8/NI10000769/Body/link/01hayashi.pdf

52 See Erik Esselstrom, *Crossing empire's edge: Foreign Ministry police and Japanese expansionism in Northeast Asia*, Honolulu: University of Hawai'i Press, 2009.

53 Hayashi Hirofumi, 'Shiberia shuppei ji ni okeru Nihon gun to "karayukisan"', *Sensou Sekinin Kenkyuu*, Vol. 24, 1999, p. 19.

54 Naoko Shimazu, *Japanese society at war: Death, memory and the Russo-Japanese war*, Cambridge; New York: Cambridge University Press, 2009, p. 90.

55 Hayakawa Noriyo, '"Juugun ianfu" seiko no rekishi teki haikei ni tsuite', *Hou no Kagaku*, Vol. 23, 1995, p. 126.

56 Onoda Hiroo, 'Watashi ga mita juugunianfu no seitai', *Seiron*, Vol. 392, 2005, pp. 142–149.

57 Koga, 'Okinawa sen ni okeru Nihon gun "ianfu" seido no tenkai(4)', p. 69.

58 Yoshimi and O'Brien, *Comfort women*, p. 61.

59 Hayashi, 'Sensou taiken ki ni miru "juugun ianfu"', p. 24.

60 Ibid., p. 25.

61 Hayashi Hirofumi, 'Rikugun ianjo kanri no ichi sokumen: Eisei sakku no koufu shiryou wo tegakari ni', *Sensou Sekinin Kenkyuu*, Vol. 1, No. 1, 1993, pp. 12–19.

62 Ibid., pp. 12–19.

63 George L. Hicks, *The comfort women*, St. Leonards, NSW: Allen & Unwin, 1995, p. 61.

64 Yasuhara Keiko, 'Bunseki ripouto: Ianfu ni tsuite', in Juugun Ianfu 110ban Henshuu Iinkai (eds), *Juugun ianfu 110ban: Denwa no mukou kara rekishi no koe ga*, Tokyo: Akaishi Shoten, 1992, p. 105.

65 Quoted in Takasaki, *100-satsu ga kataru 'ianjo', otoko no honne*, p. 48.

66 Catharine MacKinnon, *Are women human?: And other international dialogues*, Cambridge: Belknap Press of Harvard University Press, 2006, p. 114.

67   Ibid.

68   Catharine MacKinnon, 'Rape, genocide, and women's human rights', *Harvard Women's Law Journal*, Vol. 17, 1994, p. 10.

69   Chushichi Tsuzuki, *The pursuit of power in modern Japan, 1825–1995*, Oxford: Oxford University Press, 2000, p. 128.

70   Paul R. Katz, 'Germs of disaster: The impact of epidemics on Japanese military campaigns in Taiwan, 1874 and 1895', *Annales de Demographie Historique*, 1996, p. 195.

71   Atsushi Koukeshi, *Kenpei seiji: Kanshi to doukatsu no jidai*, Tokyo: Shin Nippon Shuppan Sha, 2008, p. 175.

72   Ibid., p. 121.

73   Janet Hunter, *Concise dictionary of modern Japanese history*, Tokyo: Kodansha International, 1984, p. 183.

74   MacMillan Reference Books, *Japan: An illustrated encyclopedia*, p. 1427.

75   Matsuda Toshihiko, 'Kindai Nihon shokuminchi ni okeru "kenpei kesatsu seido" ni miru "touji youshiki no sen'i": Chousen kara Kantoushuu "Manushuukoku" he', pp. 469–490, http://shikon.nichibun.ac.jp/dspace/bitstream/123456789/870/1/nk35019.pdf

76   Mark Metzler, *Lever of empire: The international gold standard and the crisis of liberalism in prewar Japan*, Berkeley: University of California Press, 2006, p. 56.

77   Edward J. Drea, *In the service of the Emperor: Essays on the Imperial Japanese Army*, Lincoln: University of Nebraska Press, 1998, p. 57.

78   Otabe Yuuji, Hayashi Hirofumi and Yamada Akira, *Kiiwaado Nihon no sensou hanzai*, Tokyo: Yuzankaku, 1995, pp. 36.

79   Ibid., p. 31.

80   Beatrice Trefalt, *Japanese Army stragglers and memories of the war in Japan, 1950–75*, London: Routledge Curzon, 2003, p. 25.

81   Yoshimi and O'Brien, *Comfort women*, p. 44.

82   Ibid., p. 57.

83   Suzuki Yuuko, 'Sekando reipu ni hoka naranai', *Sekai*, Vol. 632, 1997, p. 50.

84   Kamitsubo Takashi, *Mizuko no uta: Dokyumento hikiage koji to onnatachi*, Tokyo: Shakai Shisosha, 1993.

85   Hirota Kazuko, *Shougen kiroku juugun ianfu, kangofu: Senjou ni ikita onna no doukoku*, Tokyo: Shin Jinbutsu Ouraisha, 1975.

86   See Takasaki, *100-satsu ga kataru 'ianjo', otoko no honne*, p. 56.

87   Juugun Ianfu 110-ban Henshuu Iinkai, *Juugun ianfu 110-ban: Denwa no mukou kara rekishi no koe ga*, Tokyo: Akashi Shoten, 1992, p. 106.

88   Korean Council for Women Drafted for Military Sexual Slavery by Japan and the Research Association on the Women Drafted for Military Sexual Slavery by Japan, *True stories of the Korean comfort women*, p. 85.

89  Itou Takashi, 'Nihon kaigun ianjo', *Touitsu Hyouron*, Vol. 411, 1999, p. 56.

90  Kawada Fumiko, *Kougun ianjo no onnatachi*, Tokyo: Chikuma Shobou, 1993.

91  Onozawa, *Kindai Nihon shakai to koushou seido*, p. 255.

92  Ibid., p. 245.

93  Ibid., p. 253.

94  Saburou Ienaga, *The Pacific War: World War II and the Japanese, 1931–1945*, New York: Pantheon Books, 1978, p. 51.

95  J.A. Mangan and Takeshi Komagome, 'Militarism, sacrifice and emperor worship: The expendable male body in fascist Japanese martial culture', *The International Journal of the History of Sport*, Vol. 16, No. 4, 1999, p. 192.

96  Korean Council for Women Drafted for Military Sexual Slavery by Japan and the Research Association on the Women Drafted for Military Sexual Slavery by Japan, *True stories of the Korean comfort women*, p. 34.

97  Saburou Ienaga, *The Pacific War: World War II and the Japanese, 1931–1945*, New York: Pantheon Books, 1978, p. 53.

98  Suzuki Yuuko and Kondou Kazuko, *Onna, tennousei, sensou*, Tokyo: Orijin Shuppan Sentaa, 1989, pp. 209–210.

99  Tanikawa, *Mono iwanu shougitachi*, p. 46.

100  Ibid., pp. 56–57.

101  Tamai, *Hinomaru o koshi ni maite*, p. 122.

102  Korean Council for Women Drafted for Military Sexual Slavery by Japan and the Research Association on the Women Drafted for Military Sexual Slavery by Japan, *True stories of the Korean comfort women*, p. 43.

103  Nishino Rumiko, 'Nihon jin "ianfu" no shoguu to tokuchou', VAWW-RAC Soukai Shinojiumu, Nihon jin 'ianfu' no choushuu/taiguu/sengo, 21 September 2012, presentation handout on file with author.

104  Sheila Jeffreys, 'Prostitution', in Dusty Rhodes and Sandra McNeil (eds), *Women against violence against women*, London: Onlywomen Press, 1985, p. 68.

105  Nishino, 'Nihon jin "ianfu" no shoguu to tokuchou', VAWW-RAC Soukai Shinojiumu, Nihon jin 'ianfu' no choushuu/taiguu/sengo, 21 September 2012, presentation handout on file with author.

106  Hirota, *Shougen kiroku juugun ianfu, kangofu*.

107  Nishino, 'Nihon jin "ianfu" no shoguu to tokuchou', VAWW-RAC Soukai Shinojiumu, Nihon jin 'ianfu' no choushuu/taiguu/sengo, 21 September 2012, presentation handout on file with author.

108  Sheila Jeffreys, *The idea of prostitution*, North Melbourne: Spinifex Press, 2008, p. 200.

109  Judith Herman, 'Introduction: Hidden in plain sight: Clinical observations on prostitution', in Melissa Farley (ed), *Prostitution, trafficking and traumatic stress*, Binghamton: Haworth Maltreatment & Trauma Press, 2003, p. 2.

110   Iwata Shigenori, 'Nihonjin dansei no sei koudou to sei ishiki', *Rekishi Hyouron*, Vol. 4, No. 576, 1998, p. 30.

111   Juugun Ianfu 110-ban Henshuu Iinkai, *Juugun ianfu 110-ban*, p. 72.

112   Ibid., p. 69.

113   Takasaki, *100-satsu ga kataru 'ianjo', otoko no honne*, p. 53.

114   Ibid., p. 115.

115   Kasahara Tokushi, 'Nihon gun Nihon hei ni yoru sei bouryoku no ishiki to kouzou', *Rekishigaku Hyouron*, Vol. 849, p. 13.

116   Suzuki Masahiro, 'Sensou ni okeru dansei no sekushuariti', in Ningen to Sei Kyouiku Kenkyuu Kyougikai 'Dansei Keisei Kenkyuu' Purojekuto (eds), *Nihon no otoko wa doko kara kite doko e iku no ka: Dansei sekushuariti keisei 'kyoudou kenkyuu'*, Tokyo: Juugatsusha, 2001, p. 105.

117   Koga, 'Okinawa sen ni okeru Nihon gun "ianfu" seido no tenkai (4)', p. 64.

118   Takasaki, *100-satsu ga kataru 'ianjo', otoko no honne*, p. 99.

119   Fukuda, *Yoshiwara wa konna tokoro de gozaimashita*, p. 81.

120   See, for example, Furusawa Kiyoko, 'Higashi Timooru ni okeru Nihon gun sei dorei sei', *East Timor Quarterly*, No. 3, April 2001, http://www.asahi-net. or.jp/~ak4a-mtn/news/quarterly/number3/sexslavery3.html or Kawada Fumiko, *Indoneshia no 'ianfu'*, Tokyo: Akashi Shoten, 1997.

121   Fujino Yutaka, *Sei no kokka kanri: Bai-baishun no kin-gendaishi*, Tokyo: Fuji Shuppan, 2001, p. 288.

122   Sorano Yoshihiro, 'Kitachousen moto juugun ianfu shougen', *Ekonomisuto*, Vol. 70, No. 49, 1992, p. 34.

123   Nishino Rumiko, *Juugun ianfu no hanashi: Juudai no anata e no messeeji*, Tokyo: Akashi Shoten, 1993, pp. 59–60.

124   The Korean Council for the Women Drafted for Military Sexual Slavery by Japan, 'Bark Young Sim', http://www.womenandwar.net/bbs_eng/index.php?tbl=M0402 8&cat=&mode=V&id=7&SN=0&SK=&SW=.

125   Sorano, 'Kitachousen moto juugun ianfu shougen', p. 34.

126   The Korean Council for the Women Drafted for Military Sexual Slavery by Japan and Gang Duk-Gyung, 'From the women's volunteer labour corps to a comfort station', http://www.womenandwar.net/bbs_eng/index.php?tbl=M04028&cat=& mode=V&id=5&SN=0&SK=&SW==.

127   Itou, 'Nihon kaigun ianjo no rekishi teki hakken', p. 67.

128   Koga Noriko, 'Okinawa-sen in okeru Nihon gun "ianfu" seido no tenkai 2', *Sensou Sekinin Kenkyuu*, Vol. 61, 2008, p. 64.

129   Tanikawa, *Mono iwanu shougitachi*, p. 180.

130   Yun and Suzuki, *Heiwa o kikyuushite*, p. 19.

131   Tanikawa, *Mono iwanu shougitachi*, p. 184.

132   Mary Daly, *Gyn/ecology: The metaethics of radical feminism*, Boston: Beacon Press, 1978.

# Chapter 5

1   Janice G. Raymond, *Not a choice, not a job: Exposing the myths about prostitution and the global sex trade*, North Melbourne: Spinifex, 2013, p. 23.

2   Peipei Qiu, *Chinese comfort women: Testimonies from imperial Japan's sex slaves*, New York: Oxford University Press, 2014.

3   Chizuko Ueno (translated by Beverley Yamamoto), *Nationalism and gender*, Melbourne: Trans Pacific Press Melbourne, 2003, p. 81.

4   Suzuki Yuuko and Kondou Kazuko, *Onna, tennousei, sensou*, Tokyo: Orijin Shuppan Sentaa, 1989, pp. 207–208.

5   Yoshiaki Yoshimi and translated by Suzanne O'Brien, *Comfort women: Sexual slavery in the Japanese military during World War II*, New York; Chichester: Columbia University Press, 2000, p. 155.

6   Suzuki Yuuko, *Sensou sekinin to jendaa: 'Jiyuu shugi shikan' to Nihon gun 'ianfu' mondai*, Tokyo: Miraisha, 1997, p. 51.

7   Suzuki Yuuko, *'Jugun ianfu' mondai to seiboryoku*, Tokyo: Miraisha, 1993, p. 9.

8   Maria Höhn and Seungsook Moon (eds), *Over there: Living with the U.S. military empire from World War Two to the present*, Durham: Duke University Press, 2010, p. 42.

9   Laura Hein, 'Savage irony: The imaginative power of the "military comfort women" in the 1990s', *Gender & History*, Vol. 11, No. 2, July 1999, p. 338.

10  See Song Youn-ok, 'Nihon no shokuminchi shihai to kokka teki kanri baishun: Chousen no koushou wo chuushin ni shite', *Chousen Shi Kenkyuu Kai Ronbun Shuu*, Vol. 32, 1994, p. 60 for evidence of lack of education among both Korean and Japanese prostituted women in Korea. Korean women were mostly illiterate, but even Japanese women had mostly dropped out of primary school or just finished primary school at best.

11  Korean Council for Women Drafted for Military Sexual Slavery by Japan and the Research Association on the Women Drafted for Military Sexual Slavery by Japan (translated by Young Joo Lee; edited by Keith Howard), *True stories of the Korean comfort women: Testimonies*, London; New York: Cassell, 1995.

12  South Korean Ministry of Gender Equality and Family, 'Japanese Military Comfort Women', http://www.hermuseum.go.kr/english/sub.asp?pid=191

13  Fujinaga Takeshi, 'Shokuminchi koushou seido to Nihon gun "ianfu" seido', in Hayakawa Noriyo (ed), *Shokuminchi to sensou sekinin*, Tokyo: Yoshikawa Koubunkan, 2005, p. 32.

14  Kurahashi Masanao, *Juugun ianfu to koushou seido: Juugun ianfu mondai sairon*, Tokyo: Kyouei Shobou, 2010, p. 110.

15  Hata Ikuhiko, *Ianfu to senjou no sei*, Tokyo: Shinchousha, 1999, p. 127.

16 Seong Yeon-cheol and Gil Yun-hyung, 'China releases documents showing Japan forcibly mobilized comfort women', *The Hankyoreh*, 25 March 2014, english.hani.co.kr/popups/print.hani?ksn=629741 3/4

17 Yoshimi, *Comfort women*, p. 110.

18 Hata, *Ianfu to senjou no sei*, p. 45.

19 The Committee for Historical Facts, 'The facts', *Washington Post*, 14 June 2007, http://en.wikipedia.org/wiki/File:The_Facts_about_the_Comfort_Women.jpg

20 Fujinaga, 'Shokuminchi koushou seido to Nihon gun "ianfu" seido', p. 32. See also Hayakawa Noriyo, 'Kaigai ni okeru baibaishun no tenkai: Taiwan wo chuushin ni', *Sensou Sekinin Kenkyuu*, Vol. 10, 1995, pp. 35–43.

21 Ueno, *Nationalism and gender*, p. 81.

22 Suzuki, *Sensou sekinin to jendaa*, p. 23.

23 Fujinaga, 'Shokuminchi koushou seido to Nihon gun "ianfu" seido', p. 16.

24 Ibid., p. 38.

25 Fujinaga Takeshi, 'Shokuminchi Taiwan ni okeru Chousen jin shakukyaku gyou to "ianfu" no douin', in Osaka Sangyou Daigaku Sangyou Kenkyuujo (ed), *Kindai shakai to baishun mondai*, Osaka: Osaka Sangyou Daigaku, 2001, p. 108.

26 Song Youn-ok, 'Nihon no shokuminchi shihai to kokka teki kanri baishun', p. 87.

27 Hata Ikuhiko, 'No organized or forced recruitment: Misconceptions about comfort women and the Japanese military', *Society for the Dissemination of Historical Fact*, 2007, http://www.sdh-fact.com/CL02_1/31_S4.pdf, p. 9.

28 Tessa Morris-Suzuki, 'Addressing Japan's "comfort women" issue from an academic standpoint', *The Asia-Pacific Journal*, Vol. 12, Issue 9, No. 1, 2 March 2014, http://www.japanfocus.org/-Tessa-Morris_Suzuki/4081

29 Fujinaga, 'Shokuminchi koushou seido to Nihon gun "ianfu" seido', p. 20.

30 Ibid., p. 29.

31 Ibid., p. 30.

32 Imanishi Hajime, *Yuujo no shakaishi: Shimabara, Yoshiwara no rekishi kara shokuminchi 'koushou' sei made*, Tokyo: Yuushisha, 2007, pp. 239–240.

33 Yamashita Yeong-ae and Yun Chung-ok, *Chousenjin josei ga mita 'ianfu mondai': Asu o tomo ni tsukuru tame ni*, Tokyo: San'ichi Shobou, 1992, p. 133.

34 Ibid., p. 134.

35 Imanishi, *Yuujo no shakaishi*, p. 259.

36 Fujinaga, 'Shokuminchi koushou seido to Nihon gun "ianfu" seido', p. 33.

37 Song Youn-ok, 'Nihon no shokuminchi shihai to kokka teki kanri baishun', p. 36.

38 Yamashita Yeong-ae, *Chousenjin josei ga mita 'ianfu mondai'*, p. 139.

39 Song Youn-ok, 'Nihon no shokuminchi shihai to kokka teki kanri baishun', p. 41.

40 Ibid., p. 42.

41 Hata, *Ianfu to senjou no sei*, p. 45.

42 Song Youn-ok, 'Nihon no shokuminchi shihai to kokka teki kanri baishun', p. 59.

43  Ibid., p. 56.

44  Ibid., p. 66.

45  Ibid.

46  Ibid.

47  Ibid.

48  Matsuoka Nobuo, 'Chosen josei no rekishi ni omou', in Takahashi Kikue (ed), *Sei shinryaku o kokuhatsu suru kiisen kankou*, Tokyo: Kiisen kankou ni hantai suru onnatachi no kai, 1974, p. 35.

49  Fujinaga, 'Shokuminchi koushou seido to Nihon gun "ianfu" seido', p. 34.

50  Yamashita Yeong-ae, *Chousenjin josei ga mita 'ianfu mondai'*, p. 34.

51  Ibid., p. 158.

52  Hata, *Ianfu to senjou no sei*, p. 43.

53  Song Youn-ok, 'Nihon no shokuminchi shihai to kokka teki kanri baishun', p. 82.

54  Ibid., p. 81.

55  Ibid., p. 85.

56  Hata, *Ianfu to senjou no sei*, p. 42.

57  Ibid., p. 45.

58  See discussion in Song Youn-ok, 'Japanese colonial rule and state-managed prostitution: Korea's licensed prostitutes', *Positions*, Vol. 5, No. 1, 1997, pp. 171–219 (note that is an English translation of Song Youn-ok, 'Nihon no shokuminchi shihai to kokka teki kanri baishun', pp. 37–87). See also Chunghee Sarah Soh, 'Women's sexual labor and state in Korean history', *Journal of Women's History*, Vol. 15, No. 4, 2004, pp. 170–177.

59  See also Kawamura Minato, *Kiisen: Mono o iu hana no bunka shi*, Tokyo: Sakuhinsha, 2001.

60  Kawamura Minato, 'Kiisen no zushou gaku', in Suwa Haruo (ed), *Ajia no sei*, Tokyo: Bensey, 1999, p. 51.

61  Ibid., p. 51.

62  Fujinaga, 'Shokuminchi koushou seido to Nihon gun "ianfu" seido', p. 33.

63  Ibid., p. 36.

64  Song Youn-ok, 'Nihon no shokuminchi shihai to kokka teki kanri baishun', p. 53.

65  Ibid., p. 53.

66  Fujinaga, 'Shokuminchi koushou seido to Nihon gun "ianfu" seido', p. 42.

67  Song Youn-ok, 'Nihon no shokuminchi shihai to kokka teki kanri baishun', p. 54.

68  Yamashita Yeong-ae, 'Nationalism and gender in the comfort women issue', *Kyoto Bulletin of Islamic Area Studies*, Vol. 3–1, July 2009, p. 213, http://www.asafas. kyoto-u.ac.jp/kias/1st_period/contents/pdf/kb3_1/14yamashita.pdf

69  Song Youn-ok, 'Nihon no shokuminchi shihai to kokka teki kanri baishun', p. 70.

70  Ibid., p. 49.

71  Ibid., p. 50.

72  Ibid., p. 51.

73   Ibid., p. 53.

74   Yun Chung-ok and Suzuki Yuuko, *Heiwa o kikyuushite: 'Ianfu' higaisha no songen kaifuku e no ayumi*, Musashino-shi: Hakutakusha, 2003, pp. 19–21.

75   Ibid., pp. 19–21.

76   Brandon Palmer, *Fighting for the enemy: Koreans in Japan's war, 1937–1945*, Seattle: University of Washington Press, 2013, pp. 3 and 145.

77   Ogino Fujio, 'Toyama ken in okeru "Roumu ianfu" ni tsuite', *Sensou Sekinin Kenkyuu*, Vol. 6, 1994, p. 66.

78   The Korean Council for the Women Drafted for Military Sexual Slavery by Japan and Gang Duk-Gyung, 'From the women's volunteer labour corps to a comfort station', http://www.womenandwar.net/bbs_eng/index.php?tbl=M04028&cat=&mode=V&id=5&SN=0&SK=&SW==

79   Commission on Human Rights, Fifty-second session, 4 January 1996, *Report of the Special Rapporteur on violence against women, its causes and consequences, Ms. Radhika Coomaraswamy, in accordance with Commission on Human Rights resolution 1994/45; Report on the mission to the Democratic People's Republic of Korea, the Republic of Korea and Japan on the issue of military sexual slavery in wartime*, http://www.macalester.edu/~tam/HIST194%20War%20Crimes/documents/UN/un%20report%20on%20violence%20against%20women,%20its%20causes%20and%20conseque.htm

80   Song Youn-ok, 'Nihon no shokuminchi shihai to kokka teki kanri baishun', p. 70.

81   Ibid., p. 50.

82   Ibid., p. 53.

83   Fujinaga, 'Shokuminchi Taiwan ni okeru Chousen jin shakukyaku gyou to "ianfu" no douin', p. 107.

84   Nishino Rumiko, 'Higai sha shougen ni miru "ianfu" renkou no kyousei sei', in 'Sensou to josei he no bouryoku' Risaachi Akushon Sentaa (eds), *'Ianfu' basshingu wo koete*, Tokyo: Ootsuki Shoten, 2013, p. 38.

85   Jin Jungwon, 'Reconsidering prostitution under the Japanese occupation', *The Review of Korean Studies*, Vol. 17, No. 1, 2014, pp. 115–157.

86   Juugun Ianfu 110-ban Henshuu Iinkai, *Juuugun ianfu 110-ban: Denwa no mukou kara rekishi no koe ga*, Tokyo: Akashi Shoten, 1992, p. 89.

87   Palmer, *Fighting for the enemy*, p. 157.

88   Ibid., p. 157.

89   Juugun Ianfu 110-ban Henshuu Iinkai, *Juuugun ianfu 110-ban: Denwa no mukou kara rekishi no koe ga*, Tokyo: Akashi Shoten, 1992, p. 89.

90   Soh, 'Women's sexual labor and state in Korean history', p. 170.

91   Juugun Ianfu 110-ban Henshuu Iinkai, *Juuugun ianfu 110-ban*, p. 89.

92   Yoshimi Yoshiaki, '"Juugun ianfu" no soushutsu to Chousen soutokufu', *Sensou Sekinin Kenkyuu*, Vol. 5, 1994, p. 33.

93    Fujinaga, 'Shokuminchi Taiwan ni okeru Chousen jin shakukyaku gyou to "ianfu" no douin', p. 107.

94    Jungwon, 'Reconsidering prostitution under the Japanese occupation', pp. 115–157.

95    Delan Zhu, *Taiwan Soutokufu to ianfu*, Tokyo: Akashi Shoten, 2005, p. 91.

96    Komagome Takeshi, 'Taiwan ni okeru mikan no datsu shokuminchi ka', in Kim Pu-ja and Nakano Toshio (eds), *Rekishi to sekinin 'ianfu' mondai to 1990nen dai*, Tokyo: Seikyuusha, 2008, pp. 152–162; Komagome Takeshi, 'Taiwan shokuminchi shihai to Taiwan jin "ianfu"', in VAWW-NET Japan (eds), *'Ianfu' senji sei bouryoku no jitai I: Nihon, Taiwan, Chosen*, Tokyo: Ryokufu Shuppan, 2000, pp. 118–155.

97    Zhu, *Taiwan Soutokufu to ianfu*, p. 36.

98    Ibid., p. 67.

99    Ibid., p. 61.

100   Ibid., p. 71.

101   Ibid., p. 75.

102   Ibid., p. 62.

103   Fujinaga, 'Shokuminchi Taiwan ni okeru Chousen jin shakukyaku gyou to "ianfu" no douin', p. 99.

104   Zhu, *Taiwan Soutokufu to ianfu*, p. 32.

105   Ibid., p. 35.

106   Fujinaga, 'Taiwan ni okeru mikan no datsu shokuminchi ka', pp. 152–162; Fujinaga, 'Taiwan shokuminchi shihai to Taiwan jin "ianfu"', pp. 118–155.

107   Zhu, *Taiwan Soutokufu to ianfu*, p. 33.

108   Ibid., p. 36.

109   Fujinaga, 'Shokuminchi koushou seido to Nihon gun "ianfu" seido', p. 37.

110   Zhu, *Taiwan Soutokufu to ianfu*, p. 96.

111   Fujinaga, 'Shokuminchi koushou seido to Nihon gun "ianfu" seido', p. 38.

112   Zhu, *Taiwan Soutokufu to ianfu*, p. 34.

113   Ibid., p. 35.

114   Ibid., p. 38.

115   Ibid., pp. 44–45.

116   Fujinaga, 'Shokuminchi Taiwan ni okeru Chousen jin shakukyaku gyou to "ianfu" no douin', p. 98.

117   Fujinaga, 'Shokuminchi koushou seido to Nihon gun "ianfu" seido', p. 36.

118   Zhu, *Taiwan Soutokufu to ianfu*, pp. 62–63.

119   Shirota, *Mariya no sanka*, Tokyo: Nihon Kirisutokyoudan Shuppankyoku, 1971, pp. 35–36.

120   Zhu, *Taiwan Soutokufu to ianfu*, p. 100.

121   Ibid., p. 126.

122 Taipei Women's Rescue Foundation, 'Comfort women: Su,Yin-jiao Ah Ma', http://www.twrf.org.tw/eng/p3-service-detail.asp?PKey=aBIMaB31aBWPaB33&Class1=aBJQaB36

123 Fujinaga, 'Shokuminchi koushou seido to Nihon gun "ianfu" seido', p. 37.

124 Ibid., p. 38.

125 Fujinaga, 'Taiwan ni okeru mikan no datsu shokuminchi ka', pp. 152–162; Fujinaga, 'Taiwan shokuminchi shihai to Taiwan jin "ianfu"', pp. 118–155.

126 Fujinaga, 'Taiwan ni okeru mikan no datsu shokuminchi ka', pp. 152–162; Fujinaga, 'Taiwan shokuminchi shihai to Taiwan jin "ianfu"', pp. 118–155.

127 Fujinaga, 'Taiwan ni okeru mikan no datsu shokuminchi ka', pp. 152–162; Fujinaga, 'Taiwan shokuminchi shihai to Taiwan jin "ianfu"', pp. 118–155.

128 Fujinaga, 'Shokuminchi Taiwan ni okeru Chousen jin shakukyaku gyou to "ianfu" no douin', p. 109.

129 Hayashi Hirofumi, 'Government, the military and business in Japan's wartime comfort woman system', *The Asia-Pacific Journal: Japan Focus*, 26 January 2006, http://www.japanfocus.org/-Hayashi-Hirofumi/2332

130 Zhu, *Taiwan Soutokufu to ianfu*, p. 131.

131 Ibid., p. 169.

132 Fujinaga, 'Shokuminchi Taiwan ni okeru Chousen jin shakukyaku gyou to "ianfu" no douin', p. 109.

133 Ibid., p. 103.

134 Ibid., p. 102.

135 Ibid.

136 Fujinaga, 'Shokuminchi Taiwan ni okeru Chousen jin shakukyaku gyou to "ianfu" no douin', p. 102.

137 Ibid., p. 100.

138 Ibid., p. 101.

139 Ibid., p. 100.

140 Ibid., p. 102.

141 Ibid., p. 103.

142 Ibid., p. 108.

# Chapter 6

1 Gavan McCormack and Satoko Oka Norimatsu, *Resistant islands: Okinawa confronts Japan and the United States*, Plymouth: Rowman & Littlefield Publishers, 2012, pp. 16–17.

2 Koga Noriko, 'Okinawa sen ni okeru Nihon gun "ianfu" seido no tenkai (4)', *Sensou Sekinin Kenkyuu*, Vol. 63, 2009, p. 71.

3    Ueno Chizuko (translated by Beverley Yamamoto), *Nationalism and gender*, Melbourne: Trans Pacific Press, 2004, p. 85.

4    Yoshida Hidehiro, 'Nihon baishun shi: Henkan to sono haikei (2) Taisho/Showa shoki no baishun joukyou: Sono haikei to torishimari', *Jiyuu*, 1999, Vol. 41(12), No. 478, 140–152.

5    Hon Yun Shin, 'Okinawa sen to Chousenjin "ianfu"', in Nikkan Kyoudou 'Nihon gun ianjo' Miyakojima Chousadan (eds), *Senjyou no Miyakojima to 'ianjo'*, Okinawa: Nanyou Bunko, 2009, p. 27.

6    Itou Keiichi, 'Ianfu to heitai', in Osaka Sangyou Daigaku Sangyou Kenkyuujo (eds), *Kindai shakai to baishun mondai*, Osaka: Osaka Sangyou Daigaku, 2001, p. 20.

7    Jennifer Davies, *Sex slaves: Human trafficking*, London: RW Press, 2013.

8    Yoshida, 'Nihon baishun shi', p. 148.

9    Yoshimi Yoshiaki and translated by Suzanne O'Brien, *Comfort women: Sexual slavery in the Japanese military during World War II*, New York: Colombia University Press, 2000, p. 96.

10   Peipei Qiu, *Chinese comfort women: Testimonies from Imperial Japan's sex slaves*, New York: Oxford University Press, 2014, p. 116.

11   Takasaki Ryuuji (ed), *Hyakusatsu ga kataru 'ianjo' otoko no honne: Ajia-zensiki ni 'inanjo' ga atta*, Tokyo: Nashinokisha, 1994, p. 54.

12   Tamashiro Fukuko, 'Remembering the battle of Okinawa, forgetting the comfort women', in Muta Kazue and Beverley Anne Yamamoto (eds), *The gender politics of war memory: Asia-Pacific and beyond*, Osaka: Osaka University Press, 2012, pp. 95–114.

13   Yasuko Shinozaki, 'Okinawa no jendaa to baishun mondai', *Kumamoto Gakuen Daigaku Ronshuu 'Sougou Kagaku'*, Vol. 7, No. 1, 2000, p. 33.

14   Ibid., pp. 26, 29.

15   Mizutani Yoshiko, '"Sakanayaa" no onnatachi', in Nikkan Kyoudou 'Nihon Gun Ianjo' Miyakojima Chousadan (eds), *Senjyou no Miyakojima to 'ianjo'*, Okinawa: Nanyou Bunko, 2009, p. 155.

16   Nikkan Kyoudou, 'Nihon fun ianjo', in Miyakojima Chousadan (eds), *Senjyou no Miyakojima to 'ianjo'*, Okinawa: Nanyou Bunko, 2009, p. 153.

17   Ibid., pp. 151–152.

18   Koga Noriko, 'Okinawa-sen in okeru Nihon gun "ianfu" seido no tenkai (2)', *Sensou Sekinin Kenkyuu*, Vol. 61, 2008, p. 68.

19   Shin, 'Okinawa sen to Chousenjin "ianfu"', p. 25.

20   Shinozaki, 'Okinawa no jendaa to baishun mondai', p. 26.

21   Koga Noriko, 'Okinawa sen ni okeru Nihon gun "ianfu" seido no tenkai (1)', *Sensou Sekinin Kenkyuu*, Vol. 60, 2008, p. 48.

22   Koga, 'Okinawa sen ni okeru Nihon gun "ianfu" seido no tenkai (4)', pp. 67–68.

23   Koga Noriko, 'Okinawa sen ni okeru Nihon gun "ianfu" seido no tenkai (2)', *Sensou Sekinin Kenkyuu*, Vol. 61, 2008, p. 70.

24 Nikkan Kyoudou, 'Nihon fun ianjo'.

25 Koga, 'Okinawa sen ni okeru Nihon gun "ianfu" seido no tenkai (2)', p. 70.

26 Koga, 'Okinawa sen ni okeru Nihon gun "ianfu" seido no tenkai (4)', p. 69.

27 Koga, 'Okinawa sen ni okeru Nihon gun "ianfu" seido no tenkai (1)', pp. 49–50.

28 Ibid., p. 50.

29 Ibid.

30 Koga, 'Okinawa sen ni okeru Nihon gun "ianfu" seido no tenkai (4)', p. 68.

31 Koga Noriko, 'Okinawa sen ni okeru Nihon gun "ianfu" seido no tenkai (3)', *Sensou Sekinin Kenkyuu*, Vol. 62, 2008, p. 34.

32 Koga, 'Okinawa sen ni okeru Nihon gun "ianfu" seido no tenkai (4)', pp. 68, 70.

33 Ibid., p. 70.

34 Ibid.

35 Ibid., p. 71.

36 Koga, 'Okinawa sen ni okeru Nihon gun "ianfu" seido no tenkai (1)', p. 51

37 Koga, 'Okinawa sen ni okeru Nihon gun "ianfu" seido no tenkai (2)', p. 67

38 Koga, 'Okinawa sen ni okeru Nihon gun "ianfu" seido no tenkai (3)', p. 35.

39 See, for example, Kawada Fumiko, *Akagawara no ie: Chousen kara kita juugun ianfu*, Tokyo: Chikuma Shobou, 1987; Gima Hiroshi, *Okinawa-sen: Chousenjin gunfu to juugun ianfu: Okinawa-sen hangashuu*, Osaka-shi: Seifuudou Shoten, 1995; Fukuchi Hiroaki, *Okinawasen no onnatachi*, Tokyo: Kaifuusha; Pak Su-Nam, *Ariran no uta : Okinawa kara no shougen*, Tokyo: Aoki Shoten, 1991.

# Conclusion

1 Quoted in Kinoshita Naoko, 'For the sake of encounters with Japanese "comfort women" victims', in Iwasaki Minoru, Chen Kuan-Hsing and Yoshimi Shunya (eds), *Cultural Studies de Yomitoku Asia*, Tokyo: Serica Shobo, 2011, p. 123.

2 Mindy Kotler, 'The comfort women and Japan's war on truth', *The New York Times*, 15 November 2014, http://www.nytimes.com/2014/11/15/opinion/comfort-women-and-japans-war-on-truth.html

3 Korean Council for Women Drafted for Military Sexual Slavery by Japan and the Research Association on the Women Drafted for Military Sexual Slavery by Japan (translated by Young Joo Lee; edited by Keith Howard), *True stories of the Korean comfort women: Testimonies*, London; New York: Cassell, 1995.

4 United Nations Commission on Human Rights, *Systematic rape, sexual slavery and slavery-like practices during armed conflict: Final report submitted by Ms. Gay J. McDougall, Special Rapporteur*, 22 June 1998, p. 55, http://www.awf.or.jp/pdf/h0056.pdf

5 Asai Haruo, Murase Yukihiro and Itou Satoru (eds), *Nihon no otoko wa doko kara kite, doku e iku no ka*, Tokyo: Juutsukiya, 2001, p. 116.

6   Otsuki Nami and Hatano Keiko, 'Japanese perceptions of trafficking in persons: An analysis of the demand for sexual services and policies for dealing with trafficking survivors', *Social Science Japan Journal*, Vol. 12, No. 1, 2009, pp. 45–70.

7   M. Carael, E. Slaymaker, R. Lyerla and S. Sarkar, 'Clients of sex workers in different regions of the world: Hard to count', *Sexually Transmitted Infections*, Vol. 82, Suppl 3, 2006, pp. iii26–iii33.

8   Otsuki and Hatano, 'Japanese perceptions of trafficking in persons', p. 53.

9   Ibid., p. 53.

10  Usuki Keiko, *Gendai no ianfutachi: Guntai ianfu kara japa-yuki-san made*, Tokyo: Gendaishi Shuppankai: Hatsubai Tokuma Shoten, 1983.

11  'Kyuu Nihon gun no zangyaku sei de shin shiryou: Chuugoku/Kitsurin', *Shinbun Akahata*, 15 May 2014, http://www.jcp.or.jp/akahata/aik14/2014-05-15/2014051506_01_1.html?utm_source=dlvr.it&utm_medium=twitter

12  Hayashi Hirofumi, 'Rikugun ianjo kanri no ichi sokumen: Eisei sakku no koufu shiryou wo tegakari ni', *Sensou Sekinin Kenkyuu*, Vol. 1, No. 1, 1993, pp. 12–19.

13  M. Ui, Y. Matsui, M. Fukutomi, K. Narita, Y. Kamise and K. Yashiro. 'Factors that affect adult men's decision to hire a prostitute', *Shinrigaku Kenkyuu*, Vol. 79, No. 3, August 2008, p. 215.

14  Andrew Morrison, 'Teen prostitution in Japan: Regulation of telephone clubs', *Vanderbilt Journal of Transnational Law*, Vol. 31, No. 2, 1998, pp. 457–497.

15  Oji Tomoko, *Shoujo baishun kyoujutsu chousho: Ima, futatabi toinaosareru kazoku no kizuna*, Tokyo: Riyonsha, 1998, p. 51.

16  See database of child prostitution and pornography arrests at http://www.8peaks.jp/&#x007E;taiho38/index.php?special=deai01

17  Inoue Setsuko, *Baishunsuru otokotachi*, Tokyo: Shinhyouron, 1996.

18  Nakasato Takashi, 'Seishounen no keitai denwa nado kara no intaanetto riyou no genjyou to mondai', Working Paper, *Sougou chousa: 'Seishounen wo meguru sho mondai': Shakai teki sokumen kara*, pp. 133–148, 2009, http://www.ndl.go.jp/jp/diet/publication/document/2009/200884/32.pdf

19  'Deaikei kakarami no jiken', *Asahi Shinbun*, 17 November 2007, evening edition; 'Jidou poruno ga kyuuzou', *Nikkei Shinbun*, 15 February 2007, evening edition.

20  Anti-Pornography and Prostitution Research Group, 'Kodomotachi ni taishite nani ga dekiru no ka', *Ronbun/shiryoushuu*, Vol. 7, 2006–2007, p. 98.

21  Kaneko Yumiko, 'Chuugakukou yougo kyouin kara mita kodomo tachi no sei to sei higai', in Poruno Higai to Sei Bouryoku wo Kangaeru Kai, *Kodomo no nichijou wo torimaku sei higai*, conference proceedings, 20 November 2011, p. 13.

22  People Against Pornography and Sexual Violence, 'Manga to anime no sekai: Imada ni Nihon de ha kodomo ha seiteki taishou na no da', *Merumaga*, Vol. 25, 2014, http://paps-jp.org/mag/25/

23  Maree Crabbe and David Corlett, 'Eroticising inequality: Technology, pornography and young people', *Redress*, Vol. 20, No. 1, April 2011, pp. 11–15.

24  Mugishima Fumio, 'Poruno komikku no seishounen e no eikyou', *Seishounen Mondai*, Vol. 40, No. 11, 1993, p. 45.

25  Imanishi Hajime, *Yuujo no shakaishi: Shimabara, Yoshiwara no rekishi kara shokuminchi 'koushou' sei made*, Tokyo: Yuushisha, 2007.

26  Poruno higai to sei bouryoku wo kangaeru kai (eds), *Ima wa, mada namae no nai sei higai ga arimasu*, Tokyo: Poruno higai to sei bouryoku wo kangaeru kai, 2011.

27  Seiko Hanochi, 'A historical perspective on the Japanese sex trade', *Refuge*, Vol. 17, No. 5, 1998, https://pi.library.yorku.ca/ojs/index.php/refuge/article/viewFile/21988/20657

28  Fujino Yutaka, *Wasurerareta chiikishi o aruku: Kin-gendai Nihon ni okeru sabetsu no shosou*, Tokyo: Ootsuki Shoten, 2006.

29  Tsunoda Yukiko, *Seisabetsu to bouryoku*, Tokyo: Yuuhikaku, 2001, pp. 126–127.

30  For specific reference to the need to change Japan's legislation, see Yoshika Youko and Tomioka Emiko (eds), *Gendai Nihon no josei to jinken*, Tokyo: Akashi Shoten, 2001, p. 250.

31  Mitsuka Takeo (ed), *Gendai no baishun to jinken: Fujin no saigo no 'kakekomidera' o kangaeru*, Osaka: Osaka no Fujin Hogo Jigyou o Mamoru Kai, 1986, pp. 103, 120.

32  Takahashi Kikue and Yunomae Tomoko (eds), *Baishun, baishun*, Tokyo: Shibundou, 1986, p. 61.

33  For example, see last paragraph of Gender Equality Bureau, 'Baibaishun no genjou', http://www.gender.go.jp/teppai/sabetsu/2-5.html.

34  Wazaki Haruka (ed), *Dansei no sei ishiki ni kan suru jisshou teki kenkyuu: Sekushuariti no rekishi teki hyouzou to seifuuzoku sangyou no fiirudowaaku*, Fukushima: Fukushima ken danjo kyousei sentaa, 2005, p. 1.

35  Morita Seiya, 'Senji no sei bouryoku heiji no sei bouryoku', *Yuibutsuron Kenkyuu Nenshi*, Vol. 4, November 1999, p. 118.

36  Sheila Jeffreys, *The industrial vagina: The political economy of the global sex trade*, London: Routledge, 2009, p. 126.

37  Morita, 'Senji no sei bouryoku heiji no sei bouryoku', p. 130.

38  Ibid., p. 116.

39  Ibid., p. 18.

40  Ibid.

41  Ibid.

42  Ibid.

43  Ibid.

44  Ibid., p. 25.

45  Ibid., pp. 26–27.

46  Ibid., p. 27.

47 John Dower, 'The useful war', *Daedalus*, Vol. 119, No. 3, 1990, p. 49.

48 Ieda Shoukou, 'Bijinesu senshi no juugun ianfu tachi', *Sapio*, Vol. 5, No. 16, 1993, pp. 94–99.

49 Imanishi, *Yuujo no shakaishi*, p. 1.

50 Fujino Yutaka, *Sei no kokka kanri: Bai-baishun no kin-gendaishi*, Tokyo: Fuji Shuppan, 2001, p. 284.

51 Yayori Matsui, 'The plight of Asian migrant women working in Japan's sex industry', in Kumiko Fujimura-Fanselow and Atsuko Kameda (eds), *Japanese women: New feminist perspectives on the past, present, and future*, New York: Feminist Press at CUNY, 1995, p. 314.

52 Matsui Yayori, 'Why I oppose *kisaeng* tours', in Kathleen Barry, Charlotte Bunch and Shirley Castley (eds), *International feminism: Networking against female sexual slavery: Report of the Global Feminist Workshop to Organize Against Traffic in Women, Rotterdam, the Netherlands, April 6–15, 1983*, Rotterdam: International Women's Tribune Centre, 1984, p. 65.

53 Vera Mackie, *Feminism in modern Japan: Citizenship, embodiment, and sexuality*, Cambridge; New York: Cambridge University Press, 2003.

54 For example, see Chunghee Sarah Soh, 'Military prostitution and women's sexual labour in Japan and Korea', in Ruth Barraclough and Elyssa Faison (eds), *Gender and labour in Korea and Japan: Sexing class*, London; New York: Routledge, 2009.

55 See, for example, Sonia Ryang, *Love in modern Japan: Its estrangement from self, sex, and society*, Milton Park; New York: Routledge, 2006; Ueno Chizuko, 'Self-determination on sexuality?: Commercialization of sex among teenage girls in Japan', *Inter-Asia Cultural Studies*, Vol. 4, No. 2, 2003, pp. 317–324.

56 Sugita Satoshi, *Danken shugiteki sekushuariti: Poruno baibaishun yougoron hihan*, Tokyo: Aoki Shoten, 1999, p. 207.

57 Quoted in Kazuko Watanabe, 'The trafficking of women', in Joe Moore (ed), *The other Japan: Conflict, compromise, and resistance since 1945*, Bulletin of Concerned Asian Scholars, Armonk, NY: M.E. Sharpe, 1997, p. 314.

# Bibliography

Anti-Pornography and Prostitution Research Group. 'Kodomotachi ni taishite nani ga dekiru no ka', *Ronbun/shiryoushuu*, Vol. 7, 2006–2007.

Asai, Haruo, Murase Yukihiro and Itou Satoru (eds), *Nihon no otoko wa doko kara kite, doku e iku no ka*, Tokyo: Juutsukiya, 2001.

Askin, Kelly. 'Comfort women: Shifting shame and stigma from victims to victimizers', *International Criminal Law Review*, Vol. 1, No. 1/2, January 2001, pp. 5–32.

Atsushi, Kouketsu. *Kenpei seiji: Kanshi to doukatsu no jidai*, Tokyo: Shin Nippon Shuppan Sha, 2008.

Baldwin, Margaret. 'Split at the root: Prostitution and feminist discourses of law reform', *Yale Journal of Law and Feminism*, Vol. 5, No. 47, 1992, pp. 47–120.

Barnhart, Michael A. 'Japan's economic security and the origins of the pacific war', *Journal of Strategic Studies*, Vol. 4, No. 2, 1981, pp. 105–124.

BBC TV, *Against pornography: The feminism of Andrea Dworkin*, Sydney, N.S.W: SBS, 1992.

Beasley, William. *The rise of modern Japan: Political, economic and social change since 1850*. New York: St. Martin's Press, 2000, revised edition.

Carael, M., E. Slaymaker, R. Lyerla and S. Sarkar. 'Clients of sex workers in different regions of the world: Hard to count', *Sexually Transmitted Infections*, Vol. 82(Suppl 3), 2006, pp. iii26–iii33.

Carney, Matthew. 'Return of the samurai: Japan steps away from pacifist constitution as military eyes threat from China', *Foreign Correspondent*, Australian Broadcasting Corporation, 19 August 2014, http://www.abc.net.au/news/2014-08-19/japan-expands-their-military-amid-growing-tensions-with-china/5672932

Chai, Alice Yun. 'KOREA. Modern Period', pp. 821–824 in Helen Tierney (ed), *Women's Studies Encyclopedia*, Vol. 2, New York: Greenwood Press, 1989.

Chai, Alice Yun. 'Asian-Pacific feminist coalition politics: The chongshindae/jugunianfu ("comfort women") movement', *Korean Studies*, Vol. 17, 1993, pp. 67–91.

Chimoto, Hideki. 'Roudou toshite no baishun to kindai kazoku no yukue', in Tazaki Hideaki (ed), *Uru shintai kau shintai: Sekkusu waaku ron no shatei*, Tokyo: Seikyuusha, 1997, pp. 141–194.

Choi, H., C. Klein, M. Shin and H. Lee. 'Posttraumatic Stress Disorder (PTSD) and Disorders of Extreme Stress (DESNOS) symptoms following prostitution and childhood abuse', *Violence Against Women*, Vol. 15, No. 8, 2009, pp. 933–951.

'Clinton says "comfort women" is incorrect term', *Chosun Ilbo*, 9 July 2012, http://english.chosun.com/site/data/html_dir/2012/07/09/2012070900793.html

Crabbe, Maree and David Corlett. 'Eroticising inequality: Technology, pornography and young people', *Redress*, Vol. 20, No. 1, April 2011, pp. 11–15.

Culhane, Dara. 'Their spirits live within us: Aboriginal women in downtown eastside Vancouver emerging into visibility', *American Indian Quarterly*, Vol. 27, No. 3/4, Special Issue: Urban American Indian Women's Activism (Summer–Autumn 2003), pp. 593–606.

Cwikel, J. and E. Hoban. 'Contentious issues in research on trafficked women working in the sex industry: Study design, ethics, and methodology', *Journal of Sex Research*, Vol. 42, No. 4, 2005, pp. 306–316.

Davies, Jennifer. *Sex slaves: Human trafficking*, London: RW Press, 2013.

'Deaikei kakarami no jiken'. *Asahi Shinbun*, 17 November 2007, evening edition.

Dickinson, Frederick R. *World War I and the triumph of a new Japan, 1919–1930*, Cambridge; New York: Cambridge University Press, 2013.

Dower, John. 'The useful war', *Daedalus*, Vol. 119, No. 3, 1990, pp. 49–70.

Drea, Edward J. *In the service of the Emperor: Essays on the Imperial Japanese Army*, Lincoln: University of Nebraska Press, 1998.

Driscoll, Mark. *Absolute erotic, absolute grotesque: The living, dead, and undead in Japan's imperialism, 1895–1945*, Durham: Duke University Press, 2010.

Dworkin, Andrea. *Pornography: Men possessing women*, New York: Perigee Books, 1981.

Dworkin, Andrea. *Life and death: Unapologetic writings on the continuing war against women*, New York: The Free Press, 1997.

Dworkin, Andrea. *Scapegoat: The Jews, Israel, and women's liberation*, New York: Free Press, 2000.

Ekman, Kajsa Ekis. *Being and being bought: Prostitution, surrogacy and the split self*, Melbourne: Spinifex Press, 2013.

Enloe, Cynthia H. *Bananas, beaches & bases: Making feminist sense of international politics*, Berkeley: University of California Press, 1990.

Esselstrom, Erik. *Crossing empire's edge: Foreign Ministry police and Japanese expansionism in Northeast Asia*, Honolulu: University of Hawai'i Press, 2009.

Falconberg, Suki. 'Where in the name of all that is holy are the comfort women? An open letter to Ken Burns on "The War – An Intimate History"', 28 September 2007, http://womensspace.wordpress.com/2007/10/02/where-in-gods-name-are-the-comfort-women-an-open-letter-to-ken-burns-on-the-war-an-intimate-history/

Farley, Melissa. 'Prostitution and the invisibility of harm', *Women & Therapy*, Vol. 26, Nos. 3–4, 2003, pp. 247–280.

Farley, Melissa. *Prostitution and trafficking in Nevada: Making the connections*, San Francisco: Prostitution Research & Education, 2007.

Farley, Melissa, Emily Schuckman, Jacqueline M. Golding, Kristen Houser, Laura Jarrett, Peter Qualliotine and Michele Decker. 'Comparing sex buyers with men who don't buy sex: "You can have a good time with the servitude" vs. "You're supporting a system of degradation"', paper presented at Psychologists for Social Responsibility

Annual Meeting, 15 July 2011, Boston, San Francisco: Prostitution Research & Education, 2011.

Forbes, Mark. 'Sex city', *The Age*, 1 March 1999.

Fujime, Yuuki. *Sei no rekishigaku: Koushou seido, dataizai taisei kara baishun boushihou, yuusei hogohou taisei e*, Tokyo: Fuji Shuppan, 1997.

Fujinaga, Takeshi. 'Shokuminchi Taiwan ni okeru Chousen jin shakukyaku gyou to "ianfu" no douin', in Osaka Sangyou Daigaku Sangyou Kenkyuujo (eds), *Kindai shakai to baishun mondai*, Osaka: Osaka Sangyou Daigaku, 2001, pp. 80–115.

Fujinaga, Takeshi. 'Shokuminchi koushou seido to Nihon gun "ianfu" seido', in Hayakawa Noriyo (ed), *Shokuminchi to sensou sekinin*, Tokyo: Yoshikawa Koubunkan, 2005.

Fujino, Yutaka. *Sei no kokka kanri: Bai-baishun no kin-gendaishi*, Tokyo: Fuji Shuppan, 2001.

Fujino, Yutaka. *Wasurerareta chiikishi o aruku: Kin-gendai Nihon ni okeru sabetsu no shosou*, Tokyo: Ootsuki Shoten, 2006.

Fukuchi, Hiroaki. *Okinawasen no onnatachi*, Tokyo: Kaifuusha, 1992.

Fukuda, Toshiko. *Yoshiwara wa konna tokoro de gozaimashita: Kuruwa no onnatachi no Shouashi*, Tokyo: Bungensha, 2004.

Fukumi, Takao.*Teito ni okeru baiin no kenkyuu*, Tokyo: Hakubunkan, 1928 (reprinted 1999).

Fukuoka, Maki. 'Selling portrait photographs: Early photographic business in Asakusa, Japan', *History of Photography*, Vol. 35, No. 4, 2011, pp. 355–373.

Furusawa, Kiyoko. 'Higashi Timooru ni okeru Nihon gun sei dorei sei', *East Timor Quarterly*, No. 3, April 2001, http://www.asahi-net.or.jp/~ak4a-mtn/news/quarterly/number3/sexslavery3.html

Garon, Sheldon. *Molding Japanese minds: The state in everyday life*, Princeton: Princeton University Press, 1997.

Gender Equality Bureau, Government of Japan. 'Baibaishun no genjou', http://www.gender.go.jp/teppai/sabetsu/2-5.html

Gilead, Amihud. 'Philosophical prostitution', *Journal of Social Sciences*, Vol. 6, No. 1, 2010, pp. 85–92.

Gima, Hiroshi. *Okinawa-sen: Chousenjin gunfu to juugun ianfu: Okinawa-sen hangashuu*, Osaka-shi: Seifuudou Shoten, 1995.

Gluck, Carol. 'Introduction', in Carol Gluck and Stephen Graubard (eds), *Showa: The Japan of Hirohito*, New York; London: W.W. Norton & Company, 1992, pp. xi–lxii.

Gordon, Andrew. *A modern history of Japan: From Tokugawa times to the present*, New York; Oxford: Oxford University Press, 2003.

Hanochi, Seiko. 'A historical perspective on the Japanese sex trade', *Refuge*, Vol. 17, No. 5, 1998, https://pi.library.yorku.ca/ojs/index.php/refuge/article/viewFile/21988/20657

'Hashimoto shi "fuuzoku josei he no sabetsu da" Ishihara shi "machigattenai"', *Asahi Shinbun*, 14 May 2013, http://www.asahi.com/politics/update/0514/OSK201305140009.html

Hata, Ikuhiko. *Ianfu to senjou no sei*, Tokyo: Shinchousha, 1999.

Hata, Ikuhiko. 'No organized or forced recruitment: Misconceptions about comfort women and the Japanese military', Society for the Dissemination of Historical Fact, 2007, http://www.sdh-fact.com/CL02_1/31_S4.pdf

Hayakawa, Noriyo. '"Juugun ianfu" seiko no rekishi teki haikei ni tsuite', *Hou no Kagaku*, Vol. 23, 1995, pp. 126–130.

Hayakawa, Noriyo. 'Koushou sei to sono shuuhen: Tokyo-fu wo chuushin ni', *Sensou Sekinin Kenkyuu*, Vol. 17, 1997, pp. 51–59.

Hayashi, Hirofumi. 'Rikugun ianjo kanri no ichi sokumen: Eisei sakku no koufu shiryou wo tegakari ni', *Sensou Sekinin Kenkyuu*, Vol. 1, No. 1, 1993, pp. 12–19.

Hazama, Hiroshi. *Keizai taikoku o tsukuriageta shisou: Koudo keizai seichouki no roudou eetosu*, Tokyo: Bunshindou, 1996.

Hayashi, Hirofumi. 'Sensou taiken ki ni miru "juugun ianfu"', *Sensou Sekinin Kenkyuu*, Vol. 5, 1994, p. 31.

Hayashi, Hirofumi. 'Japanese comfort women in Southeast Asia', *Japan Forum*, Vol. 10, No. 2, 1998, pp. 211–219.

Hayashi, Hirofumi. 'Shiberia shuppei ji ni okeru Nihon gun to "karayukisan"', *Sensou Sekinin Kenkyuu*, Vol. 24, 1999, pp. 65–75.

Hayashi, Hirofumi. 'Government, the military and business in Japan's wartime comfort woman system', *The Asia-Pacific Journal: Japan Focus*, 26 January 2006, http://www.japanfocus.org/-Hayashi-Hirofumi/2332

Hayashi, Hirofumi. 'Japanese military comfort houses and Overseas Chinese "comfort women" in South-east Asia (summary)', http://www.geocities.jp/hhhirofumi/eng05.htm

Heilemann, Tammy and Janaki Santhiveeran. 'How do female adolescents cope and survive the hardships of prostitution? A content analysis of existing literature', *Journal of Ethnic and Cultural Diversity in Social Work*, Vol. 20, No. 1, 2011, pp. 57–76.

Hein, Laura. 'Savage irony: The imaginative power of the "military comfort women" in the 1990s', *Gender & History*, Vol. 11, No. 2, July 1999, pp. 336–372.

Henson, Maria Rosa. *Comfort women: Slave of destiny*, Metro Manila: Philippine Center for Investigative Journalism, 1996.

Herman, Judith. 'Introduction: Hidden in plain sight: Clinical observations on prostitution', in Melissa Farley (ed), *Prostitution, trafficking and traumatic stress*, Binghamton, NY: Haworth Maltreatment & Trauma Press, 2003, pp. 1–12.

Hicks, George L. *The comfort women*, St. Leonards: Allen & Unwin, 1995.

Hirai, Kazuko. 'Zasshi ni hyoushou sareta Nihonjin "ianfu" kara miete kuru mono', presentation handout on file with author 29 September 2012, VAWWRAC Soukai Shimpojiumu, 'Nihon jin "ianfu" no higai jitai ni semaru!'.

Hirai, Kazuko. 'Nihon gun "ianjo" kara senryou gun "ian shisetsu"/"akasen" e', presentation handout at VAWRACC Soukai Shimpojiumu, 'Nihon jin "ianfu" no choushuu/taiguu/sengo', 21 September 2013.

Hirao, Hiroko. 'Senji ka "Shina tokou fujo" no ki', *Sensou Sekinin Kenkyuu*, Vol. 61, 2008, pp. 10–19.

Hirota, Kazuko. *Shougen kiroku juugun ianfu, kangofu: Senjou ni ikita onna no doukoku*, Tokyo: Shin Jinbutsu Ouraisha, 1975.

Höhn, Maria and Seungsook Moon (eds), *Over there: Living with the U.S. military empire from World War Two to the present*. Durham: Duke University Press, 2010.

Horner, Emily. 'Kamishibai as propaganda in wartime Japan', *Storytelling, Self, Society*, Vol. 2, Issue 1, No. 2, 2005, pp. 21–31.

Hunter, Janet. *Concise dictionary of modern Japanese history*, Tokyo: Kodansha International, 1984.

Hunter, Janet. 'Women's labour force participation in interwar Japan', *Japan Forum*, Vol. 2, No. 1, 1990, pp. 105–125.

Hunter, Susan Kay. 'Prostitution is cruelty and abuse to women and children', *Michigan Journal of Gender and Law*, Vol. 95, 1993, pp. 1–14.

'Ianfu mondai, fuuzokugyou wo meguru Hashimoto shi no hatsugen youshi', *Asahi Shinbun*, 13 May 2013, http://www.asahi.com/politics/update/0514/OSK201305130144.html?ref=reca

Ieda, Shoukou. 'Bijinesu senshi no juugun ianfu tachi', *Sapio*, Vol. 5, No. 16, 1993, pp. 94–99.

Ienaga, Saburou. *The pacific war: World War II and the Japanese, 1931–1945*, New York: Pantheon Books, 1978.

'If we don't face our past, we're bound to repeat the same mistakes.' Japanese wartime medical orderly reports on army's role in maintaining 'comfort women' system, David McNeill introduction, Matsumoto Masayoshi testimony (Japanese and English transcript and video of testimony), translation by Miguel Quintana, http://www.japanfocus.org/-David-McNeill/4202

Inoue, Setsuko. *Baishunsuru otokotachi*, Tokyo: Shinhyouron, 1996.

Imanaka, Yasuko. 'Guntai to koushou seido', in Hayakawa Noriyo (ed), *Shokuminchi to sensou sekinin*, Tokyo: Yoshikawa Koubunkan, 2005.

Imanishi, Hajime. *Yuujo no shakaishi: Shimabara, Yoshiwara no rekishi kara shokuminchi 'koushou' sei made*, Tokyo: Yuushisha, 2007.

Imamura, Shouhei, Imamura Productions and Kino International Corporation. *Karayuki-san, the making of a prostitute*, New York, NY: Kino International, 1980.

Itou, Takashi. 'Nihon kaigun ianjo no rekishi teki hakken', *Toitsu Hyouron*, Vol. 411, 1999, pp. 64–75.

Itou, Keiichi. 'Ianfu to heitai', in Osaka Sangyou Daigaku Sangyou Kenkyuujo (eds), *Kindai shakai to baishun mondai*, Osaka: Osaka Sangyou Daigaku, 2001.

Iwata, Shigenori. 'Yobai to kaishun', *Nihon Minzoku Gaku*, Vol. 158, No. 186, 1991, pp. 74–112.

Iwata, Shigenori. 'Nihon dansei to sei koudou to sei ishiki: 1910–1930 nendai wo chuushin ni', *Rekishi Hyouron*, Vol. 4, 1998, pp. 28–39.

Japan Women for Justice and Peace. 'What is "comfort women"?', http://nadesiko-action.org/wp-content/uploads/2013/01/nadeshiko_zWeb.pdf

Jeffreys, Sheila. 'Prostitution', in Dusty Rhodes and Sandra McNeil (eds), *Women against violence against women*, London: Onlywomen Press, 1985.

Jeffreys, Sheila. *The spinster and her enemies: Feminism and sexuality, 1880–1930*, North Melbourne: Spinifex Press, 1997.

Jeffreys, Sheila. *The idea of prostitution*, North Melbourne: Spinifex Press, 2008.

Jeffreys, Sheila. *The industrial vagina: The political economy of the global sex trade*, London: Routledge, 2009.

Jeong, Nam-Ku. 'Inside Japan's growing xenophobic right-wing', *The Hankyoreh*, 9 June 2013, http://www.hani.co.kr/arti/english_edition/e_international/591008.html.

'Jidou poruno ga kyuuzou', *Nikkei Shinbun*, 15 February 2007, evening edition.

Jungwon, Jin. 'Reconsidering prostitution under the Japanese occupation', *The Review of Korean Studies*, Vol. 17, No. 1, 2014, pp. 115–157.

Juugun Ianfu 110-ban Henshuu Iinkai. *Juuugun ianfu 110-ban: Denwa no mukou kara rekishi no koe ga*, Tokyo: Akashi Shoten, 1992.

'Kaigai de baishun suru Kankokujin josei, Nihon 5man nin Beikoku 3man nin, Beiou de shakai mondai ka', 28 May 2012, http://news.searchina.ne.jp/disp.cgi?y=2012&d=0528&f=national_0528_040.shtml

Kamitsubo, Takashi. *Mizuko no uta: Dokyumento hikiage koji to onnatachi*, Tokyo: Shakai Shisosha, 1993.

Kampf, Antje. 'Controlling male sexuality: Combating venereal disease in the New Zealand military during two world wars', *Journal of the History of Sexuality*, Vol. 17, No. 2, May 2008, pp. 235–258.

Kaneko, Yumiko. 'Chuugakukou yougo kyouin kara mita kodomo tachi no sei to sei higai', in Poruno Higai to Sei Bouryoku wo Kangaeru Kai, *Kodomo no nichijou wo torimaku sei higai*, conference proceedings, 20 November 2011 pp. 13–19.

Kano, Mikiyo. 'The problem with the "comfort women problem"', *Ampo: Japan-Asia Quarterly Review*, Vol. 24, No. 2, 1993, pp. 42–63.

Kanzaki, Kiyoshi. 'Shoujo geisha no jinshin baibai', *Heiwa*, Vol. 1, 1955, pp. 78–81.

Kanzaki, Kiyoshi. *Baishun: Ketteiban Kanzaki repouto*, Tokyo: Gendaishi Shuppankai, 1974.

Katz, P. R. 'Germs of disaster: The impact of epidemics on Japanese military campaigns in Taiwan, 1874 and 1895', *Annales de Demographie Historique*, 1996, pp. 195–220.

Kawada, Fumiko. *Akagawara no ie: Chousen kara kita juugun ianfu*, Tokyo: Chikuma Shobo, 1987.

Kawada, Fumiko. *Kougun ianjo no onnatachi*, Tokyo: Chikuma Shobou, 1993.

Kawamura, Minato. 'Kiisen no zushou gaku', in Suwa Haruo (ed), *Ajia no sei*, Tokyo: Bensey, 1999.

Kawamura, Minato. *Kiisen: Mono o iu hana no bunka shi*, Tokyo: Sakuhinsha, 2001.

Kawada, Fumiko. *Indoneshia no 'ianfu'*, Tokyo: Akashi Shoten, 1997.

Kelly, Joan. *Women, history and theory: The essays of Joan Kelly*, Chicago: University of Chicago Press, 1984.

Kempadoo, Kamala. 'Globalization and sex workers' rights', *Canadian Women's Studies*, Vol. 22, No. 3/4, 2002/2003, p. 143. http://pi.library.yorku.ca/ojs/index.php/cws/article/viewFile/6426/5614

Khan, Yoshimitsu. 'Schooling Japan's imperial subjects in the early Showa period', *History of Education: Journal of the History of Education Society*, Vol. 29, No. 3, 2000, pp. 213–223.

Kim, Il Myon. *Nihon josei aishi: Yuujo, jorou, karayuki, ianfu no keifu*, Tokyo: Gendaishi Shuppankai, 1980.

Kim, Il Myon. *Guntai ianfu: Senso to ningen no kiroku*, Tokyo: Tokuma Shoten, 1992.

Kim, Pu-ja and Song Youn-ok. *'Ianfu', senji seibouryoku no jittai*, Tokyo: Ryokufuu Shuppan, 2000.

Kinoshita, Naoko. 'For the sake of encounters with Japanese "comfort women" victims', in Iwasaki Minoru, Chen Kuan-Hsing and Yoshimi Shunya (eds), *Cultural studies de Yomitoku Asia*, Tokyo: Serica Shobo, 2011, pp. 108–131.

Kinoshita, Naoko. 'Victimization of Japanese "comfort women": Opinions and redress movements in the early 1990s', in The Tokai Foundation for Gender Studies (ed), *Gender studies*, Nagoya: The Tokai Foundation for Gender Studies (14), 2011, pp. 89–113.

Koga, Noriko. 'Okinawa sen ni okeru Nihon gun "ianfu" seido no tenkai (2)', *Sensou Sekinin Kenkyuu*, Vol. 61, 2008, pp. 64–71.

Koga, Noriko. 'Okinawa sen in okeru Nihon gun "ianfu" seido no tenkai (4)', *Sensou sekinin kenkyuu*, Vol. 63, 2009, pp. 62–81.

Komagome, Takeshi. 'Taiwan shokuminchi shihai to Taiwan jin "ianfu"', in VAWW-NET Japan (eds), *'Ianfu' senji sei bouryoku no jitai I: Nihon, Taiwan, Chosen*, Tokyo: Ryokufu Shuppan, 2000, pp. 118–155.

Komagome, Takeshi. 'Taiwan ni okeru mikan no datsu shokuminchi ka', in Kim Pu-ja and Nakano Toshio (eds), *Rekishi to sekinin 'ianfu' mondai to 1990nen dai*, Tokyo: Seikyuusha, 2008, pp. 152–162.

Korean Council for Women Drafted for Military Sexual Slavery by Japan and the Research Association on the Women Drafted for Military Sexual Slavery by Japan (translated by Young Joo Lee; edited by Keith Howard). *True stories of the Korean comfort women: Testimonies*, London; New York: Cassell, 1995.

Kotler, Mindy. 'The comfort women and Japan's war on truth', *The New York Times*, 15 November 2014, http://www.nytimes.com/2014/11/15/opinion/comfort-women-and-japans-war-on-truth.html

Kurahashi, Masanao. *Kita no karayukisan*, Tokyo: Kyouei Shobou, 1989.

Kurahashi, Masanao. *Juugun ianfu mondai no rekishiteki kenkyuu: Baishunfugata to seiteki doreigata*, Tokyo: Kyouei Shobou, 1994.

Kurahashi, Masanao. *Juugun ianfu to koushou seido: Juugun ianfu mondai sairon*, Tokyo: Kyouei Shobou, 2010.

Kusama, Yasoo. *Jokyuu to baishoufu*, Tokyo: Nihon Tosho Sentaa, 1982.

'Kyuu Nihon gun no zangyaku sei de shin shiryou: Chuugoku/Kitsurin', *Shinbun Akahata*, 15 May 2014, http://www.jcp.or.jp/akahata/aik14/2014-05-15/2014051506_01_1.html?utm_source=dlvr.it&utm_medium=twitter

Langton, Rae. *Sexual solipsism: Philosophical essays on pornography and objectification*, Oxford: Oxford University Press, 2009.

Limoncelli, Stephanie. *The politics of trafficking: The first international movement to combat the sexual exploitation of women*, Stanford: Stanford University Press, 2010.

Lone, Stewart. 'The Japanese military during the Russo-Japanese War, 1904-05: A reconsideration of command politics and public images', STICERD/International Studies, Discussion Paper No. IS/98/351, 1998, http://www.russojapanesewar.com/aspects.pdf

Lone, Stewart. *Provincial life and the military in imperial Japan: The phantom samurai*, Abington: Routledge, 2010.

Mackie, Vera. 'Militarized memories and sexual silences: Writing about military prostitution in the Second World War', *Japanese Studies*, Vol. 16, 1996, pp. 62–68.

Mackie, Vera. *Feminism in modern Japan: Citizenship, embodiment, and sexuality*, Cambridge; New York, Cambridge University Press, 2003.

MacKinnon, Catharine. 'Rape, genocide, and women's human rights', in Alexandra Stiglmayer (ed), *Mass rape: The war against women in Bosnia-Herzegovina*, Nebraska: University of Nebraska Press, 1994.

MacKinnon, Catharine. 'Rape, genocide, and women's human rights', *Harvard Women's Law Journal*, Vol. 17, 1994.

MacKinnon, Catharine. *Are women human? And other international dialogues*, Cambridge, MA: Harvard University Press, 2007.

MacKinnon, Catharine. 'Sexual abuse as sex inequality', in Catharine MacKinnon (ed), *Women's lives, men's laws*, Cambridge: Harvard University Press, 2007.

MacKinnon, Catharine. 'Trafficking, prostitution, and inequality', *Harvard Civil Rights-Civil Liberties Law Review*, Vol. 46, 2011, pp. 271–309.

MacMillan Reference Books. *Japan: An illustrated encyclopedia*, Tokyo: Kodansha, 1993.

Mangan, J. A. and Takeshi Komagome. 'Militarism, sacrifice and emperor worship: The expendable male body in fascist Japanese martial culture', *The International Journal of the History of Sport*, Vol. 16, No. 4, 1999, pp. 181–204.

Masuda, Sayo (translated by G. G. Rowley). *Autobiography of a geisha*, New York: Columbia University Press, 2003.

Masutomi, Masasuke. 'Gotaiten to geigi mondai', *Kakusei*, October 1915.

Matsuda, Toshihiko. 'Kindai Nihon shokuminchi ni okeru "kenpei kesatsu seido" ni miru "touji youshiki no sen'i": Chousen kara Kantoushuu "Manushuukoku" e', http://shikon.nichibun.ac.jp/dspace/bitstream/123456789/870/1/nk35019.pdf

Matsugu, Miho. 'In the service of the nation: Geisha and Kawabata Yasunari's snow country', in Martha Feldman and Bonnie Gordon (eds), *The courtesan's arts: Cross-cultural perspectives*, New York: Oxford University Press, 2006, pp. 243–255.

Matsui, Yayori. 'Why I oppose *kisaeng* tours', in Kathleen Barry, Charlotte Bunch and Shirley Castley (eds), *International feminism: Networking against female sexual slavery: Report of the Global Feminist Workshop to Organize Against Traffic in Women, Rotterdam, the Netherlands, April 6–15, 1983*. Rotterdam: International Women's Tribune Centre, 1984.

Matsui, Yayori. 'The plight of Asian migrant women working in Japan's sex industry', in Kumiko Fujimura-Fanselow and Atsuko Kameda (eds), *Japanese women: New feminist perspectives on the past, present, and future*, New York: Feminist Press at CUNY, 1995.

Matsuoka, Nobuo. 'Chosen josei no rekishi ni omou', in Takahashi Kikue (ed), *Sei shinryaku o kokuhatsu suru kiisen kankou*, Tokyo: Kiisen Kankou ni Hantai suru Onnatachi no Kai, 1974.

Matsumura, Toshio. 'Biruma no tokoro "juugun ianfu"', *Doko*, No. 1589, 1999, pp. 18–22.

McCormack, Gavan and Satoko Oka Norimatsu. *Resistant islands: Okinawa confronts Japan and the United States*, Plymouth: Rowman & Littlefield Publishers, 2012.

McDougall, Gay. *Systematic rape, sexual slavery and slavery-like practices during armed conflict: Final report*. Geneva: UN, 1998.

McLelland, Mark. *Love, sex, and democracy in Japan during the American occupation*, New York: Palgrave Macmillan, 2012.

Metzler, Mark. *Lever of empire: The international gold standard and the crisis of liberalism in prewar Japan*, Berkeley: University of California Press, 2006.

Mikanagi, Yumiko. 'Women, the state, and war: Understanding issue [*sic*] of the "comfort women"', *Kokusai Kirisutokyou Daigaku Shakai Kagaku Jaanaru*, Vol. 48, 2002, pp. 37–54.

Millet, Kate. *Sexual politics*, New York: Ballantine, 1970.

Mitsuka, Takeo (ed). *Gendai no baishun to jinken: Fujin no saigo no 'kakekomidera' o kangaeru*, Osaka: Osaka no Fujin Hogo Jigyou o Mamoru Kai, 1986.

Mizutani, Yoshiko. '"Sakanayaa" no onnatachi', in Nikkan Kyoudou 'Nihon Gun Ianjo' Miyakojima Chousadan (eds), *Senjyou no Miyakojima to 'ianjo'*, Okinawa: Nanyou Bunko, 2009.

Moon, Katharine. *Sex among allies: Military prostitution in U.S.-Korea relations*, New York: Columbia University Press, 1997.

Moon, Katharine. 'South Korean movements against militarized sexual labor', *Asian Survey*, Vol. 39, No. 2, 1999, pp. 310–327.

Moon, Katharine. 'Resurrecting prostitutes and overturning treaties: Gender politics in the "anti-American" movement in South Korea', *The Journal of Asian Studies*, Vol. 66, No. 1, February 2007, pp. 129–157.

Moran, Rachel. *Paid for: My journey through prostitution*, Melbourne: Spinifex Press, 2013.

Morita, Seiya. 'Senji no sei bouryoku heiji no sei bouryoku', *Yuibutsuron Kenkyuu Nenshi*, Vol. 4, November 1999, pp. 113–140.

Morita, Seiya. 'Pornography, prostitution, and women's human rights in Japan', in Christine Stark and Rebecca Whisnant (eds), *Not for sale: Feminists resisting prostitution and pornography*, North Melbourne: Spinifex, 2004, pp. 64–84.

Morita, Seiya. 'Poruno to ha nani ka, poruno higai to ha nani ka', in Poruno Higai to Sei Bouryoku wo Kangaeru Kai (eds), *Shougen: Gendai no sei bouryoku to poruno higai*, Tokyo: Tokyo-to Shakai Fukushi Kyougikai, 2010, pp. 50–51.

Morrison, Andrew. 'Teen prostitution in Japan: Regulation of telephone clubs', *Vanderbilt Journal of Transnational Law*, Vol. 31, No. 2, 1998, pp. 457–497.

Mugishima, Fumio. 'Poruno komikku no seishounen e no eikyou', *Seishounen Mondai*, Vol. 40, No. 11, 1993.

Muta, Kazue. 'The new woman in Japan', in Margaret Beetham and Ann Heilmann (eds), *New woman hybridities: Femininity, feminism, and international consumer culture, 1880–1930*, London: Routledge, 2004.

Najita, Tetsuo. *Japan: The intellectual foundations of modern Japanese politics*, Chicago; London: University of Chicago Press, 1974.

Nakasato, Takashi. 'Seishounen no keitai denwa nado kara no intaanetto riyou no genjyou to mondai', Working Paper, *Sougou chousa: 'Seishounen wo meguru sho mondai': Shakai teki sokumen kara*, pp. 133–148, 2009, http://www.ndl.go.jp/jp/diet/publication/document/2009/200884/32.pdf

'New NHK head's "comfort women" remark stirs controversy', *Japan Today*, 26 January 2014, http://www.japantoday.com/category/national/view/new-nhk-heads-comfort-women-remark-stirs-controversy

Nishino, Rumiko. *Juugun ianfu no hanashi: Juudai no anata e no messeeji*, Tokyo: Akashi Shoten, 1993.

Nishino, Rumiko. 'Nihonjin ianfu: Dare ga dono youni choushuu sareta ka', in VAWW-NET Japan (eds), *Nihon gun sei dorei sei wo sabaku 2000nen josei kokusai senpan houtei no kiroku: Jisshou sareta senji seibouryoku ni okeru higai to kankeisei*, Vol. 3/4, Tokyo: Rokufu Shuppan, 2000.

Nishino, Rumiko. 'Naze ima, Nihon jin"ianfu" nano ka?', presentation handout on file with author, 29 September 2012, VAWWRAC Soukai Shimpojiumu, 'Nihon jin 'ianfu' no higai jitai ni semaru!'.

Nishino, Rumiko. 'Higai sha shougen ni miru "ianfu" renkou no kyousei sei', in 'Sensou to josei he no bouryoku' Risaachi Akushon Sentaa, *'Ianfu' basshingu wo koete*, Ootsuki Shoten, 2013, pp. 23–42.

Norma, Caroline and Melinda Tankard Reist (eds), *Prostitution narratives: Stories from survivors of the sex trade*, Melbourne: Spinifex Press, 2016.

Office to Monitor and Combat Trafficking in Persons, *Trafficking in persons report 2009*, http://www.state.gov/g/tip/rls/tiprpt/2009/123136.htm

Ogino, Fujio. 'Toyama ken in okeru "roumu ianfu" ni tsuite', *Sensou Sekinin Kenkyuu*, Vol. 6, 1994, pp. 64–67.

Oji, Tomoko. *Shoujo baishun kyoujutsu chousho: Ima, futatabi toinaosareru kazoku no kizuna*, Tokyo: Riyonsha, 1998.

Olsen, Frances. 'Statutory rape: A feminist critique of rights analysis', *Texas Law Review*, Vol. 63, No. 3, 1984, pp. 393–394.

Onoda, Hiroo. 'Watashi ga mita juugunianfu no seitai', *Seiron*, Vol. 392, 2005, pp. 142–149.

Onozawa, Akane. *Kindai Nihon shakai to koushou seido: Minshuushi to kokusai kankeishi no shiten kara*, Tokyo: Yoshikawa Koubunkan, 2010.

Onozawa, Akane. 'Shiryou ni miru Nihonjin "ianfu" no choushuu no jitai', in presentation notes on file with author, 29 September 2012, VAWW-RAC Soukai Shinpojiumu, 'Nihon jin 'ianfu' no higai jitai ni semeru!'.

Orihara, Minami and Gregory Clancey. 'The nature of emergency: The Great Kanto Earthquake and the crisis of reason in late imperial Japan', *Science in Context, Suppl. Witness to Disaster: Earthquakes and Expertise*, Vol. 25, No. 1, March 2012, pp. 103–126.

Otabe, Yuuji, Hayashi Hirofumi and Yamada Akira. *Kiiwaado Nihon no sensou hanzai*, Tokyo: Yuzankaku, 1995.

Otsuki, Nami and Hatano Keiko. 'Japanese perceptions of trafficking in persons: An analysis of the demand for sexual services and policies for dealing with trafficking survivors', *Social Science Japan Journal*, Vol. 12, No. 1, 2009, pp. 45–70.

Paku, Su-Nam. *Ariran no uta*, Tokyo: Aoki Shoten, 1991.

Palmer, Brandon. *Fighting for the enemy: Koreans in Japan's war, 1937–1945*, Seattle: University of Washington Press, 2013.

Park, Hyun. 'Bill related to comfort women passed in US Congress', *The Hankyoreh*, 17 January 2014, www.hani.co.kr/arti/english_edition/e_international/620209.html

People Against Pornography and Sexual Violence, 'Manga to anime no sekai: Imada ni Nihon de ha kodomo ha seiteki taishou na no da', *Merumaga*, Vol. 25, 2014, http://paps-jp.org/mag/25/

Phillipps, Jeremy. 'City and empire – Local identity and regional imperialism in 1930s Japan', *Urban History*, Vol. 35, No. 1, 2008, pp. 116–133.

Pilzer, Joshua. 'Music and dance in the Japanese military "comfort women" system: A case study in the performing arts, war, and sexual violence', *Women and Music: A Journal of Gender and Culture*, Vol. 18, 2014, pp. 1–23.

Poruno Higai to Sei Bouryoku wo Kangaeru Kai (eds), *Ima wa, mada namae no nai sei higai ga arimasu*, Tokyo: Poruno Higai to Sei Bouryoku wo Kangaeru Kai, 2011.

Qiu, Peipei, Zhiliang Su and Lifei Chen. *Chinese comfort women: Testimonies from imperial Japan's sexual slaves*, New York: Oxford University Press, 2014.

Ramseyer, Mark. 'Indentured prostitution in Imperial Japan: Credible commitments in the commercial sex industry', *The Journal of Law, Economics, & Organization*, Vol. 7, No. 1, 1991, pp. 89–116.

Ramseyer, Mark and Frances Rosenbluth. *The politics of oligarchy: Institutional choice in Imperial Japan*. Cambridge: Cambridge University Press, 1998.

Raymond, Janice G. *Not a choice, not a job: Exposing the myths about prostitution and the global sex trade*, North Melbourne: Spinifex, 2013.

Ruff-O'Herne, Jan. *50 years of silence*, Sydney: Editions Tom Thompson, 1994.

Ryang, Sonia. *Love in modern Japan: Its estrangement from self, sex, and society*, Milton Park; New York: Routledge, 2006.

Saga, Junichi. *Memories of silk and straw: A self-portrait of small-town Japan*. Tokyo; New York: Kodansha International; distributed in the U.S. through Harper & Row, 1987.

Sato, Barbara. *The new Japanese woman: Modernity, media, and women in interwar Japan*, Durham and London: Duke University Press, 2003.

Schencking, Charles. *The Great Kanto Earthquake and the chimera of national reconstruction in Japan*, New York: Columbia University Press, 2013.

Senda, Kakou. *Juugun ianfu*, Tokyo: Koudansha, 1993.

Seong, Yeon-cheol and Gil Yun-hyung. 'China releases documents showing Japan forcibly mobilized comfort women', *The Hankyoreh*, 25 March 2014, english.hani.co.kr/popups/print.hani?ksn=629741 3/4

Shared Hope International. 'Japan: Culture and crime promote commercial markets of sexual exploitation', http://www.sharedhope.org/files/demand_japan.pdf

Shimazu, Naoko. *Japanese society at war: Death, memory and the Russo-Japanese war*, Cambridge; New York: Cambridge University Press, 2009.

Shimojuu, Kiyoshi. *Miuri no nihonshi: Jinshin baibai kara nenki boko e*, Tokyo: Yoshikawa Kobunkan, 2012.

Shimokawa, Koushi and Hiroki Hayashi. *Yuukaku o miru*, Tokyo: Chikuma Shobou, 2010.

Shin, Hon Yun. 'Okinawa sen to Chousenjin "ianfu"', in Nikkan Kyoudou 'Nihon gun ianjo' Miyakojima chousadan (eds), *Senjyou no Miyakojima to 'ianjo'*, Okinawa: Nanyou Bunko, 2009.

Shinozaki, Yasuko. 'Okinawa no jendaa to baishun mondai', *Kumamoto gakuen daigaku ronshuu 'sougou kagaku'*, Vol. 7, No. 1, 2000, pp. 159–216.

Shirota, Suzuko. *Mariya no sanka*, Tokyo: Nihon Kirisutokyoudan Shuppan Kyoku, 1971.

Shu, Tokuran (Delan Zhu). *Taiwan soutokufu to ianfu*, Tokyo: Akashi Shoten, 2005.

Silverberg, Miriam. 'The modern girl as militant', in Gail Bernstein (ed), *Recreating Japanese women, 1600–1945*, Berkeley, Los Angeles; Oxford: University of California Press, 1991, pp. 239–266.

Silverberg, Miriam. 'The cafe waitress serving modern Japan', in Stephen Vlastos, *Mirror of modernity: Invented traditions of modern Japan*, Berkeley: University of California Press, 1998.

Silverberg, Miriam. *Erotic grotesque nonsense: The mass culture of Japanese modern times*, Berkeley: University of California Press, 2007.

Smethurst, Richard. *A social basis for prewar Japanese militarism: The army and the rural community*, Berkeley: University of California Press, 1974.

Smith, Kerry Douglas. *A time of crisis: Japan, the great depression, and rural revitalization*. Cambridge: Harvard University Asia Center; distributed by Harvard University Press, 2001.

Soh, Chunghee Sarah. 'The Korean "comfort women": Movement for redress', *Asian Survey*, Vol. 36, No. 12, 1996, pp. 1226–1240.

Soh, Chunghee Sarah. 'From imperial gifts to sex slaves: Theorizing symbolic representations of the "comfort women"', *Social Science Japan Journal*, Vol. 3, No. 1, April 2000, pp. 59–76.

Soh, Chunghee Sarah. 'Women's sexual labor and state in Korean history', *Journal of Women's History*, Vol. 15, No. 4, 2004, pp. 170–177.

Soh, Chunghee Sarah. 'The Korean "comfort women" tragedy as structural violence', in Wook Gi-Shin, Soon-Won Park and Daqing Yang (eds), *Rethinking historical injustice and reconciliation in northeast Asia*, New York: Routledge, 2007, pp. 17–35.

Soh, Chunghee Sarah. *The comfort women: Sexual violence and postcolonial memory in Korea and Japan*, Chicago: University of Chicago Press, 2008.

Soh, Chunghee Sarah. 'Military prostitution and women's sexual labour in Japan and Korea', in Ruth Barraclough and Elyssa Faison (eds), *Gender and labour in Korea and Japan: Sexing class*, London; New York: Routledge, 2009.

Song, Youn-ok. 'Nihon no shokuminchi shihai to kokka teki kanri baishun: Chousen no koushou wo chuushin ni shite', *Chousen Shi Kenkyuu Kai Ronbun Shuu*, Vol. 32, 1994, pp. 37–87.

Song, Youn-ok. 'Japanese colonial rule and state-managed prostitution: Korea's licensed prostitutes', *Positions*, Vol. 5, No. 1, 1997, pp. 171–219.

Sorano, Yoshihiro. 'Kitachousen moto juugun ianfu shougen', *Ekonomitsuto*, Vol. 70, No. 49, 1992, pp. 548–553.

Snitow, Ann Barr, Christine Stansell and Sharon Thompson. *Powers of desire: The politics of sexuality*, New York: Monthly Review Press, 1983.

'Stop undermining Kono statement', *Japan Times*, 25 June 2014, http://www.japantimes. co.jp/opinion/2014/06/25/editorials/stop-undermining-kono-statement/#.VFNosfnLe4E

Study Team on the Details Leading to the Drafting of the Kono Statement etc. *Details of exchanges between Japan and the Republic of Korea (ROK) regarding the comfort women issue – From the drafting of the Kono Statement to the Asian Women's Fund*, 20 June 2014, http://www.mofa.go.jp/files/000042171.pdf

Sugisaka, Keisuke. *Tobita no ko: Yuukaku no machi ni hataraku onnatachi no jinsei*, Tokyo: Tokuma Shoten, 2013.

Sugita, Satoshi. *Danken shugiteki sekushuariti: Poruno baibaishun yougoron hihan*, Tokyo: Aoki Shoten, 1999.

Suzuki, Masahiro. 'Sensou ni okeru dansei no sekushuariti', in 'Ningen to Sei' Kyouiku Kenkyuu Kyougikai 'Dansei Keisei Kenkyuu' Purojekuto (eds), *Nihon no otoko wa doko kara kite doko e iku no ka: Dansei sekushuariti keisei 'kyoudou kenkyuu'*, Tokyo: Juugatsusha, 2001, pp. 108–117.

Suzuki, Tessa Morris. 'Freedom of hate speech; Abe Shinzo and Japan's public sphere', *The Asia-Pacific Journal*, Vol. 11, Issue 8, No. 1, 25 February 2013, http://www.japanfocus.org/-Tessa-Morris_Suzuki/3902

Suzuki, Tessa Morris. 'Addressing Japan's "comfort women" issue from an academic standpoint', *The Asia-Pacific Journal*, Vol. 12, Issue 9, No. 1, 2 March 2014, http://www.japanfocus.org/-Tessa-Morris_Suzuki/4081

Suzuki, Tessa Morris. 'Letters to the dead: Grassroots historical dialogue in East Asia's borderlands', in Tessa Morris Suzuki, Morris Low, Leonid Petrov and Timothy Y. Tsu, *East Asia beyond the history wars: Confronting the ghosts of violence*, London: Akashi Shoten, 2014.

Suzuki, Yuuko. *Chousenjin juugun ianfu: Shougen Showa shi no danmen*, Tokyo: Iwanami Shoten, 1991.

Suzuki, Yuuko. *'Jugun ianfu' mondai to seiboryoku*, Tokyo: Miraisha, 1993.

Suzuki, Yuuko. 'Ima, mimi kakete kioku kizumu toku', *Human Rights*, Vol. 111, 1997, pp. 20–27.

Suzuki, Yuuko. 'Sekando reipu ni hoka naranai', *Sekai*, Vol. 632, 1997, pp. 48–53.

Suzuki, Yuuko. *Sensou sekinin to jendaa: 'Jiyuu shugi shikan' to Nihon gun 'ianfu' mondai*, Tokyo: Miraisha, 1997.

Suzuki, Yuuko and Kondou Kazuko. *Onna, tennousei, sensou*, Tokyo: Orijin Shuppan Sentaa, 1989.

Tabuchi, Hiroko. 'Women forced into WWII brothels served necessary role, Osaka mayor says', *The New York Times*, 13 May 2013, http://www.nytimes.com/2013/05/14/world/asia/mayor-in-japan-says-comfort-women-played-a-necessary-role.html?_r=0

Taipei Women's Rescue Foundation. 'Comfort women: Su, Yin-jiao Ah Ma', http://www.twrf.org.tw/eng/p3-service-detail.asp?PKey=aBIMaB31aBWPaB33&Class1=aBJQaB36

Takahashi, Kikue. *Sei shinryaku o kokuhatsu suru kiisen kankou*, Tokyo: Kiisen Kankou Ni Hantai Suru Onnatachi No Kai, 1974.

Takahashi, Ryuuji (ed). *Hyakusatsu ga kataru 'ianjo' otoko no honne: Ajia-zen'iki ni 'inanjo' ga atta*, Tokyo: Nashinokisha, 1994.

Takahashi, Kikue and Yunomae Tomoko (eds), *Baishun, baishun*, Tokyo: Shibundou, 1986.

Takasato, Suzuyo. *Okinawa no onnatachi: Josei no jinken to kichi guntai*, Tokyo: Akashi Shoten, 1996.

Takayasu, Yae. 'Onna no Rabauru kouta', in Senchuu-ha group (eds), *Zoku senchuu-ha no yuigon*, Tokyo: Kai Shobou, 1979.

Tamai, Noriko. *Hinomaru o koshi ni maite: Tekka shoufu, Takanashi Taka ichidaiki*, Tokyo: Gendaishi Shuppanka, 1984.

Tamashiro, Fukuko. 'Remembering the battle of Okinawa, forgetting the comfort women', in Muta Kazue and Beverley Anne Yamamoto (eds), *The gender politics of war memory: Asia-Pacific and beyond*, Osaka: Osaka University Press, 2012, pp. 95–114.

Tanaka, Yuki. *Japan's comfort women: Sexual slavery and prostitution during World War II and the US occupation*, London; New York: Routledge, 2002.

Tanikawa, Mitsue. *Mono iwanu shougitachi: Sapporo yuukaku hiwa*, Sapporo-shi: Miyama Shobou, 1984.

The Committee for Historical Facts. 'The facts', *Washington Post*, 14 June 2007, http://en.wikipedia.org/wiki/File:The_Facts_about_the_Comfort_Women.jpg

The Leap Organization. 'Excerpt from Dr. Suki Falconberg's book…', http://www.leapnonprofit.org/Phil%20article%20Suki%20Falconberg.htm

Tipton, Elise. *Modern Japan: A social and political history*, London: Routledge, 2002.

Tipton, Elise. 'Cleansing the nation: Urban entertainments and moral reform in interwar Japan', *Modern Asian Studies*, Vol. 42, No. 4, 2008, pp. 705–731.

Tomioka, Emiko and Mutsuko Yoshioka. *Gendai Nihon no josei to jinken*, Tokyo: Akashi Shoten, 2001.

Trefalt, Beatrice. *Japanese army stragglers and memories of the war in Japan, 1950–75*, London: RoutledgeCurzon, 2003.

Tsunoda, Yukiko. *Seisabetsu to bouryoku*, Tokyo: Yuuhikaku, 2001.

Tsuzuki, Chushichi. *The pursuit of power in modern Japan, 1825–1995*. Oxford: Oxford University Press, 2000.

Ueno, Chizuko and 'Self-determination on sexuality?: Commercialization of sex among teenage girls in Japan', *Inter-Asia Cultural Studies*, Vol. 4, No. 2, 2003, pp. 317–324.

Ueno, Chizuko. (translated by Beverley Yamamoto). *Nationalism and gender*, Melbourne: Trans Pacific Press, 2004.

Ui, M., Y. Matsui, M. Fukutomi, K. Narita, Y. Kamise and K. Yashiro. 'Factors that affect adult men's decision to hire a prostitute', *Shinrigaku Kenkyuu*, Vol. 79, No. 3, August 2008, pp. 215–223.

UNESCO. 'Nomination form International Memory of the World Register Archives about "Comfort Women": The Sex Slaves for Imperial Japanese Troops', http://www.unesco.org/new/fileadmin/MULTIMEDIA/HQ/CI/CI/pdf/mow/nomination_forms/china_comfort_women_eng.pdf

United Nations Commission on Human Rights. *Report of the Special Rapporteur on violence against women, its causes and consequences, Ms. Radhika Coomaraswamy, in accordance with Commission on Human Rights resolution 1994/45; Report on the mission to the Democratic People's Republic of Korea, the Republic of Korea and Japan on the issue of military sexual slavery in wartime*, 4 January 1996, http://www.awf.or.jp/pdf/h0004.pdf

Ward, Vanessa B. 'A Christian challenge: Chou Takeda Kiyoko and feminist thought in modern Japan', *Women's History Review*, Vol. 21, No. 2, 2012, pp. 281–299.

Wilson, Sandra. 'Rethinking the 1930s and the "15-Year War" in Japan', *Japanese Studies*, Vol. 21, 2001, pp. 155–164.

Watanabe, Kazuko. 'Trafficking in Women's Bodies, Then and Now: The Issue of Military "Comfort Women"', *Peace & Change*, Vol. 20, 1995, pp. 501–514.

Wazaki, Haruka (ed). *Dansei no sei ishiki ni kan suru jisshou teki kenkyuu: Sekushuariti no rekishi teki hyouzou to seifuuzoku sangyou no fiirudowaaku*, Fukushima: Fukushima Ken Danjo Kyousei Sentaa, 2005.

Yamashita, Yeong-ae and Yun Chung-ok. *Chousenjin josei ga mita 'ianfu mondai': Asu o tomo ni tsukuru tame ni*, Tokyo: San'ichi Shobou, 1992, pp. 128–167.

Yamashita, Yeong-ae. 'Nationalism and gender in the comfort women issue', *Kyoto Bulletin of Islamic Area Studies*, Vol. 3–1, July 2009, pp. 208–219.

Yasuhara, Keiko. 'Bunseki ripouto: Ianfu ni tsuite', in Juugun Ianfu 110ban Henshuu Iinkai (eds), *Juugun ianfu 110ban: Denwa no mukou kara rekishi no koe ga*, Tokyo: Akaishi Shoten, 1992, pp. 87–108.

'Yegeurina'. 'There is no such thing as voluntary or involuntary: Can it really ever be a choice?' in *Salim Center* (translated by Yunmi Lee), booklet (self-published, on file with author).

Yoon, Bang-Soon L. 'Imperial Japan's comfort women from Korea: History & politics of silence-breaking', *Journal of Northeast Asian History*, Vol. 7, No. 1, 2010, pp. 5–39.

Yoshimi, Yoshiaki and translated by Suzanne O'Brien. *Comfort women: Sexual slavery in the Japanese military during World War II*, New York: Colombia University Press, 2000.

Yoshimi, Yoshiaki. '"Kouno danwa" to "ianfu" seiko no shinsou kyuumei', in Risaachi Akushon Sentaa (eds), *'Ianfu' basshingu wo koete*, Tokyo: Ootsuki Shoten, 2013, pp. 2–22.

Yoshimi, Yoshiaki. '"Kouno danwa" wo dou kangaeru ka', in Sensou to Josei he no Bouryoku Risaachi Akushon Sentaa (ed), *'Ianfu' basshingu wo koete: 'Kouno danwa' to Nihon no sekinin*, Tokyo: Otsuki Shoten, 2013.

Yoshimi, Yoshiaki. 'Nihon baishun shi: Henkan to sono haikei (2) Taisho/Showa shoki no baishun joukyou: Sono haikei to torishimari', *Jiyuu*, Vol. 41, No. 12, Issue 478, 1999, pp. 140–152.

Yoshimi, Kaneko. *Baishou no shakaishi*, Tokyo: Yuuzankaku, 1984.

Yoshimi, Yoshiaki. '"Juugun ianfu" no soushutsu to Chousen soutokufu', *Sensou Sekinin Kenkyuu*, Vol. 5, 1994, pp. 32–36.

Yun, Chung-ok and Suzuki Yuuko. *Heiwa o kikyuushite: 'Ianfu' higaisha no songen kaifuku e no ayumi*, Musashino-shi: Hakutakusha, 2003.

Zhu, Delan. *Taiwan Soutokufu to ianfu*, Tokyo: Akashi Shoten, 2005.

# Index

CPSIA information can be obtained
at www.ICGtesting.com
Printed in the USA
LVOW13*1618170217

524635LV00008B/155/P

9 781472 512475